Winning Website Sales Letters

*How To Create An Opening That Pulls Prospects In... A Message
That Sells Them... And An Offer They Simply Can't Refuse*

Copyright © Robert Boduch
Success Track Communications
thesuccesstrack@gmail.com

Published by:

Success Track Communications
Pickering, Ontario
L1W 2T8
Canada
email: thesuccesstrack@gmail.com

For free updates, special bonus reports & more, please visit:
http://www.bizprofitbuilder.com

Winning Website Sales Letters

How To Create The Opening That Attracts Them...The Message That Sells Them... And The Offer That Gets More Prospects To Buy NOW!

Table Of Contents

Introduction -- 10

Why Write Your Own Sales Letters? -- 13
22 Valuable Insights You'll Acquire By Reading This Book -- 15

Phase I

1.   Keys To Successful Online Sales Letters -- 17

Understanding The Culture Of The Internet -- 17
Building An Online Business Is About Building Relationships -- 18
Understanding The Online Audience -- 19
Target Your Approach -- 20
Direct Marketing With A Twist -- 21
Credibility Is Everything -- 23
Strategy Is More Important Than Creativity -- 24
Think The Way Your Market Thinks -- 25
Provide Value For Your Prospect's Time -- 26
Make An Instant Connection With Your Target Audience -- 26
Consistently Deliver The Information Your Audience Wants -- 27
Keep Your Purpose In Mind As You Write -- 28
Always Stay One Step Ahead -- 29

2.   Why People Buy and How To Get More To Buy From You -- 30

The Controlling Force That Directs Your Prospect's Actions -- 30
103 Specific Pain/Pleasure Reasons Why Anyone Would Be Interested In Buying Your Product -- 33
People Buy When Offered A "Magic" Solution -- 35
People Buy When You Hit Their Hot Buttons -- 37
People Buy On Emotion -- 39

People Buy When The Experience Gives Them An Emotional High -- 40
People Justify Buying With Logical Reasoning -- 41
People Buy Unique Advantages And Special Benefits -- 43
People Buy When They're Offered Great Value -- 44
People Buy From Credible Sources They Can Trust -- 48
People Buy When Fear Is No Longer A Factor -- 49
People Buy When The Message Resonates -- 50
People Buy Solutions To A Pressing Problem -- 51
People Buy When It's Easy To Obtain The Benefits They Want -- 52
People Buy Because You Deliver Instant Gratification -- 53
People Buy Better Alternatives -- 53
People Buy Convenience -- 54
People Buy When GivenThe Right Solution At The Right Time -- 55
People Buy Results, Not Products -- 55
People Buy Due To The Special Incentives Offered -- 56

3. Why People Don't Buy -- 58

People Don't Buy Exaggerated Claims -- 58
People Don't Buy From Amateur Marketers -- 59
People Don't Buy From Over-Designed Sites -- 59
People Don't Buy From Clever, Catchy, Or Humorous Ad Copy -- 60
People Don't Buy When They're Uncertain -- 60
People Don't Buy If The Product Isn't A Good Fit -- 61
People Don't Buy If They Feel They're Being Pushed -- 62
People Don't Buy What They Need - They Buy What They Want -- 62
People Don't Buy When There's No Clear Cut Advantage -- 63
People Don't Buy Again If They Weren't Satisfied The First Time -- 63

4. Emotions Are Key -- 65

Why Emotional Copy Sells More Products -- 65
The Number One Key To Writing With Emotion -- 66
How To Be Sure You're Addressing The Right Emotion -- 67
How To Write Emotional Copy -- 67
Qualities Of Emotionally Charged Copy -- 68
Other Ways To Inject Emotion -- 70

Key Points To Remember About Writing With Emotion -- 72

5.   The Sales Letter Plan -- 74

The Purpose Of A Plan -- 74
Identify Your Goals and Objectives -- 75
Define Your Market -- 77
Identify Your Competitor's Strengths and Weaknesses -- 78
Get To Know Your Product Inside-Out -- 79
Determine Your Strongest, Most Unique Selling Advantages -- 81
Create An Irresistible Offer -- 83
Add A Strong Guarantee -- 84
Build A Case In Favor Of Your Product -- 85
Outline The Order Process -- 86
The Ultimate Sales Letter Plan Worksheets -- 87

6.   Sales Letter Templates -- 97

Why Use A Sales Letter Template or Formula? -- 97
The A.I.D.A. Formula For Writing Effective Ads -- 97
Alternate Sales Letter Formulas By Noted Copywriters -- 99
The Two Most Important Steps Of Any Formula -- 101
Additional Elements Of Power and Persuasion -- 102

Phase II

7.   Start Your Sales Letter With A Powerful, Attention-Grabbing Headline -- 105

The Purpose Of The Headline -- 106
Why Headlines Are So Important Online -- 108
The Role Benefits Play In Headlines -- 109
How To Get Started Writing A Great Headline -- 110
The Most Effective Headline Formats For Website Sales Letters -- 111
How To Create A Winning Headline In Just Minutes -- 113
Powerful Headline Words and Phrases -- 115
How To Make A Good Headline Even Stronger -- 123

How To Write An Emotional Headline -- 124
What Kind Of Things Do Successful Headlines Offer? -- 125
Where Else Do These Headline Ideas Apply? -- 127
Key Points To Keep In Mind When Creating Sales Letter Headlines -- 127
Simple Enhancements To Make Your Headline Impossible To Miss -- 128
How To Be Sure Your Headline Is Effective -- 129
How Long Should A Sales Letter Headline Be? -- 132

8. How To Create A Riveting Opening That Intrigues, Invites, and Compels Prospects To Read On -- 134

What Makes The Opening So Important? -- 134
Why Are Openings So Difficult To Write? -- 135
The Best Way To Get Started -- 136
Do Salutations Help? -- 137
Tried and True Techniques For Creating Riveting Openings -- 139
How Opening Paragraphs Encourage Further Reading -- 140
How The Headline and Opening Work Together -- 141
How Long Should The Opening Be? -- 142
The 3 Crucial Tasks Successful Openings Complete -- 143
The Quickest Way To Create A Magnetic Opening -- 143
Where Most Openings Go Wrong -- 144
Examples Of Effective Opening Lines -- 145

9. Successful Sales Copy Is All About Buyer Benefits -- 149

What Exactly Are Benefits Anyway? -- 149
What About Features? -- 149
Which Benefits Should Be Included? -- 151
The Easiest Way To Turn Features Into Benefits -- 151
Why Benefits Are So Important -- 152
How To Reveal Your Product's Benefits For Maximum Impact -- 154
In What Order Should Benefits Be Presented? -- 155
Should The Benefits Of Bonus Material Be Unveiled Too? -- 156
How To Make Writing Body Copy Easier -- 156
How To Uncover Features That Can Be Converted Into Benefits -- 159
Is It Ever Acceptable To Stretch The Truth? -- 160
Using Bullet Points To Present Your Benefits -- 162

Keys To Successful Bullets -- 164
How To Write Provocative, Interest-Arousing Bullets -- 165
More Examples Of Effective Bullet Copy -- 166
Where To Find Rich Sources Of Bullet Point Material -- 169
Great Lead-Ins For Powerful Bullets -- 170

10.   Build Your Case With Solid Proof -- 173

Why Proof Is Such An Important Element -- 173
How Other People's Experience Helps Influence New Customers -- 174
Additional Ways To Build Credibility -- 175
How Perception Affects Your Results -- 176
Other Factors That Come Into Play -- 177
The Kind Of Proof That Matters Most To Prospects -- 178
How Your Reputation Serves You Online -- 178
What Makes Some Testimonials Better Than Others -- 179
Where To Best Place Your Customer Testimonials -- 181
How To Overcome The Fears That Concern Prospects -- 182
Why Testimonials Are Such Valuable Marketing Tools -- 184
Premium Quality Testimonials -- 185
Other Methods For Building Credibility -- 186

11.   Creating Irresistible Offers -- 187

Offers Defined -- 187
The Kinds Of Items To Include In Your Offers -- 187
Why A Summarized Offer Is So Important -- 188
Key Points To Remember When Compiling An Offer -- 188
Knowing Your Market Is Crucial -- 189
What Makes An Offer Totally Irresistible? -- 190
How To Convert Your Offer Into Direct Sales -- 191
How To Improve A Good Offer To Make It A Great Offer -- 192
What Is It About Offers That Make Them So Important? -- 192
Background Information For Building A Stronger Offer -- 194
What About Free Offers? -- 195
Additional Factors To Keep In Mind -- 196
Why Bother With An Offer Anyway? -- 198
What Incentives Should Your Offer Include? -- 198

How To Take A Basic Product And Create An Irresistible Offer -- 199

12. How To Craft A Powerful Guarantee   202

Why Having A Guarantee Is Important -- 202
What A Strong Guarantee Tells Prospects About You -- 203
Is A Standard Guarantee Okay… Or Do You Need More? -- 203
The Most Appealing Types Of Guarantees -- 204
How To Draw Attention To Your Guarantee -- 207
Make An Impact With An Elaborate Promise -- 208
How To Make Your Guarantee Seem Like An Ironclad Promise - Without
Sounding Like A Legal Document -- 209

13. Closing The Sale -- 213

How To Go For The Sale Every Time -- 213
How To Win New Customers Without Being Pushy -- 215
What Action Do You Want Prospects To Take? -- 216
What Else Can Be Done To Convert Prospects Into Customers? -- 216
How To Reassure Cautious Prospects -- 217
The Best Methods To Sustain Interest Through To The Order Form -- 218
Additional Closing Techniques -- 219
How To Avoid Losing The Sale -- 220
Tips For Creating A Stronger, More Influential Close -- 221

14. Add A Powerful P.S. -- 223

Why The P.S. Is Such An Important Component -- 223
How Prospects Typically Read A Sales Letter -- 223
What's Wrong With Most P.S.'s? -- 224
How To Utilize A Postscript For Maximum Effectiveness -- 225
How To Make It Even Better -- 225
Key Ingredients Of Successful P.S.'s -- 226
How To Make Sure Your P.S. Pulls Prospects In -- 228
What About Content? -- 228
Examples of Effective P.S.'s -- 229
What About Multiple P.S.'s - Do They Actually Work? -- 231

Examples of Multiple P.S.'s -- 232
Information You Shouldn't Include In Your P.S. -- 233
Key Points To Keep In Mind -- 234
How Long Should The P.S. Be? -- 235
How Prospects View P.S.'s -- 236

15. Creating An Order Form The Finalizes The Sale -- 237

Making The Transition From Sales Letter To Order Form -- 237
The Lead Component -- 238
Is An Order Form Headline A Necessity? -- 238
What's The Best Way To Launch Order Form Copy? -- 239
How To Improve The Responsiveness Of Your Order Form -- 241
Elements Worth Repeating -- 243
How To Make Your Order Form More Universally Acceptable and User-Friendly -- 243
What Variable Options Should Be Included On The Order Form? -- 245
How The Order Form Can Reassure Anxious Customers -- 245
Where Some Order Forms Go Wrong -- 247
Problems With Secure Options and Third Party Providers and How To Overcome Them Quickly, Easily, And At Zero Cost -- 247

Phase III

16.   Review, Revise & Edit For More Effective Copy -- 249

Easy Ways To Spot Errors -- 249
How To Minimize Editing Time -- 250
Other Things To Look Out For At The Editing Stage -- 251
Simple Ideas For Improving Readability and Flow -- 256
Specific Ways To Emphasize Key Points -- 257
How To Make Reading Your Sales Letter A Less Daunting Task -- 258
How To Strengthen Your Bullet Points -- 259
Remember Your Purpose While Editing -- 260

17. Design Enhancements -- 261

Sales Letter Design 101 -- 261
The First Thought You Want Entering Your Prospect's Mind -- 262
Why It's So Important To Avoid Fancy Designs Altogether -- 263
How To Make A Basic Sales Letter More Visually Appealing -- 264
What Else Should You Keep In Mind When Organizing Your Site? -- 265
Simple Techniques To Aid Readability -- 266
Which Areas Should Definitely Be Emphasized? -- 267
What About Graphics? -- 268
What About Text? -- 269
Fine Tuning Your Design and Layout -- 272
How To Target Different Groups With Your Sales Letter -- 273
Testing Is A Major Key To Success -- 274

18. Common Mistakes -- 275

Lack Of Preparation -- 275
Presenting A Confusing Message -- 276
Wasting Your Visitor's Time -- 276
Lacking Credible Proof -- 277
Not Being Clear About What It Is You're Offering -- 278
Uninspiring Copy That Focuses On The Product -- 278
A Short Message That Doesn't Do An Adequate Selling Job -- 279
Failing To Pull Prospects In From The Start -- 280
A Weak Close -- 281
A Site That Doesn't Facilitate Easy Buying -- 282
A Sales Letter That Doesn't Effectively Calm Prospect Fears --282
A Lack Of Uniqueness -- 283

Conclusion -- 284

Introduction

If you're looking for a step-by-step process to craft a compelling online sales letter - than this book is for you. Inside you'll find valuable insights, techniques, and a step-by-step method to turn your product into profit by creating a message with irresistible appeal to your target market. It's about using words for maximum impact, so you can sell more of your products or services online.

Ask any direct marketing veteran and they'll tell you the sales letter is the heart and soul of every package. It's the number one tool of choice among copywriters. Now you can apply many direct response secrets accrued over the years to let your words do the selling online - 24 hours a day and around the world.

The explosive growth of the Internet - particularly the World Wide Web - has created an unprecedented marketing opportunity. Suddenly, marketers everywhere can market their goods and services to a global audience, without the need for a traditional store or print catalogue... and all the high costs associated with these methods.

Today you don't even need an office to establish a moneymaking enterprise. On the web, all you really need is an adequate presence, a steady stream of qualified traffic, and a persuasive sales letter. Of course, it's fundamental to have a top-quality product and to direct your message to an identifiable market segment. But that's the case with any business you start - online of offline.

The foundational key to marketing success is to help people solve their problems or satisfy their desires. When you give them what they want, you immediately attract attention and interest because that's what your prospects are already thinking about -- and magnetically drawn towards.

Providing you with the tools to help you craft a powerful and persuasive sales letter is the purpose of this book. If you follow the steps I suggest, you'll soon acquire the ability to write effective sales copy. The more letters you write, the more skill you'll develop and the easier it gets to influence prospects to buy.

Some people simply don't have the time to learn new skills. Others couldn't be bothered mastering the ins and outs of persuasive copywriting. Still others don't think they have the language skills to craft a moneymaking sales letter.

That's why copywriters exist... to serve these people. But if you can't afford the fees of a competent professional, you needn't worry. Help has arrived - now it's up to you to use it. Reading and memorizing this material will help somewhat. But the real gains are made only by applying these ideas in the world of online marketing.

Look, the simple fact is... if you can carry on a conversation with a friend ... you can write a letter. And if you've ever had to convince somebody to 'buy' into your point of view -- you know what it takes to sell. It takes passion, belief, enthusiasm, and persuasion. Successful sales letters influence and persuade in a friendly, one-on-one, conversational manner.

"It is insight into human nature that is the key to the communicator's skill. For whereas the writer is concerned with what he puts into his writings, the communicator is concerned with what the reader gets out of it. He therefore becomes a student of how people read or listen."

-- William Bernbach

Traditional copywriting is essentially "salesmanship in print". Online it's more like "salesmanship in pixels". Though many serious prospects will print out your letter for easier reading, it first appears as nothing more than a collection of pixels on the prospect's computer screen.

Anyone can learn to write an effective online sales letter. It makes no difference what your background is - you could be a professional, tradesman, author, inventor, hobbyist, or homemaker. What does matter is that you have identified a hungry market and have a quality product -- one that offers buyers the help they seek to make life better in some way.

The knowledge and expertise you're about to acquire isn't a quick-fix. It's not an instant solution. Nor is it something to tuck inside a drawer, or leave on your bookshelf - only to gather dust.

Use this book as a practical tool and valuable resource and you'll acquire priceless skills - skills that can serve you well for a lifetime.

According to the late Gary Halbert, who was somewhat of a legend in copywriting circles…

> *"The most valuable skill you can have in today's world... if... you want to become independently wealthy... is... the ability to write a great sales letter."*

These principles, ideas, and strategies can serve you for many years to come. They can and will help you sell virtually any good product designed to address the market's problems and desires.

Many of these ideas have been adapted and adopted from the direct response industry and they work just as well online. They're tried and true techniques that have worked for years and will continue to do so.

How can I be so sure?

While technologies and applications have continually changed… human nature hasn't. We still yearn for the same emotional rewards our forefathers did.

Yes, this book is about marketing online and generating sales directly from a website. But as high-tech as the web seems… it's important to remember that you're still communicating with a living, breathing human being. You're communicating with an individual - someone with their own hopes and fears.

"Advertising is, actually, a simple phenomenon in terms of economics. It is merely a substitute for a personal sales force - an extension, if you will, of the merchant who cries aloud his wares."

-- Rosser Reeves

Powerful and persuasive salesmanship is a one-on-one communication - regardless of the level of sophistication used to deliver the message.

I've spent a large part of the past 6 years writing online sales letters for a variety of clients. Additionally, I've been privileged to discuss what makes a successful online sales letter with numerous colleagues, clients, and marketers.

These experiences have helped me develop a 'system' that has worked over and over again, in many different markets. Now I offer it to you.

In Phase I, you'll learn what it takes to create a great online sales letter. Then, you'll uncover the major reasons why people buy… and why they don't. Unveiled next is the *Ultimate Sales Letter Planner* to help you establish your own outline - an important first step to writing a powerful sales letter.

Phase II takes you through the process of crafting a moneymaking sales letter - starting with the headline and ending with the P.S. You'll discover why the headline is the most important part of every sales letter and how to create an appealing headline that grabs attention… and how to write a powerful opening that pulls prospects in. Next, you'll master the skill of crafting benefit copy and how to prove your claims to the audience. You'll then learn how to build an irresistible offer and rock-solid guarantee. Finally, it's a matter of closing the sale, adding a provocative P.S. and creating an order form that's quick and easy for buyers.

In Phase III, you'll learn how to turn your rough draft into a finished sales letter. Here, you'll learn how to polish it up to make your letter even stronger. This process involves both editing and basic design enhancements. This section ends with a discussion of common mistakes and how to avoid them - as well as an online sales letter checklist.

Why Write Your Own Sales Letters?

No one else understands your product the way you do. If you've been in business for a while, or you've spent months in product development, chances are you know everything there is to know about your product. For someone else to gain this kind of intimate knowledge -- it would take months, perhaps even years.

To understand your product enough to sell it in quantity means someone else would need to invest substantial time in research. That's part of the reason why copywriters charge what they do. A sizable chunk of the total fee from a reputable copywriter covers the time it takes to get the writer "up to speed" on your product, it's advantages, the marketplace, unique selling points, competition, etc.

There's no way around it. If you want gold, you've got to dig for it. And if you want results - you better do your research first.

You already have the knowledge and first-hand experience. This gives you an obvious advantage from the start. You'll save time and money by transferring your "inside information" into appealing copy, rather than have someone else first do the in-depth research for you.

Another advantage to writing your own web copy is that it gives you your own distinctive voice. It injects your own style and personality into the letter helping you connect with your reader - something you can use to your advantage in subsequent sales efforts.

In reality, no one cares as much about your product and your success as you do. Your business is your investment and only you will feel the full effect of the results produced. As a copywriter, I take each assignment seriously. I put my heart and soul into my work and give it my best shot every time out. But the truth is… I never have as much riding on the outcome as does the entrepreneur or business owner who hired me.

If you've looked around, chances are you've discovered a mountain of material already published on writing sales copy. But what's different about this text is its exclusive focus on website sales letters. This book isn't about selling by email… and it's not about creating "killer" direct mail packages either. It's about how anyone -- including you -- can take an idea and craft it into a compelling online sales letter that pulls in cash-paying customers to your website - even if you've never written a winning sales letter before.

With my step-by-step process, you won't have to struggle to crank out a great moneymaking letter. You won't have to spend grueling hours locked away in isolation hoping and praying for the words to flow naturally and persuasively.

Just knock off one step at a time. I'll share with you the ideas, techniques, tactics, strategies, secrets, and shortcuts I've learned along the way. When you're done, you wont just have an effective sales letter - you'll have acquired valuable asset - a skill -- that can bring you a steady stream of customers, cash flow, and profits for many years to come.

My system isn't a radical departure from proven direct-response methods… far from it. It merely simplifies the process so anyone can follow along, understand the concepts and then apply them to their own online letters. Following my format makes the actual writing a breeze. It organizes your thinking, thereby creating a planned and prioritized sales presentation.

The key to any huge task is to first simplify it.

Break it down into smaller manageable tasks. Crafting winning sales letters is no different. That's where this system shines -- by breaking down each aspect of sales letter writing into a series of simple steps. It makes writing much easier and fun to do. With each step, you'll not only gain new skills, but valuable experience too.

Please note - I've used the masculine pronoun when referring to prospects and customers throughout this volume. It was done so as a matter of grammatical convenience and consistency -- nothing more. Prospects and customers come in both genders. My objective is to help you, whether you are a man or a woman. Just remember that the value is in the information -- not in the method of delivery.

22 Valuable Insights You'll Acquire By Reading This Book

1. How to tackle any marketing project from the start to ensure your success

2. Key distinctions about online prospects and how you should approach them

3. Crucial information you need to gather before writing

4. The 3 things online prospects ask themselves when they arrive at your site

5. Specific reasons why people buy… and why they don't

6. How to cut through the clutter of competing messages and reach prospects where they live

7. A simple way to outline your sales letter to make it easier to write

8. The mindset to adopt whenever you write sales copy

9. Templates/ formats to help you conceptualize the process of selling with words

10. How to write a powerful, super-effective headline whenever you want

11. Easy prospect-pulling ways to start your letter

12. How to uncover small distinctions and turn them into huge benefits

13. Simple, super-fast ways to write intriguing and compelling bullets

14. The best method for proving any claim with a single paragraph

15. How to take any product and create an offer with magic appeal

16. Surefire techniques for strengthening your letter with a risk-free guarantee

17. How to close sales through the written word

18. What to say in your P.S. to ensure continued prospect interest

19. How to craft an order form that encourages and facilitates sales

20. A simple method for spotting glaring errors before launching your letter

21. Quick and easy design techniques to give your message more appeal

22. Common website sales letter pitfalls and how to easily avoid them

Phase I

Keys To Successful Online Sales Letters

"Primarily writing good copy is essentially the same no matter where it's presented but writing for the Internet requires one important distinction. That distinction is less verbiage with more impact."

-- Charlene Rashkow

Understanding The Culture Of The Internet

To make the most of your website sales letter you need to understand the Internet, its culture, and the people who use it on a regular basis. It's one huge smorgasbord of information and opportunity -- one that grows larger every single day.

New websites are being launched at an enormous rate. You can find just about anything online including the good, the bad, and the utterly tasteless. The choices truly are mind-boggling.

For the consumer, it's a rich resource of information and a way of bringing the world home, via their computer screens. For businesses, it's a dirt-cheap tool for reaching previously inaccessible customers and markets.

Many offline businesses have an online presence as well. It's just another tool in their respective arsenals. Still, other businesses are being created exclusively for the web. It's also a chance to add convenient at-home shopping to virtually any product or service.

With millions of people already online and more added daily, it's not surprising that new sales-oriented websites are popping up at an alarming rate. For the consumer, this means even more choices, making it more challenging to spend a limited amount of cash. For businesses, it means increased competition.

Despite the growing competition, setting up a sales-generating site has massive appeal worldwide. It seems that everyone and their cousin already has at least one website. Yet, some of the simplest sites are among the most successful. Yes, it is possible to succeed with a mini-site -- if you do it the right way.

Marketing on the Internet is about gently wooing prospects - pulling them inside your site, as opposed to 'pushing' a product upon them.

Doing business online means selling in a virtual environment. Buying and selling online is a totally new concept -- a major shift from traditional shopping. Since most people naturally resist change, you face an added challenge when marketing to the unseasoned online prospect.

The most effective way to win over new online prospects is to make your offer more tangible, real, and credible. Make it easy for buyers to envision exactly what they're getting and let them know when they'll get it. Create an ordering process that's fun, easy and natural - one that simulates buying from a catalogue, direct mail piece, infomercial, or the shopping channel. Give your audience something they can touch - something that makes the whole process of buying online more like the real world they're used to.

Traditionally, the lure of the Internet has been due to the vast resources freely available to anyone with a telephone line and computer. Surfers quickly get used to this unlimited accessibility to massive amounts of information, free of charge. A fair amount of it is useless junk, but for many, the lure of anything 'free' is too tempting to resist.

One approach is to tap into this tradition and provide helpful information on your site in addition to your sales copy. You don't have to give away the store by any means… but by feeding the frenzy, you're apt to be more accepted in the online marketing world.

Building An Online Business Is About Building Relationships

Marketing is largely a process of building relationships - regardless of the media or method. But the online population seems particularly sensitive to 'in your face' marketing. Respect this reality, or you'll pay a hefty price.

Think of your business as an on-going enterprise. Yes, you want to gener-ate sales immediately… but more importantly, you want to build a successful business. Real riches come not from first-timers, but from your repeat customers and the referrals those customers send your way. This can only happen when you've truly satisfied the customer initially - where he willingly becomes an advocate of your business.

Selling online is about doing everything in your power to persuade targeted prospects to make a purchase. But this can never be done at the expense of a relationship. So if you use deception, trickery or shady practices to get the sale, you cannot create long-term customer success and without this, you will imminently fail.

Understanding The Internet Audience

Why are people online? What is it they want to get out of their Internet experience?

According to a survey conducted by the Pew Research Center, nearly 75% of users went online to seek out information. The type of information most sought had to do with their hobbies, special interests, and purchases they were planning for the near future. 64% visited travel related websites... while 62% went to weather sites. 54% sought data and information about health and medicine... while just over 50% conducted educational research.

What does this tell you as a marketer? It says that once online, people are goal directed. They seek out certain things of interest to them personally. If you want to succeed, you better cater to the wishes of the marketplace. This means giving them what they want, when they want it. It's all about facilitating the search by getting straight to the heart of the matter.

People don't want to be entertained... anyone can get their fill of entertainment from television. Forget flash introductions and splash pages - that only eats up precious time. Instead, help people get the information they seek immediately. Give them clear, attractive benefits, backed up by real data. Make it easy for prospects to comparative shop. Give them the solutions they want, backed by logical straight talk. Make it easy for visitors to convince themselves. Quick, easy information of relevance - with no fluff and no filler -- that's the way to serve the online user.

People today are time-poor. Evolutionary changes in the workplace have resulted in heavier workloads and higher stress levels. There just isn't enough time between work, family obligations, and chores to do all the things they'd really like to do in their busy lives.

Yet the available choices of new products and services keep multiplying at a rapid pace. Everyday exciting new products are unveiled -- right before your eyes --fueling temptations and unleashing desires.

When consumers do get online, they want to make the most of their experience. They're in complete control of the surfing experience. They know what they want and are acutely aware when it's not delivered quickly. Online consumers make fast decisions about how and where they'll spend their time. Just because a visitor shows up at your site, doesn't mean he'll still be there 10 seconds later.

Cater to their 'wants' and you have a fighting chance of sustaining attention and interest. Eliminate any possible obstruction or time-waster. Make it fun, fast and easy to explore your website. Respect the time and intelligence of your visitors. They're in control and they know it. With unlimited choices just a click away, if you don't feed those 'wants' immediately, they'll quickly go elsewhere.

Target Your Approach

Though there are hundreds of millions of people connected to the Internet, only a fraction of these people are prime targets for your offer. It's self-defeating to think otherwise. If you're one of those people who figure you've got something that nearly everyone would love to own - think again. If your product is directed at the general marketplace, you need to re-frame your proposition.

What works best online is a targeted approach to marketing. Narrow your niche. Find those who are best suited to your solution. You want capable, eager and qualified prospects only.

Target marketing is precision marketing. You simply find an untapped, under-filled or poorly served market that already exists and shape your offer to fit like a glove to those already established desires. It's simply a matter of identifying those people whose hunger hasn't been adequately satisfied - people who are likely interested in your unique solution and have the means to acquire it.

Online users seek information related to their interests. Do-it-yourself home renovators visit sites that help with their kitchen, bath, basement, and deck building projects. They're most interested in new products and helpful information to make these repairs and upgrades to their homes. Camping enthusiasts plan and book trips online. Home gardeners look for tips on growing bigger, juicier tomatoes than the neighbor next door.

What market do you serve? Identify your niche and then make a commitment to dominate it. Make your unique product the ultimate solution for that specific market and ignore the others. By doing so, you'll make an impact on those who can benefit the most from whatever it is you offer. You can still target separate markets, but do so with separate websites that cater exclusively to each.

Direct Marketing With A Twist

The best model for website sales letters is direct mail. Why? Direct response marketing is all about getting an immediate response, not building an image. Direct marketing strives for maximum measurable returns on a minimum investment - every time out. With your online sales letters, you should also strive for a sale (or response) right away.

If you fail to win an immediate reply, chances are the prospect will forget about your offer and never order at all. In direct mail, however, the prospect has your letter, order form, envelope, brochure and lift letter in hand. It's something he can easily place on the coffee table and pick up again later, when he's ready to seriously consider ordering. Each piece in the package has the capability to grab interest, increase desire and convince the prospect to buy.

But online, you don't have that luxury. For the prospect to go back and read your letter, he must either print it out on his own paper and using his own ink and burning his own money... or he needs to make a conscious decision to return to your site later. Sure, book-marking might make it somewhat easier to return, but if the page is merely placed among hundreds of other favorites, there's a good chance your page will be over-looked altogether.

So the main disadvantage of online sales letters vs. off-line, is that they only exist as pixels on the user's screen - unless or until the prospect decides to print it. Even then, your sales letter gets printed on familiar paper -- usually of the plain white variety - so there's no chance of creating the same 'feel' or special effect that a multiple-piece direct mail package can.

But the obvious advantage is the cost savings. Online there's no postage, traditionally the single most expensive element of any direct marketing campaign. Since your sales letter exists only in cyberspace, there's no printing cost whatsoever. Additionally, you never have to worry about how much material you can stuff into an envelope without exceeding standard postage costs. In direct marketing, exceeding the limit by even a slight margin can be devastating to your entire campaign by multiplying actual costs.

Online, the amount of space available is virtually unlimited. You can include as many pages and go into as much detail as you want. Additional space can always be acquired at a very reasonable cost. The challenge is that the online prospect has a limited attention span… so your letter needs to keep him on the edge of his seat or he's gone elsewhere.

It's no surprise than that so many have been attracted to the Internet as a means of marketing products and services. It has a worldwide reach and the cost of setting up business is a tiny percentage of what it would take to set up in the real world. It's an open invitation to every breed of marketer to jump in and take advantage of this huge opportunity. The result is that for some, the web has become a massive new avenue for advertising. They attempt to entice people by delivering a barrage of messages in the hope that one 'sticks'. Or they employ glitz and flash with the mistaken belief that they can somehow trick people into paying attention to their message and buying their product.

Truth is… this approach would never fly in the real world of bricks and mortar businesses. It would be a complete waste of money to even try. But because it's so cheap to set up shop on the web, some take a "let's try it" approach. They simply don't understand the online environment and the low tolerance of users for such an approach.

Credibility Is Everything

People buy from those they know, like, and trust. To succeed online, you need to create a comfortable environment where prospects can get a feel for who you are and what you're all about. It's important that you establish credibility at every opportunity and help foster good feelings about doing business with you.

The proliferation of products and services online has inevitably led to an increase in frauds and cheats. Media stories bring some of the larger scams to light… but only after hundreds or thousands of people have been victimized. Buyers have their guard up as a matter of self-protection. It's not a case of being innocent until proven guilty. Online, you're suspect from the beginning and need to earn the trust of consumers before they'll ever buy from you.

Visitors arrive at your site presumably due to your lead generation efforts. They're interested, but unsure. Perhaps they've never heard of you. The fact that you live half way around the world is another cause for concern. Your job is to alleviate any uncertainty and make visitors feel comfortable about you, your product and business.

When you know your market and you communicate such an understanding, your prospects soon develop an affinity towards you.

Talk to your prospect as a friend. Be warm and personal. Tell them the way it is in a straightforward and truthful manner. Don't beat around the bush. Be direct and forthright - the same way you'd communicate with a friend. Show you care. Demonstrate a knowledge and respect for your audience and they'll be inclined to like you too.

Trust begins with a professional presence -- and that begins with your own domain name. It's shocking to me how many marketers attempt to sell products from a site that clearly exposes their amateur status. Domain names cost only a few dollars for a full year's use. And professional web hosting can be had for just $10 a month - or even free in some cases. So there's absolutely no need for anyone to be marketing products from a free site that also advertises their service on what should be your property. Get your own domain and find an affordable host that doesn't demand an advertising banner or pop-up window promoting their services on your site. That's all it takes to get started on the right foot.

Make full use of endorsements, testimonials, and associations. Give people something that's a little easier for them to accept and believe - like the comments of a recognized authority who has used your product.

Project an image of stability. Let people know you've been in business for x-number of years and show them your real world business address and facilities. Give them something they can relate to -- something that makes you seem like a real, legitimate business with a physical location somewhere on planet earth. It's comforting and reassuring for prospects to know that yours is a real legitimate business.

Strategy Is More Important Than Creativity

Creativity doesn't sell. It's not the creativity and design skill that go into your web site that makes a difference - it's the appeal of your message. Sure, you may get a lot of people commenting on your beautiful layout, choice of colors, fancy enhancements, and so on. But *fancy* and *beautiful* don't sell. Whatever doesn't contribute directly to sales is a waste of time, money, effort, and megabytes.

A proven online strategy is to target a specific market, deliver powerful and unique benefits -- and then introduce a truly irresistible offer. Those three elements alone account for 90% of the effectiveness of any website sales letter. That means 90% of your effort and time should focus on these key elements and only 10% of your time should be allotted to layout and design.

Visitors show up at your site with certain expectations. You've already piqued their interest, whet their appetite, or aroused their sense of curiosity to get them there in the first place. They anxiously anticipate a payoff. It's like walking into a restaurant -- you go there with the expectation of receiving a meal. Everybody does. Now, your visitors are looking for that special something to quench their thirst and satisfy their hunger. So now is the time to feed those freshly activated emotional drivers.

True prospects arrive in search of something - they don't just land on your site by accident. You triggered a spark… now it's a matter of turning that spark of interest or curiosity into a burning desire to buy now. The best way to accomplish this goal is to use proven techniques of targeting a hungry market, unveiling your most appealing benefits and introducing an offer that's too good to resist.

Think The Way Your Market Thinks

Give your prospects exactly what they want. Help them solve a particular problem. Provide an edge that will bring them closer to the magical result they dream of. Pile on benefit after benefit, so they clearly understand the tremendous value they get when they purchase from you.

Make your presentation exclusively for that particular group. If you're marketing to dog owners, resist the temptation to include the owners of different kinds of pets. Shape your offer to fit the market. Dog owners generally wouldn't be interested in knowing your product was also perfect for cats too. In fact, making such a revelation could actually harm sales. Your product might then be perceived as a 'generic' item, rather than a specific solution for a specific category of prospect.

Present your strongest benefits… then, mention the features that make key benefits possible. Provide credible proof that your product delivers what you say it does. Introduce an enticing offer and tell your prospect the exact steps he needs to take next to be able to enjoy all those promised benefits for himself.

Give your prospect all the information he could possibly need to make an intelligent decision. Leave no question unanswered… no stone unturned.

But how you go about it is equally important. Make your key components the most visually dominating parts of your copy. Use headlines, sub-headings, bullet points and frames to suggest important points - points that shouldn't be missed.

Provide Value For Your Prospect's Time

Marketing online means catering to an audience. With time at a premium, anything that wastes the precious resource of time is quickly shunned. It's crucial that you stay on target with your message. Look out for any area where you might have drifted off course. If you go off on a tangent, you're inviting the prospect to click away -- and that's exactly what he'll do.

Maintain a benefit-laden focus. When you're revealing benefits, you're discussing what the reader gets. In essence, you're talking about the reader, so you have his undivided attention. But shift gears for a moment and you may never recover. Launch into a spiel about how wonderful your company is and suddenly you've turned off your previously riveted reader.

Make it easy for readers to get your essential message by starting with the benefits of greatest importance to prospects. Highlight key points and sections of your sales letter. Make it fast, easy, convenient, and pleasurable to order from you. Maintain a prospect-centered approach and you're much more likely to retain readership and interest - essential prerequisites to getting the order.

Make An Instant Connection With Your Target Audience

Since people ultimately buy from those they know, like and trust, make an effort to establish rapport early on. Strive to make a connection with your prospect from the start. Your lead-generation ads and marketing pieces should be in alignment with the first screen of your sales letter. This tells the prospect he's arrived at the correct location, thus justifying his presence there.

First impressions are critical. If you fail to make a quick connection, your prospect will venture off to another site. Perception is everything. Exist for your prospect. Be agreeable and open - like a friend. Maintain a commitment to helping solve your prospect's problem and getting him closer to wherever he wants to go.

Perception begins as the first screen of your sales letter loads on the user's screen. You need to reach out to prospects right away - beginning with the headline.

Not only must your words be relevant and of crucial importance to your target market, your message must also appear easy to read. This means organizing the information and providing adequate spacing. It also means highlighting key areas -- without overdoing it. Online, you can use plenty of white space to make your message appear easy, understandable, and not intimidating in the least. This usually isn't an option in traditional direct mail as there's only so much space you can utilize without exceeding standard postage costs.

Short paragraphs with adequate spacing in between is quite appealing to the eye.

It tells readers 'this is quick and easy - keep reading'. It's also a good idea to avoid really long sentences. Short paragraphs, short (though somewhat varied) sentences, and short words make for easy, effortless reading.

Consistently Deliver The Information Your Audience Wants

In the online world, people travel with one hand on the trigger. The *trigger* in this case is their mouse - the one tool that puts the surfer in total control of their online experience. It's a good idea to construct your sales letter with this in mind. Bore your reader for just a second and chances are, he'll be gone forever.

Capture and sustain reader interest from the headline through to the post-script. Make your message compelling, intriguing, and interesting. Get right to the point without delay. Write each line and paragraph as though its purpose was to lead the reader to the next.

Let one compelling thought flow smoothly into the next. Continuously deliver the payoff in the form of benefits and helpful information. Instant and consistent delivery of what the prospect wants to hear is the only way to ensure that he reads on.

Provide as much information as needed to get the sale. Keep it energizing, upbeat and always about the prospect and what your product does for him.

Demonstrate your key points in interesting ways. Use metaphors the reader can relate to. Tell a compelling story to dramatize your ultimate benefit.

Keep Your Purpose In Mind As You Write

You're there to # 1 - make a sale and... #2 - forge a relationship.

The primary purpose of your sales letter is to get the sale. You want to secure a commitment from your prospect to buy. To this end, you need to understand the prospect's problems and aspirations and determine how your product delivers the ultimate solution. Presenting your unique benefits, prove them, and follow up with a strong offer -- loaded with enticement. Make the value of your offer worth many times the asking price.

Gain the attention of your target group of prospects and fuel their interest with your new discovery that will make their lives better in some way. Give them plenty of reasons for taking action now and make it exceptionally easy to order.

It's also important to remind prospects about the cost of inaction. If they fail to decide in favor of action, they're voting in favor of the status quo. Nothing will change in their lives until they change by taking action. That's the message you need to drive home in your letter.

Conduct your business with an eye to the future. Avoid any temptation to grab a quick buck and move on. Establish a sense of stability and a sterling reputation... and your business will grow on its own.

As new prospects continue to arrive at your website, they'll do so with a preconceived opinion of you. Continually delight customers and word quickly spreads. But fail to deliver what you promise or make yourself unavailable to customers and you'll soon feel the effects of a major backlash. Exceed your customer's expectations and they might pass the word on to a few close friends. But anger them and you can bet they'll tell anyone who will listen. And in the online world, this happens in record speed as word spreads like wildfire.

Nurture customers. Serve them well. Be there when they need you. Show them respect and appreciation and you'll be well on you way to success.

Simply treat people as you'd like to be treated. The golden rule still reigns supreme.

Always Stay One Step Ahead

One thing's for sure, the more successful you become online… the more competitors will try to take advantage of your success for their own gain. In the online world, competitors can literally spring up overnight and start taking customers away from you instantly. The more successful you are, the bigger the target you become.

If you want to maximize your returns and protect your business, you need to be aware of who your competitors are and what they're doing.

Your best bet is to create and sustain an element of exclusivity. Add a special feature, unique benefit, or an additional product or service -- one that would be difficult for others to duplicate.

Know what unique advantages are most appealing to prospects and stay informed about your competitors as best you can. Constantly think of new ways to add even more value, benefit, and exclusivity to your package. That way, when you need to bump up your offer even more, you'll have several ways to do it.

Why People Buy... And How To Get More Of Them To Buy From You

"Let's get right down to the heart of the matter. The power, the force, the overwhelming urge to own that makes advertising work, comes from the market itself, and not from the copy. Copy cannot create desire for a product. It can only take the hopes, dreams, fears and desires that already exist in the hearts of millions of people, and focus those already existing desires on to a particular product. This is the copy-writer's task: not to create this mass desire - but to channel and direct it."

-- Eugene Schwartz

The Controlling Force That Directs Your Prospect's Actions

Two controlling forces direct everything your prospect does. Every action taken is an action to move them away from pain... or towards pleasure. Pain and pleasure govern everything human beings do.

Your objective is to incite action; to get your prospect to place an order. To do this, you need to be aware of the forces of pain and pleasure currently dominating his thought processes and affecting his life.

Every action taken is based on the basic biological need to avoid pain... and/or a desire to gain pleasure. No one buys life insurance for the pleasure of paying large monthly premiums for the next 25 years. They buy insurance to minimize the pain and suffering of their surviving loved ones.

What fundamental force fuels the sales of homes, accessories, cars, clothing, movies, books, CD's and millions of other products? It's the pleasure... or rather the perceived pleasure that ownership of these things bring.

Become aware of the underlying impact of pain and pleasure. These forces are silently at work driving the decisions of your prospects and customers.

'Pain' and 'Pleasure' will continue to be a major force in your customer's life in the years ahead. Your ability to anticipate future specifics of pain and pleasure can have a dramatic effect on your business. If you can tap into this power at its most basic level, not just now, but down the road as well -- you'll touch a nerve with your audience and gain a receptive ear for your message.

"A good ad should be like a good sermon: it must not only comfort the afflicted, it also must afflict the comfortable."

-- Bernice Fitz-Gibbon

What is your prospect and customer thinking about? What problem, worry, anxiety, or fear is foremost on their mind? How does your product reduce or eliminate this problem? Understanding your market's greatest problem is a primary step to offering the optimum solution and profiting like never before.

What does your prospect or customer most desire? What is it that he or she would love to have, see, do, visit, enjoy, or profit from? Uncover this primary want and you've just discovered the way to get the undivided attention of those you wish to serve.

The best strategy to use really depends on your product and market. If you're marketing a product that reduces eye-strain for computer users, you have a problem, or pain to solve. If you're selling vacation packages to Las Vegas, the motive for your audience is pure fun and games.

Your mission is to tap into your prospect's natural desire to avoid pain and to gain pleasure. But while you're at it, you must understand that your prospect is apprehensive about the decision to buy and needs all the re-assurance you can provide.

According to Robert Collier, one of the all-time great copywriters, these are the 6 major motives for human action:

Love
Gain or Greed
Duty
Pride
Self-Indulgence
Self-Preservation

Joe Karbo, author of *The Lazy Man's Way To Riches* composed this list of 4 major motivators:

Immortality
Recognition
Romance
Reward

Refer to either list. What motive(s) drives your prospect? Choose the dominant appeal that's most likely to get the attention of your prospects -- and keep them interested and actively involved so they continue reading and ultimately buy.

Health foods, supplements, safety equipment, and insurance are obvious markets for the Self-Preservation or Immortality angle.

For a financial planner, stockbroker, business trainer, or restaurant franchisor, the promise of Gain or financial Reward is likely the strongest carrot one could dangle for these specific targets.

Dating services use the lure of Love and Romance to attract new clients.

Beauty treatments, massage services, vacation packages and ice cream parlors could successfully appeal to the desire for Self-Indulgence.

Now let's take this one step further.

Beyond the major motives for action are specific reasons people read every word of your message and ultimately buy your product.

Following are 103 emotional appeals to help you identify the best specific approach to use in your sales letter.

This list represents a wide range of reasons why prospects respond to individual appeals. These are the specific things prospects want - to move them towards pleasure and take them away from pain.

103 Specific Pain/ Pleasure Reasons Why Anyone Would Be Interested In Buying Your Product

To make money
To save money
To achieve comfort
To enjoy health
To live longer
To be popular
To satisfy curiosity
To gain pleasure or enhance enjoyment
To feel clean
To be praised and admired
To be in style
To satisfy an appetite
To own beautiful possessions
To attract the opposite sex
To be an individual, independent
To emulate others
To take advantage of opportunities
To get a surprise
To be successful
To make work easier
To gain prestige
To be sociable
To express creativity
To be efficient or more efficient
To protect oneself and family
To protect the future of one's family
To be a good parent
To be liked
To be loved
To express a personality
To be in fashion
To fulfill a fantasy
To be up-to-date with the latest trend
To own attractive things
To collect valuable things
To satisfy the ego

To be "first" at something
To enjoy exotic tastes
To live in a clean environment
To be strong and healthy
To renew vigor and energy
To find new and rare things
To be more beautiful or attractive
To win the affection of others
To satisfy sexual desires
To bring back pleasant memories
To be lucky
To feel important
To gain knowledge
To improve ones own appearance
To be recognized as an authority
To enhance leisure
To do things well
To get a better job
To be your own boss
To gain social acceptance
To keep up with others
To appreciate beauty
To be proud of possessions
To resist the domination of others
To relieve boredom
To gain self-respect
To win acclaim
To win advancement
To seek adventure
To satisfy ambition
To be among the leaders
To gain confidence
To get on the bandwagon
To get something for nothing
To gain self-assurance
To have safety in buying something else
To protect reputation
To "one-up" others
To relax
To replace the obsolete

To add fun or spice to life
To be in style
To conserve natural resources
To protect the environment
To make others happy
To find love
To feel intelligent
To be benevolent
To be part of a group
To prepare for the future
To feel wanted, appreciated and valuable
To work less
To save time
To have security in old age
To overcome obstacles
To avoid shortages
To avoid criticism
To avoid loneliness
To take their mind off their troubles
To avoid personal injury
To avoid damages
To avoid physical pain
To avoid loss of reputation
To avoid loss of money
To avoid trouble
To prevent unemployment
To avoid embarrassment
To get rid of aches and pains
To escape drudgery
To gain freedom from worry
To escape shame
To avoid effort
To protect possessions

People Buy When Offered A "Magic" Solution

Imagine the perfect solution to your prospect's dilemma. If you could offer magic to your customer, what would that 'magic' entail? What ideal scenario can you envision that would make your customer's life easier, hassle-free, or better in some way?

Your mission is to find utopia… and present your product as the next best thing. You want to get as close to 'magic' as you can without being ridiculous or absurd. Deliver the ultimate solution - something close to magical, even miraculous - without crossing the line. Paint a glorious picture of what is achievable, while maintaining believability.

The idea here is to add a dose of rationale and logic to your sales presentation while injecting as much magical appeal into it as possible.

Get your prospect's mindset away from the harsh reality of present circumstances and into a place of 'magic'… where their specific problems are solved forever and their dreams are fulfilled in style.

Magical solutions take your prospect out of pain and into pleasure. They produce results that seem effortless… solid gains without risk or investment… instant solutions without the hassles.

Simply do this (whatever your product entails) and "magic" happens.

There's the hard way… and then there's magic. They're at opposite ends of the scale. One method involves effort, energy, time, sweat, money, or risk. The other is simply a remote control device that instantly takes buyers where they want to go at the push of a button.

The closer you get to the side of magic, the more appeal your offer has and the easier it is to close the sale. That is… as long as the magical solution remains on the side of the believable.

Here's an example…

To the frustrated, repeat dieter who has tried everything yet now finds himself heavier than before, the magic solution would have to be in stark contrast to any other he's tried. Another radical diet plan seems like the same old approach many have suggested before. A healthier diet combined with regular exercise seems to work. But anything that requires persistent effort and discipline isn't likely to have much appeal in the marketplace. On the other hand, special beverages, pills and equipment that supposedly does the exercising for you, would have plenty of "magic appeal". It's an instant, easy solution that doesn't require any work or risk.

Now let's say that you've written a book for the weight loss market... but your methods are hardly revolutionary -- and require some basic lifestyle changes. How can you add magic to your product?

Here are a few ways to add "magic" to a weight loss information product:

> Make it incredibly easy to get started with your program
> Break it down into baby-steps that require very little effort
> Focus on one lifestyle change at a time
> Give buyers positive actions they can take while still sitting on the couch
> Show them how they can actually lose weight and enjoy their favorite desserts
> Give them fun, fast and simple ways to shed excess pounds without knowing it
> Suggest foods that speed up the body's metabolism such as hot peppers
> Suggest so-called "negative calorie" foods like celery that burn up more calories than they take on through chewing and digestion

Now, if your weight loss book was already complete, these ideas could just as easily be applied to bonus products offered as part of the package. Add magical appeal to your products and sales will soar.

People Buy When You Hit Their Hot Buttons

Understanding your market is the most important key to creating copy that sells. If you want to get through to people and really make a difference in their lives through your product, than you must get on the same wave-length.

You need to penetrate the prospective customer's mindset and connect with their thoughts. Making that connection is imperative to being heard. Tap into the existing thoughts, concerns, worries, or aspirations of your prospect -- and do so effectively -- and you'll instantly gain an attentive ear.

Know the specifics of your market. Delve deep into the issues facing these people on a daily basis. Become one of them through empathy and under-standing. When you fully understand your market on a cellular level, it's much easier to connect and communicate effectively.

Hot buttons are triggers that clearly and decisively address the issues that are most important to prospects. Hot buttons are the benefits, advantages, and incentives that make prospects 'hot' for your product or offer.

As an example...

Lets say you owned a small roofing business, and you were in the market for accounting software. What hot buttons might appeal to you?

- Easy to use without the need for years of computer experience
- Quick installation and set up
- Technical support by telephone - 24 hours a day/7 days a week
- Simple electronic filing of sales tax, employee deductions, and income tax
- Satisfaction guarantee
- Overnight shipping via FedEx or UPS

Each individual point might be very important and appealing. And if this software package were customized specifically for roofers, it would have even more magical, hot button appeal. That's the key. This particular product could easily become the program of choice for roofers because of its specific design for the roofing industry market.

A tailor-made solution would speak in standard roofing industry terms. It would help estimate prices and accurately tabulate real costs by the job, day, week, or month. In short it would save days of toil and reams of paperwork, while substantially improving accuracy. It would truly be a tool of indispensable value to the roofing contractor.

Hot button appeals are powerful when marketers take the time to assess the real *wants* of the marketplace - the 'wants' that no one else has bothered to address.

When you give people exactly what they seek, it makes it very difficult for them to resist the powerful temptation to buy.

"Yes, I sell people things they don't need. I can't, however, sell them something they don't want. Even with advertising. Even if I were of a mind to."

-- John O'Toole

Emotions come into play. Hot buttons evoke emotional responses. When you touch a nerve with your proposed solution to a problem, or aid to a dream, you fuel a compelling desire to get it and to get it now. Desire expands exponentially -- as one hot button is stacked upon another.

Each niche has different hot buttons that you must address if you want success. What appeals to one specific market might not appeal to another.

People Buy On Emotion

The fact that your prospect's pain and pleasure radar is on guard continuously, presents an opportunity for you -- the marketer. Emotions rule. All you have to do is move prospects away from a state of pain and into a feeling of pleasure.

Deliver the payoff your product offers. Let them experience all the joys of ownership in their imaginations. Make it vivid. Bring it to life with sensory appeals. Allow them to see, hear, smell, taste, and touch the actual benefits your product offers. Give them every opportunity to put themselves in the picture, happily using the product. Empower prospects by facilitating the experience of ownership.

Let them see first hand how your product enhances their life in some way. What is it about your product that makes performing a specific task, easier, faster, more effective, more satisfying, or less stressful? Give them everything you've got - everything that can make a difference.

Everyone wants the best life possible -- it's this universal desire to which we're all attuned. Let them 'feel' the end results they'll get when they actually own your product.

The more painful and pressing the problem, the more appeal any solution has to prospects. The stronger the appeal, the greater the number of potential customers you'll draw to your offer.

People buy benefits -- not products. Benefits put the prospect into the picture. Benefits give relevance and usefulness to a product. Benefits are the emotional payoff the buyer gets out of the deal.

Allowing prospects to experience the perceived benefits and advantages strengthens the desire to buy. It turns wants into desires and strong cravings. When your prospect wants it badly enough, he'll find a way to overcome any obstacle -- including price -- to get it.

"You can say the right thing about a product and nobody will listen. You've got to say it in such a way that people will feel it in their gut. Because if they don't feel it, nothing will happen."

-- William Bernbach

People Buy When The Shopping Experience Gives Them An Emotional High

Get prospects into a mental state of pure enjoyment and your chances of making the sale shoot skyward. When people are feeling good, they want to stay in that zone of emotional pleasure. Your challenge is to get them into that feel good state - to make the online experience with you one of satisfaction and enjoyment.

Much of their shopping experience while at your website involves navigating, checking out your links, reading your sales copy and (hopefully) proceeding to the order form.

In traditional retailing, there's the whole experience of going to a particular shop… experiencing the ambiance… seeing exciting new items for the first time… and browsing around until the "perfect" product is found. Sensory involvement comes into play. Smart merchants create selling environments that evoke good feelings through sight, sounds, scents, and tasty free samples.

Online, you don't have the benefit of creating an appealing physical environment - yours is a virtual store, existing only in cyberspace. But what you do have are words… and the careful use of words alone can create positive feelings that drive sales. Words are your most valuable tools.

Words command attention and build interest. Words influence and persuade. Words make you money.

Sure, you could use music files and flashy graphics on your website, but these distract and annoy prospects more than they help enhance their experience. Not only that… these files take time to download, particularly on slower computers. Your visitor is left staring at a blank or half-filled screen, waiting for it to fully load. How long will it take until these frustrated folks flee, never to return again?

Shape your prospect's environment with picture words that trigger glorious visuals and powerful, positive emotions. Create an emotional high for prospects as they envision themselves enjoying or profiting from the promised benefits.

Your success in selling online is directly dependent on your ability to take whatever it is you offer and transform it into positive energy and pleasurable feelings experienced by your prospect. Get them to experience an emotional high and they'll be much more willing to spend money at your site.

Why?

Prospects buy simply because they want to hold on to these enjoyable thoughts and feelings. The obvious way to do that is to acquire the product - the same product whose descriptive copy set off these feelings in the first place.

People Justify Buying With Logical Reasoning

People buy on emotion… and justify with logic. Of course, some purchases require little or no 'justification'. If you're selling a low cost product like a how-to book and the price is within the realm of a "pocket change" expense -- logic may not factor into the buying decision at all. But if you were selling a $5000 personal development seminar, you'd be well advised to add plenty of logic into your sales argument. After all… There's much more at stake. Prospects will want to think about it longer.

There are logical reasons and there are emotional reasons. Emotional reasons are crucial to stimulating interest and fueling a strong desire to buy. Logical reasons assure the buyer that the decision to purchase is a sound one.

Emotional reasons are benefit-related… like the feeling of pride and accomplishment you get to experience firsthand while driving the new sports car awarded to you -- for having reached your first year's sales target as a new distributor.

"Soon after a hard decision something inevitably occurs to cast doubt."

-- R. Fitzhenry

Logical reasons are based on cold, hard reality and straightforward facts. The business opportunity that offers the car is a 100% legitimate business -- therefore the entire registration fee is a tax-deductible expense, so the actual net cost to you is zero.

Now, combine emotional reasons with logical reasons...

"Get started in your own profitable business today! Follow our simple, but proven plan and you too could be driving your very own shiny new bright red Mazda RX-8 in 8 months or less -- just like Jeanne Smith and Joe Howe did!

Get started today -- all it takes is a modest investment of $99. Plus, the official receipt you get makes your business investment 100% tax-deductible, so your actual cost is ZERO! Think about it -- virtually unlimited earning capability… with the legal tax deductions only a business owner can claim. What are you waiting for?"

Logical arguments make perfect sense in the clear light of day. It's back-up support for emotionally charged benefits. Logical reasons for buying are rationalizations that reassure customers that their decision to purchase is a sound one.

Not providing logical reasons for buying can actually increase customer returns. Prospects buy when they're 'in heat' for your promised benefits. After the excitement and anticipation of these benefits starts to fade, questions begin to arise. The newly converted buyer soon begins second-guessing himself and starts to question the validity of his purchase. It could be the result of self-analysis, or…as is often the case, the effect of comments, questions, or concerns voiced by another - often a spouse, or business partner.

People Buy Unique Advantage And Special Benefits

What is it about your offer that makes it truly unique? You've got to have something that sets you apart. Without an individual advantage, you won't stand out from the crowd. Your widget will be perceived as being pretty much like every other widget in the marketplace. There's no differentiation - no distinguishing factors to make you the overwhelming favorite.

Strive to create a "wow!" response from prospects as they discover your site and your solution. Let them revel in the rare find they've uncovered as they come across the solution they've long been seeking. Make your benefits special and more desirable.

Provide an unusual advantage - something that makes your offer more valuable than any other option available -- online or offline. Add a new twist to your product. Make it do more in less time or with greater ease. Give it additional perceived value and make this value a major selling point. Add an exclusive feature - something that's only available from one source -- you.

But just adding uniqueness to your product isn't enough. Your exclusive advantage must be something that makes a noticeable difference to the prospect - not to you.

If it doesn't grab prospects as clearly being advantageous or more beneficial than other options, find something else that has more appeal. Make the advantage obvious and clearly discernible -- something that will give prospects an edge or a greater return on their financial investment.

Creating a unique marketplace advantage shouldn't be limited to products alone. You can also boost sales by making it easier, faster, safer, smarter, or better to buy from you.

How?

Streamline the process and save people time. Do everything in your power to serve them in a quick and efficient manner. Make it a "no-brainer" to order quickly, securely, and easily - like Amazon does.

People Buy When They're Offered Great Value

Few can resist outstanding value. Give your customers more bang for their buck. Don't just sell a product... offer a complete package. Totally overwhelm buyers with value and word quickly spreads. Deliver more than any logical person could ever expect - that's how you shoot your sales through the roof... that's how you create a "wow!" response... and that's how your reputation spreads and you profit like crazy from additional referral sales.

The value overload approach is the exact opposite of the discount offer. Discounting is less effective as a marketing tool. Once you start discounting, it's tough to stop. When you're selling comparable products to you competition, it's easy to get pulled into the price-cutting game. But it's a dangerous game to play... one that will likely leave you wounded and bloody from the business battlefield.

There's always someone who willingly cuts prices even further until there's virtually no profit left. And without profits, you cannot survive. Best to avoid going there altogether.

A far better strategy is to pack on the extras. Give far more in "use value" to customers than you ask from them in "cash value". Stack the deck decidedly in their favor. Give them much more than anyone could logically expect to get. Make your total package worth 5, 10, or 20 times what you actually charge for it.

This need not cost you a fortune - in fact, to spend a lot of money here really defeats the purpose. What you want to do is create a series of low-cost/ high-perceived value products and the best and easiest way to do this is with information products.

Information can be packaged in many forms. Information can be sold as physical products like books, booklets, fact sheets, reference guides, special reports, audio or video cassettes, and DVD's. Information can also be supplied in electronic formats like real audio, video clips, MP3's, membership websites, or downloadable PDF files.

Here's an example of an offer that's overloaded with value:

Items You Get:	*Actual Market Value*
1. How To Get Rich With Your Website (8 tapes & manual)	$247.00
2. Unlimited Duplication/Marketing License to: How To Get Rich With Your Website	$2,500.00
3. How To Get A Million Dollars In Free Advertising On The Internet (8 tapes & manual)	$195.00
4. Unlimited Duplication/Marketing License to: How To Get A Million Dollars In Free Advertising On The Internet	$2,500.00
5. 42 Ultimate Secrets To Making Money Online (8 tapes & manual)	$195.00
6. Unlimited Duplication/Marketing License to: 42 Ultimate Secrets To Making Money Online	$2500.00
7. Surefire Success Marketing tool Kit	$997.00
8. Turn-Key Web Sites For Items #1, #3, & #5	$1,997.00
9. Guaranteed Merchant Account Package	$195.00

Special Bonus Product - Internet Wealth Secrets CD Rom -- Complete with Unlimited Duplication/

Marketing License: $997.00

TOTAL VALUE OF PACKAGE: $12,323.00

Your Total Investment If You Reserve Before July 31: $1,497

As you can see, the combination of the full package makes the offer much more enticing.

Struggling for ways to offer additional value? Consider these:

- Free telephone or personal email access to an expert (you)
- Booklet of famous, inspirational, or motivational quotes
- Free periodic service call (free annual PC tune-up, or complimentary oil changes with new car purchase)
- Booklet or report of with Frequently Asked Questions (FAQ's)
- Workshop apron provide free with woodworking tools
- Free critiques of current advertising and sales materials
- Ezine or newsletter subscription
- Gift certificates offering discounts on other products you carry
- Official membership documentation and special privileges such as access to exclusive special events and offers
- Special Report offering 101 ways to use your product
- Video tape demonstrating new kitchen device with easy recipes
- Bonus coupons offering extended memberships or upgraded pack ages at substantial discounts
- Checklists, Summary Cards and Cheat Sheets

Whether your bonus information products are hard copy or digital versions, you can pack lots of value inside by delivering the things inquiring minds want to know. Give them an inside look and expose your trade secrets. Share helpful ideas or provide training they just can't get anywhere else -at any price. Offer tons of real and perceived value and you'll give your audience another good reason to buy from you.

It's not the actual price of your product or service that matters most, it's the value buyers get in return. It's the payoff that makes it worthy of the price.

Offer more than others do and the perceived value of your product increases accordingly. You could be selling identical name-brand products as many other online businesses. What makes you different and gives you a clear and distinct advantage over your competitors is the extra value you add to the whole package.

Added value could mean free delivery or 24-hour technical support. It could be the bonus manual that you supply with your software product, or the 3-year guarantee you offer, instead of the industry standard 1-year guarantee. Build more versatility into your product… or make it last longer. Additional uses for the same product… or extending the life cycle of your product makes it more valuable to buyers.

There are plenty of ways to add value to whatever it is you're selling. Here are a few to further illustrate this concept further:

- Gift-wrapping
- Helpful, informative articles
- Multiple-purpose packaging
- Informative newsletters or ezines
- Information sheets
- Special reports
- Maintenance or set-up tips provided for each product model
- Offering more of your main product (13 bagels with every dozen ordered, instead of the usual 12)
- Email or telephone technical support services
- Accessibility to private, information-based web sites
- Premiums or small bonus gifts

It's important to employ value-added bonuses customers really want. Give them extras they place a high value upon. It doesn't do much good to offer something of negligible appeal… or a product they could easily get elsewhere for free.

Be careful about spending too much on bonus items though. Stick to low cost/ high value items such as information, in all its various forms. It doesn't have to cost a lot to create a high degree of desire. Often these value-added premiums can be acquired at an extremely low cost, but the perceived value they add to the purchase can be worth a hundred times the cost or more. And that's exactly what you want.

People Buy From Credible Sources They Can Trust

"Any seeming deception in a statement is costly, not only in the expense of the advertising but in the detrimental effect produced upon the customer, who believes she has been misled."

-- John Wanamaker

Know that you are being judged from the start. Even before your prospect arrives at your website, they have preconceived notions, questions, concerns, and doubts.

Prospects enter your "space" questioning your credibility. They're looking to poke holes in your sales argument and they generally mistrust you from the very beginning. Prospects don't just buy into whatever you're saying -- they question it all.

Everyone has had the experience of being burned before. Somewhere along the lines in a previous transaction your prospect was ripped off and taken advantage of. Naturally this created a deep, long lasting wound. Your prospect doesn't want to repeat the experience -- or the pain.

Knowing your prospects tendency to doubt most sales claims, what can you do to counterattack this disbelief and increase sales? Answer: become an expert or authority in your field and provide all the back-up proof you can.

We all tend to believe the experts, specialists, and authority figures. Look at the reverence given to people in positions of power - doctors, judges, world leaders and other high-powered government officials.

Positioning yourself as an expert and proving that claim beyond any shadow of a doubt makes your words far more believable.

Instead of questioning what you say, prospects are more likely to merely accept it as the truth. This gives you a huge edge in perception. After all, you're no longer someone off the street trying to make a sale. Instead, you're a respected individual of high standing, specialized knowledge, and expertise - someone who should be listened to.

People Buy When Fear Is No Longer A Factor

Remove the fear prospects feel when considering a purchase and your chances of making the sale shoot sky high. No matter how good your offer sounds, unless your prospect is familiar with your business, there's always going to some fear involved. No one wants to make a bad purchase. Instead, everyone wants to be assured that they've done the right thing by placing an order.

What does your prospect fear?

> *Losing money*
> *Making a bad purchase*
> *Being ripped off*
> *Spending more than is necessary*
> *Providing a deposit, then waiting endlessly*
> *Having no recourse of action*
> *Doing business with a shady vendor*

Here's how can you reduce or eliminate specific fears that may be holding your prospects back from making a purchase:

Fear of getting a product of inferior quality - Prove your claims with plenty of testimonials.

Fear of sending money to an unknown source - Expose more of yourself and your business by providing credibility boosters such as affiliations, big-name clients, and a brief bio or introduction. Let them know you mean business and that you're there to serve people.

Fear of not getting what they thought they were getting -- Offer a straight-forward, clear, hassle-free, money-back guarantee.

Fear of spending more money than they really want to - Offer to match, or beat any other price, within a specified time limit. This assures buyers that you've done everything possible to trim the fat from your price -- giving them the maximum value possible.

Fear of making the wrong decision - Again, a strong money-back guarantee is your best bet. Make buying a safe, risk-free experience.

Fear of doing business with the wrong type of vendor - Establish a site that looks professional. Stress the number of customers served, years in business, etc. Convey stability and a history of success.

Methodically answer every objection your prospect could possibly present. Knock off each concern, one-by-one. Acknowledge the fears… then, overcome them. Use logic to explain your position as it reflects a sensible and business-like approach.

Start with a quality product and present it as though you care. Be serious, not shoddy in the appearance and presentation of your website. Introduce your product as a viable alternative solution to your prospect's problem. Deliver your argument in clear, coherent, easy-to-understand, simple everyday English. Show that you're an established entrepreneur, one with an image of professionalism - the opposite of the here today -- gone tomorrow, fly-by-night operation everyone fears when entering into a new business relationship.

Use the words of others to enhance your reputation and quietly sell prospects on you and your product. Prospects are naturally skeptical of your claims. They tend to believe third party opinions more, as long as they appear real. It's crucial that you don't edit your customer feedback for this reason. If it looks too polished or "doctored", believability comes into question.

The more you can minimize the effect of fear and the more you can make it a non-issue, the more products you'll sell. It's as simple as that.

People Buy When The Message Resonates

When prospects feel understood and listened to - they respond favorably. The sooner you can make this connection with your audience, the more likely it is you'll gain an interested and attentive ear. Give your prospect something he or she wants - a solution out of pain, or a shortcut to a pleasurable state of being.

Communicate in a way that grabs the attention and interest of your specific, targeted audience. Touch on the needs, wants, and frustrations experienced by the individual you wish to reach. These are the issues that occupy your prospects thoughts.

When you address these in a solution-oriented way, you very quickly capture attention. You'll gain an instant rapport as the prospect feels that finally, there's someone who understands his plight and can offer a workable solution. With such a connection already established, your message stands a much better chance -- not just of getting through, but of being welcomed and accepted.

With a foundation of trust already established, your prospects feel as if they know you because you know them. Without first establishing this kind of resonance, your message is just another in the crowd. It's more 'noise' to be avoided. But reveal your understanding of the issues and show how much you care about making life better for your prospect and you'll be rewarded with more business.

Here's an example...

A tool expert unveiling a new, time saving attachment for a circular saw would surely command the attention of carpenters, renovators, and building contractors. Why? The expert is seen as someone who understands the industry, the challenges of the job, and the functions of the accessory as it relates to the professional user on a daily basis.

People Buy Solutions To A Pressing Problem

It's not the physical item itself carefully packaged inside a box that buyers want - it's what they get as a result of buying the product. It's the perceived benefit they ultimately obtain that triggers the purchase. It's the thing that fixes their particular problem.

The key is to first find those who are experiencing the problem your product solves. Timing is crucial. If your solution is presented to the prospect at a time when the level of frustration is high, he'll do almost anything to reduce his pain and suffering. Your solution seems to be just the ticket. Your product offers an ideal, quick fix.

Marketing is about finding hungry markets… and then supplying the ultimate solution to help buyers experience less pain and more pleasure.

While mired in pain, your prospect wants an easy way out - a simple solution. Give him what he wants at the exact moment he realizes he must have it… and the sale is in the bag. It's about being in the right place at the right time, not about manipulation to get what you want. Help enough frustrated prospects get what they want and you'll surely get what you want in the long run. But remember to keep it uncomplicated.

The best solutions are fast and easy to implement. They're useful and interesting… and they have a far-reaching, long-term payoff. Short-term solutions may help customers feel better fast, but the good feelings soon wear off leaving the buyer more frustrated than before. Short-term solutions may very well improve one's emotional state, but relief is only temporary. It's like taking a pill to treat a symptom; the pain may subside for a while, but it soon rears its ugly head yet again.

People Buy When It's Easy To Obtain The Benefits They Want

One thing you must do in every ad, marketing piece and sales letter is to make it exceptionally easy for interested prospects to take the next step towards a purchase.

Stay on track with a single, coherent message -- something prospects can easily follow. Guide them gently from your headline, through your body copy and then on to the order page. Make it exceptionally easy to place an order in very little time and with almost no effort on their part.

Build a site that's easy to navigate… create a presentation that's sound and sensible and not confusing in the least. After all… if you confuse them… you'll lose them.

Make it impossible to dispute your clear logic. Give prospects something they can easily agree to. Get them into an agreeable spirit and mode. This is an important entry point to eventually closing the sale. Win agreement early on and prospects are less likely to disagree with you later. Baby-step them through the buying process. The more agreeable your information is, the less likely they are to challenge it and the more likely they are to place an order because doing so seems to be an easy answer.

People Buy Because You Deliver Instant Gratification

Nobody wants to wait anymore. Have you noticed this trend? Our society is moving at a much faster pace than it did years ago. It seems that advancement brings about many more choices. The problem is… there are simply too many demands on everyone's time these days.

Because time is at a premium, any delay is costly. There are only so many hours in a day… and days in a week. Naturally, many people gravitate towards anything that has the potential to save time. There's the express line at the grocery store… drive through dry cleaners and coffee shops… and automated banking machines and drivers license renewal kiosks. Online banking saves the time of waiting in line for a teller, as does online ticket purchases to shows and concerts.

How does your online solution save prospects time and deliver instant gratification?

Email makes delivering written content instantaneous. Real time merchant accounts allow for orders to be processed and shipped at the buyer's convenience -- any hour of day or night.

Instant delivery mechanisms allow hungry prospects to satisfy their cravings immediately, without the kind of delays common to traditional delivery channels. Instant gratification gives buyers exactly what they want, now. No longer is it necessary to have to wait for the payoff. Now, prospect's can simply click their mouse… and put an end to their pain and anxiety - fast and forever.

People Buy Better Alternatives

What makes your product a better choice in the marketplace? Give prospects a better alternative. Make your differences stand head and shoulders above all other available options. Extra advantages give people solid reasons for doing business with you -- as opposed to someone else.

Save your buyers time and money. Give them a solution that's easier to implement, or has fewer side effects. Make your product more versatile with multiple applications. Gives your buyers the results they want for less money, time, and effort - and make these advantages clear in your sales letter.

Adding a new twist to an existing product can make yours more appealing. Anything *new* has natural human appeal. We're conditioned to be on the lookout for the latest and greatest developments and we've come to expect upgrades, improvements, new versions and editions on a regular basis.

When your product is clearly the better choice, more buyers will naturally gravitate towards you - as long as you educate them about your unique attributes.

People Buy Convenience

Convenience is about service. Make it easy to navigate throughout your site and to read your information. Organize the details so it's effortless to find the information prospects want. Design your site to make it quick and easy to fulfill the 'wants' of your market.

Your objective is to get visitors to react to your sales message by proceeding to your order page and completing the transaction. As simple, straightforward and painless as you can make it… you're still faced with a formidable task.

Imagine your prospect as someone who's unwilling to move a muscle for anything - even for something as great as your product. A pressing problem weighs heavily on his mind. A genuine, viable solution would help solve the dilemma, but he's tired, stressed out, and easily distracted. Finding a solution is a daunting task - one that could take weeks, or months.

Now, picture your prospect's delight when he arrives at your site. Suddenly, there in everyday English, right before his eyes is the answer to his specific problem. It's the remedy he's been looking for all along.

The key lies in being in the right place at the right time -- when the prospect is ready to take action. You're there when your prospect is thinking about a solution. That's what offering convenience is all about.

Not only do you promise to give the buyer what he wants... but you also make it exceptionally easy to get it. Minimum clicks... minimum time... minimum effort... and maximum payoff. It's an ideal answer - the perfect solution.

Embrace convenience every step of the way. Consider your prospect's total experience with your business. Examine every facet including shopping, delivery of information, ordering, and payment options. Look also at your customer service, technical support, exchange and upgrade options... and make those as convenient and hassle-free as possible for the customer.

Make your copy easy to read without effort or strain. Stick to one message only and lead prospects sequentially to the order page.

People Buy When Given The Right Solution At The Right Time

Timing is another key to getting more folks to buy from you. You've got to 'strike while the iron's hot'. It's about getting your message in front of prospects while they're most anxious for a solution.

The guy selling umbrellas to outdoor concert-goers as the heavy downpour begins, is in the right place at the right time. The more obvious the immediate need... the greater the frustration... or the deeper the desire... the more likely it is you'll gain an enthusiastic ear and a new customer.

It's all about targeting your communications and reaching a market that's already hungry for what you have to offer. Tapping into an existing market is a much more expedient way to succeed than trying to 'create' a market by educating customers.

People Buy Results, Not Products

Results are what everyone wants. It's the payoff they get as a result of buying the product, not the product itself. If you're selling 'products' it's going to be long, hard struggle up success mountain. Focus instead on the results - the pleasurable benefits -- buyers get and you can take the express elevator to the top.

The potential for positive results is what triggers strong emotions. It's these emotions that dominate your prospect's mind and drive his behavior and actions. Results are the appealing carrot dangling before his eyes. It's there to be claimed - well within reach.

Stress *results* and the act of selling gets easier. It's exciting for prospects when they can envision themselves on the other side of the fence -- using, enjoying, or profiting from whatever you offer. You don't have to push your product on anyone. Show them the results that are possible to attain -- just as others have done before -- and you'll help them sell themselves on your product.

The more effective you are at enabling prospects to see themselves in the picture getting the same kind of results, the more you'll sell. You want your prospect to feel that the same kind of end result is well within grasp.

People Buy Due To The Special Incentives Offered

Incentives are all the things you include in your offer to stimulate response and sales. Bonus products, guarantees, introductory offers, and special payment plans are strong incentives, designed to better serve buyers and give them more than their money's worth.

The purpose of incentives is to make your sales proposition so overwhelming in the buyer's favor that placing an order today is the only intelligent action to take. To do anything else would mean missing out on your life changing, "deal of the decade".

Incentives are little nudges designed to get your slothful prospect out of a state of fear, doubt, and inaction into one of confidence, hope, and positive action. Your mission in assembling a power pack of incentives is to get prospects to swing into 'buying mode' and the best way to do that is to load on the positive rewards, bonuses, and assurances to make your offer a dandy - one that no sane prospect could, in good conscience, refuse.

Provide an overload of buyer incentives and you weaken the force field of inertia by magnetically pulling prospects towards you. The more appealing the incentives, the more you stack the deck in favor of action -- the stronger the pull of the magnet. Incentives overcome reasons for not buying.

What elements could be considered incentives?

> *Great value ($100 worth for $10)*
> *Special Pricing*
> *Volume Discounts*
> *Bonus Gifts, Accessories, and Information Products*
> *Guarantees and Warranties*
> *Fast, Easy Searching, Shopping, and Ordering*
> *Quick, Easy, No-Hassle Returns or Exchanges*
> *Exclusivity or Status such as a special membership*
> *Enjoyable Overall Buying Experience*
> *Solves A Problem - The Exact Problem Plaguing the Customer*
> *Convenience - Acquiring Product, Shopping Experience, Actual Use*
> *Rare Offer or Opportunity*
> *Back Up Support or Long-Term Added Value*
> *An Easy First Step -- Test Drive or Trial Run*

Incentives trigger action... and the stronger the incentives -- the greater the inclination to buy.

Pack your sales message with as many high-demand incentives as you possibly can. Make prospects want what they sense they need. Emphasize what they'll lose out on by not taking action immediately. Get them to feel the pain of another missed opportunity.

Why People Don't Buy

*"The only way to get someone to do what you want them to do
is to get them to want to do it."*

-- John Yeck

Knowing what makes prospects turn the other way is just as important as knowing what makes them buy. Often it's the little things that cost you sales - pages that take too long to load... links that don't work the first time... even simple spelling mistakes can cost you sales.

Once you've completed your sales letter, it's well worth reviewing in search of anything that could be turning prospects away from your proposition. Spot the potential pitfalls before launching your sales letter. Have others review your work as well. You'll be glad you took the time to do this the minute you spot the first potential obstruction.

People Don't Buy Exaggerated Claims

Most people view advertising with a high level of skepticism. They take whatever claims they read and hear with a grain of salt. They suspect marketers will do just about anything to make the sale. Many do. But you'd be well advised to stay on the straight and narrow. Any claim that cannot be backed up 100% should be eliminated from your copy.

If you stretch the truth even a little, you know it. If you know you're exaggerating, many prospects will pick up on that subtle signal through your communication. If they suspect a fabricated tale, they'll never trust you with their money. But there is a simple solution: don't lie.

Use all the enticement and powers of persuasion you can generate. But never cross the line. If you do and you're found out, the marketplace will never trust you again. Remember, your mission should be success over the long term. You're not merely interested in making a sale today... you want to foster a lifelong relationship with each and every customer.

It's important that your message appears credible. Avoid the use of multiple exclamation marks (!!!) and adjectives -- often these are signs of an over-hyped message. It's the kind of 'in-your-face' hard selling that doesn't go over well on the web.

People Don't Buy From Amateur Marketers

You could have the hottest, most desirable product -- perfectly suited to your target consumer. But when prospects arrive at your website, they see flashing images, colors that blend, rather than contrast… numerous pop-up windows and banners… and a general lack of organization. All are signs of an amateur marketer at work.

If you look the part, that's how you'll be judged. What's worse is that the opinion people get from their first exposure to your site gets transferred directly to your product. A shoddy presentation suggests that the product may also suffer from the same kind of flaws. It may be unfair… but this is the kind of association that can easily develop.

Spelling mistakes, typos, unreadable type, and confusing links must be corrected beforehand. Make it easy for prospects to get your essential message, clearly - cleanly. That means an organized path that ultimately leads to a natural conclusion. It also means legible type of at least 10 points - and a color that strongly contrasts with the background. To do otherwise will brand you an amateur, discredit your marketing message, and turn off many would-be buyers.

People Don't Buy From Over-Designed Sites

"Great designers seldom make great advertising men, because they get overcome by the beauty of the picture - and forget that merchandise must be sold."

-- James Randolph Adams

It's easy to get wrapped up in the technology -- to want to use these newly discovered tools and acquired skills on your website. But don't let technology get in the way of your sales message.

Slick, overproduced websites might appeal to the designer's sense of pride, but they do little to sell prospects on your goods. You're better off to keep it simple, direct, and clear. Save the bells and whistles for the used car dealer down the street. Adding additional elements to make your site look more attractive only adds to page load times. The longer it takes to load, the lower the number of visitors who'll stick around waiting.

It's information that online users want - not fancy graphics and design. Use your layout and design to facilitate an efficient delivery of the information your prospects want to know about.

People Don't Buy From Clever, Catchy, Or Humorous Ad Copy

Prospects don't visit your site to get a chuckle. They aren't there to be entertained. They're not amused by catchy headlines, teaser copy, or unusual graphics. Save these for the corporations who pour millions into "creative" television spots that satisfy egos and win awards… but fail to attract large numbers of buyers. The reality is that as direct-response tools, often these ads fail miserably.

Any of these approaches actually diminishes the effect of your sales letter. It takes the focus off the message and drops it squarely on the technique or method of delivery.

It's a safer bet and always a more effective approach to stick to those benefits most appealing to your target market. You have but one opportunity to impact your prospect's life and generate a response. Why waste the opportunity trying to be cute or funny? That doesn't make any sense. You want response and the most likely way to ensure a good response is to follow simple direct response techniques.

People Don't Buy When They're Uncertain

Uncertainty creates uneasiness. If you're product is new in the marketplace, you've got to work harder to prove it's worthiness to prospects.

Solicit user feedback and use that feedback in the form of testimonials in your sales letter. Let prospects know that others have thoroughly tested your product and the results fully support your advertising claims.

If prospects are hesitant to buy because they're not yet comfortable with you or your business, give them more information. Add a brief bio and a few photographs. Show your 'bricks and mortar' business where all orders are received and shipped. Mention the affiliation or association you share with your market. Help your prospect get comfortable with you. Put him at ease. Answer the most common questions on a separate Frequently Asked Questions (FAQ) page. The more they know, like and respect about you, the more they'll trust you.

Ease any concern over credit card use online by providing safe and secure ordering options. This is less of an issue today than it used to be as many more services are available. A secure order form is an obvious answer... but not the only one. Telephone and fax ordering is still preferred by some people. Give them the option so they can choose the ordering method they prefer.

One option I've used problem-free for years is secure email ordering. It's very simple. Just advise buyers to submit their credit card details in two separate emails. In the first email, they send the first two sets of numbers. For a Visa order, it would look like this: xxxx xxxx. The second email follows with the last two sets of numbers and the expiry date - xxxx xxxx 03/12. Of course you'll need their name and complete mailing address too.

This system has worked like a charm and doesn't require anything beyond a simple email address. With this system, a hacker would have to intercept two separate messages and be able to put them together to steal the information - a highly unlikely scenario.

People Don't Buy If The Product Isn't A Good Fit

Targeting your market is a fundamental step to success. The only people who'll ever buy from your sales letter are those to whom the benefits appeal. If they're not a good prospect to begin with, no amount of persuasive copy will ever convince them to fork over their dough. That's why all your lead generation efforts should be directed at 'grade-A' prospects only -

those most interested, capable, and likely to buy. Other 'traffic' won't lead to sales very often.

You want only qualified prospects to arrive at your site based on their predetermined interest. Then it's up to your sales letter to close the deal. Remember, good quality prospects arrive with high expectations, interest, and excitement. But that doesn't mean they're about to spend any money. You need to fuel their interest and propel their desire to the level where they simple must have what you're offering. Move them with your words every step of the way.

Make sure any purchase is the right one from the customer's perspective. You want delighted customers... not disappointed ones. That's why it's so important to avoid trickery and deceit at all costs. It's not just about making the sale today... but about making the sale stick (no refund) and acquiring a long-term customer.

People Don't Buy If They Feel They're Being Pushed

You've got to realize that your prospect is in control of the buying process. Selling online means pulling readers inside in an inviting way.... not pushing your product upon them in an attempt to generate revenue.

Pushing products creates a feeling among prospects that you're trying to gain an upper hand, trying to take control of the situation. Trying to control prospects is pointless. It only instills a sense of fear... and a fearful prospect will never buy.

Guide them. Provide a road map that directs them to their desired destination. Give them the opportunity and lead the way. Let them know they're in total control and the fear melts away.

People Don't Buy What They Need -- They Buy What They Want

Needs are uninspiring and unemotional.

'Wants' on the other hand, are the driving force behind all but the most rudimentary of purchases. Get your prospect to want it and you've moved much closer to a sale.

"No matter how much they NEED what you're selling, if they don't WANT it, they won't BUY it!"

-- John Counsel

Needs are purely logical... while wants are emotional. Remember, it's emotions that are the driving force. Whenever the two -- logic and emotion -- come into conflict, emotion invariably wins.

You could sell on emotion alone. But anything beyond the petty cash or pocket change expenditure would be difficult to sell using just logic. The most effective approach is to employ a combination of both emotion and logic.

People Don't Buy When There's No Clear Cut Advantage

Offering the same thing that's readily available from numerous other sources is not the most effective route to online success. You've got to offer something more. If not, why should anyone take a chance on buying from you - an unknown entity?

If prospects already have an established supplier, there's no need to find another -- unless of course, they're unhappy for some reason. If they can meet their shopping requirements from another source, perhaps one that's close by or better known, there's little incentive to venture out online in search of another source.

You need to offer more - something special... something unique... a clear-cut benefit or extra advantage. If it's not very appealing to at least check out your offer, no one will.

People Don't Buy Again If They Weren't Satisfied The First Time

Can you remember being disappointed with a particular buying experience? What kind of feelings did the experience leave behind?

Chances are, you'll never go back to buying again from the same source and you've probably shared your experience with others. One bad experience can cost untold thousands of dollars in lost revenue over the years. Yet, this is a common problem online - even amongst corporations and big-names who should clearly know better.

Personally, in the past year, I've had at least 3 such experiences online. One business never shipped all the products I was promised in the offer. When this was brought to their attention... they offered an excuse and another promise to deliver. Still nothing.

On another occasion, I was overcharged. The merchant in this case was using a third-party billing arrangement and suggested I contact this organization instead. I never was compensated and vowed to never buy from this individual again.

The third disappointment occurred with a downloadable software program. When I couldn't get it to work properly on my system, I contacted the seller. At this point I was given the contact information for the technical person behind the product, whom I was assured would help.

As it turned out, I could never reach this individual. Fortunately, I was able to solve the problem myself after spending an extra hour or so trying various options. What's interesting to me is that the seller never bothered to follow up to ensure that I was satisfied. A little ironic I thought, since this particular firm stresses its "superior" customer service in their ads. It may be a minor point... but it certainly changed my view of the company.

Think about all the possible reasons why prospects might not buy from you. Develop a plan to counter act all such reasons and excuses. Convince them that your way is a better way for them to go.

It's important that you take the time to address all customer service issues and handle them in a sound, professional manner. Give prospects one small reason to not buy and they'll seize it. Inaction is always easier than action - regardless of the payoff. People establish their own comfort zones and bad habits that are often extremely difficult to break. The challenge is to make your offer so alluring that it helps move even the most sluggish of prospects into a buying frenzy. Fix your faults first.

Emotions Are Key

"Everyone -- no exceptions - responds to well-written, persuasive, emotionally based copy. Not everyone can write it, that's why copywriters are often paid so much, but no one can escape its power."

-- Dr. Joe Vitale

Why Emotional Copy Sells More Products

As humans, we're governed by our emotions. Emotions are experienced as feelings and the way we feel determines the actions we're willing to take.

Consciously, we're aware of an action that needs to be taken. We need to carry the trash out to the curb. We need to get that assignment completed before the impending due date. And we need to do something about those pesky weeds in the garden. But until we feel like doing it -- until the motivation is sufficient to make us want to do it -- most of us will simply put it off, even indefinitely.

Why? Human beings are driven by emotion. It's the persistent desire to experience pleasure and the need to avoid pain that dictates what we do in a given situation. If it seems too painful, we avoid it like the plague. That is… until further avoidance would cause even more pain. Then we tend to take the least painful route.

When the promise of a pleasurable payoff is dangled before your prospect, he's naturally pulled towards it. Emotional copy triggers an emotional response. The key is to tap into an existing desire. The moment you hit the right hot button, your prospects emotions become activated and aroused.

Emotions clearly are the driving force of behavior. People react to emotional copy. It grabs prospects and excites their senses. Emotionally charged copy engages and involves prospects by fueling their already existing fires of desire. It always produces a reaction when it's in alignment with the prospect's problems, anxieties, fears, goals, hopes, dreams, and aspirations.

The deciding factor in any buying situation is always emotional. People live with their emotions on their sleeve and are naturally drawn towards compatible opportunities that help them experience more of the good feelings and less of the bad. They decide to buy or not to buy based on emotion -- only to later justify it with the smallest measure of logic. Most sales are made with 90% emotion and only 10% logic. So, infusing your sales copy with a healthy dose of emotion is crucial to making an impact on any audience.

The Number One Key To Writing With Emotion

Purpose, passion, and enthusiasm makes your writing come alive. True passion cannot be faked... it has to be sincere. And a sincere desire to help your prospect get what he wants has magical appeal in the marketplace. When you truly care about your prospect and you fully believe in your product 100% -- you quite naturally command an attentive audience. Readers sense your sincerity and are pulled towards your message and are much more receptive to your words.

You've got to care about the people you serve. You've got to want to help them. And when you're so enthused and confident in your product, those feelings are literally transferred through your words to the heart and soul of the prospect.

Writing with emotion is much easier when you understand the market you serve. Understanding the specific emotional motivators of your reader makes it easy to hit the target with your copy. You'll develop an instant rapport because of your understanding of the prospect's problems and desires. Then, it's just a matter of transferring your feelings about your 'found' solution with 100% conviction. Do so and you'll automatically be writing emotional copy - copy that will definitely have an impact on the reader.

Connect *needs* with *wants*. Merge the two of them. Make the need a powerful want so prospects are not only inclined to take action - but, compelled to do so. Needs are logical... wants are emotional. Convert the need into something more desirable. Now you have something that appeals to prospects and lures them to action. Without fueling the desire, you won't move a lot of product out the door.

How To Be Sure You're Addressing The Right Emotion

Clearly identify the problems and desires of your reader and you'll have uncovered the key to tapping into their dominant emotional hot button.

No one reads your sales letter or buys from you without a compelling reason to do so. The reason is the problem, anxiety, worry, or deeply rooted desire. The reason is always emotional. It's the 'symptom' prospect's want to address and it's this thought that is first and foremost on their minds as they arrive at your sales page.

Knowing the symptom common to your market is fundamental to offering the ultimate answer or problem-solving solution. Without a pain-inducing problem or the imagined pleasure that comes with a goal attained - you don't have a market. There's no emotional target to which you can address your message, no symptom to command your cure.

Fortunately, we thrive on progress, advancement, growth, and expansion on every front. It's human nature to want new and better things and to constantly improve our lives in some way. There's no shortage of problems or desires. It's simply a matter of identifying the specific hot buttons of your target market and hitting them hard and fast in your sales copy.

How To Write Emotional Copy

A sound understanding or your prospect's current conditions or circum-stances gives you the background to craft a compelling sales message. Where they are now in their lives is at the opposite end of the scale from where they want to be. The purpose of your product and offer is to bridge the gap.

Current Circumstances -- Desired Results

When you arrive on the scene via your sales letter, your prospect is on the left side of the scale. He might feel frustrated, stressed out, annoyed, or disappointed. In general, he feels pain.

"The philosophy behind much advertising is based on the old observation that every man is really two men - the man he is and the man he wants to be."

-- William Feather

What would take him out of this painful state and into one of bliss is your magical solution. Where your prospect is now is not where he wants to be. He wants to be at the other end of the scale - where pleasure exists and pain is nothing but a distant memory.

Here the problem is solved and the desire fulfilled. Your mission is to help the prospect escape the pain of the present and express-route them to the other side - where pleasure abounds.

Sell the *magic* and you'll be selling with emotion. Get the prospect to realize how close he is to what he really wants. Create a scenario not just of possibility, but one of probability. Getting to the side of magic must be easy, relatively fast, and risk free. It has to appear within comfortable reach. Fill your prospect with hope and then carve the path straight to the goal.

Qualities of Emotionally-Charged Copy

Emotional copy makes an instant connection with your prospect because it promises the answer he seeks. Hard-hitting emotional copy quickly triggers desires deep within. Strong, on-target emotional copy grabs the prospect by the jugular. He senses immediately that your message is different, relevant, important and just the thing he's been searching for. Emotional copy is engaging copy - something that sustains the prospects keen attention and interest.

This should come as no surprise, as you simply uncovered an existing desire and addressed it with precision and persuasive power. Good copy makes the ultimate result appear attainable. It comes across as a strong promise that's readily accepted and believed.

Effective emotional copy is active copy. It involves prospects, activates their senses and fuels their hopes and dreams.

A purely logical statement has a plain vanilla quality about it. It's straight-forward and bland. It just sits there on the screen or printed page. But inject emotion into it and your copy comes to life. It touches the reader in a special way and fans the flame of desire that's been simmering, like a dormant volcano that's now ready to erupt in a fury.

Let's take a look at two different markets- the business opportunity market and the weight loss market - and see how an emotional meaning differs from a logical one.

Business Opportunity Market

Appeal: To Make Money

Logical interpretation:
> Improve financial future
> Increase net worth
> Make a career change
> Pay off debts

Emotional Interpretation:
> Earn Unlimited Income
> Achieve Financial freedom
> Live your dreams
> Achieve new status
> End your money worries forever - even get rich
> Have all the "toys" you want - cars, boats, home electronics, and a beautiful home
> Vacation several times a year

Weight Loss Market

Appeal: Lose Weight Now

Logical appeal:
> Improve your overall health
> Lower your risk of heart attack and stroke

Save money by spending less on food

Emotional appeal:
    Look fabulous in a bathing suit
    Turn heads at the beach
    Look wonderful for that special occasion (wedding, anniversary, graduation, reunion, etc.)
    Listen to what others say about you now
    Be admired by others - particularly those of the opposite sex
    Feel good about yourself
    Accomplish something on your own
    Buy a whole new wardrobe - get the latest fashions and look fabulous wearing them
    Look years younger

Which appeal has more *magic* in it?

I think you'll agree that although the logical reasons may be sound and true, most people would be more motivated to action by the emotional appeals presented.

Think of the copy you could write using the points classified as 'emotional'. These naturally evoke images and help you paint the most enticing of scenarios. The logical points might be every bit as important -- even more so - but what gets people to read your copy and respond is emotionally charged, benefit-oriented copy.

Other Ways To Inject Emotion

Use fear to trigger anxiety and compel prospects into action. Let them know that you can only help them if they're willing to help themselves by taking action. Convey the details about the exciting benefits that can be theirs - but only through action now. Remind prospects about everything they'll miss out on should they fail to seize the opportunity. Hint at their current pain. Agitate it just a little. Be clear about your positive alternative… and place the responsibility of a brighter future squarely on their shoulders. Give them everything they want to achieve all they desire… but be clear about what they need to do to get it.

Create a desire to find out more about your proposition. Plant the seed of possibility. Tempt, tease, and tantalize your prospects. Give them a sample of what you have to offer... and lure them inside. Use ellipses -- a series of 3 dots (...) -- to set the stage and create a feeling of anticipation and suspense. Give them just enough to activate a powerful emotional trigger and then shift gears ever so slightly. It's not about deception but about capturing and securing your audience's attention before you unveil your entire package.

Inject feeling and emotion with action words. Talk about the prospect getting, enjoying, feeling, experiencing, or profiting from the benefits you offer. Anything you can preface with the word 'you' puts the prospect clearly in the picture.

Consider these alternates for your sales copy:

You win
You uncover or discover
You benefit from
You earn
You reap
You obtain
You enjoy
You discover
You have
You learn
You secure
You end up with
You achieve
You luxuriate
You reach
You mingle
You lounge
You travel
You build
You garner
You find
You profit from
You gain access to

All of the words from the list above that follow "you" are verbs - action words. Activate your copy using words like these. They involve the reader and trigger mental pictures of the promised reward. Prospects love to hear about themselves. This kind of a phrase appeals to prospects because it's always about them and what they get from a given proposition. The "you get" phrase or any other like it ensures that what follows is a prospect benefit.

Communicate with energy, intensity, and enthusiasm. Do this and you're communicating with emotion. Enthusiasm is contagious. It's the fuel that turns a spark of desire into a raging flame. Enthusiasm evokes the kind of positive emotions humans crave. Positive feelings lead to action and action is the name of the game.

Key Points To Remember About Writing With Emotion

1.   Use emotional copy often. Remember, prospects buy on emotion and only later justify with logic. It may take lots of emotion to win the sale… but only a small amount of back up to justify it.

2.   Increase the intensity of your emotional copy to a feverish pitch. Don't hold back. Lay it on the line for maximum impact. You want to be absolutely certain that the emotional appeal has done its job.

3.   The more genuine your enthusiasm - the more likely it is that you'll influence prospects with your words. Prospect's have an innate ability to sniff out the artificial. They don't buy it. Sincerity comes from the heart. If it's not sincere -- it's perceived as hype.

4.   Appeal to the "greed gland" whenever possible. This isn't just a business opportunity appeal that works, most like to get as much in their basket for as little cash outlay as possible. The magic of a strong offer is its appeal to the greed gland. The more you can bundle into your package, the more likely it is you'll overcome fear and inertia and get the sale.

5.   Organize your information for maximum emotional appeal. Gather all the facts, figures, data, experiences, and customer stories and arrange them to fit the existing "wants" of your market.

6.   Make visiting your site a pleasurable experience for everyone. Allow every prospect to feel your enthusiasm and eagerness to serve. Make it so they not only satisfy their hunger and get the benefit of your product when they buy… but that they also feel great about the overall experience

"You see with your eyes. You hear with your ears.
But you listen with your emotions."

-- Bob Proctor

The Sales Letter Plan

"The secret of getting ahead is getting started. The secret of getting started is breaking your complex and overwhelming tasks into small manageable tasks, and then starting on the first one."

-- Mark Twain

The Purpose Of A Plan

Anxious to get started writing your sales letter? Good. I strongly urge you to begin with a plan. With a simple plan or outline in place, you'll be armed with all the essentials you need to create a powerful and persuasive piece.

It doesn't matter what your writing project is - book, report, or sales letter. Planning makes life easier. It organizes your thoughts. It gives you a roadmap to follow so you're never stuck at a dead end. A sales letter plan forces you to think things through up front -- before you write -- making the actual writing much easier and giving it a smoother flow.

Planning facilitates productivity. It forces you to think clearly and focus on the important areas, while providing an overview of the project. There's no question -- a sound plan does work in your favor.

When you get right down to it, a sales letter plan helps you:

- Gather Important Information
- Organize and Assess All Available Data
- Assemble Key Sales Letter Components
- Prioritize Benefits Based On Their Appeal To Prospects
- Confirm That The Important Ingredients Are All Present Before You Begin

A sales letter plan simplifies the actual writing. It gives you concrete material from which to work. It naturally dictates the direction you take, and it enables you to follow along a road map to the successful completion of your sales letter.

The more detailed your plan, the easier it is to write compelling sales copy. With a plan, you're never left wondering what to write next. All the essential information is right before your eyes -- making it quicker and easier to form interesting and persuasive copy.

"When it comes to writing copy, far too much attention is paid to the actual writing and far too little is paid to ferreting out facts about that which the copywriter is trying to sell."

-- Gary Halbert

Planning isn't just a means to an end, however. Yes, having a completed sales letter plan in front of you is very important. But the hidden value of your plan lies in the thinking processes that go into completing it. As even the most basic of plans takes shape, you'll discover valuable ideas, key points, and concepts to employ. A plan literally forces you to think things through ahead of time.

After you've used this method to write a few sales letters, you'll see how getting it all recorded on paper helps you tremendously.

Crafting a sales letter plan does take time -- perhaps this is why so few do it. But the time and effort expended always pays a worthwhile dividend. A plan gives you direction, power, and focus. It puts you on a straight path towards your goal.

Identify Your Goals and Objectives

Step one of your sales letter plan is to state your goals and objectives.

What are your priorities? What kind of measurable results do you desire and how do you plan to get there?

Getting clear about what it is that you want is an important first step. When you're clear about the target, reaching it is much easier. Knowing what it is you seek gives you a target to aim for - a large, stationary target. When you're not crystal clear about your goal, it's an uphill battle. It's as though you're trying to hit a moving target, and you're never quite sure where you stand.

Choose a number. Not just any number… but a figure you feel is attainable. Since your sales efforts are an ongoing process rather than a one-shot campaign, you can set your sales goals by the month or year.

As an example, you might choose 100 sales per month, or 1200 per year. With a $97 product, that's $9,700 in monthly sales… or $116,400 for the year.

Set a target for both sales and the percentage of conversions. You'll have many times more visitors than actual buying customers. Not everyone buys, in fact, most don't. To generate one sale, you might need to attract 10, 50, or 500 visitors to your sales page - depending on the variables involved. Converting one in ten represents a conversion percentage of 10% -- one in five hundred means your conversion rate is .2%. The lower the number of visitors you require to achieve your goal, the higher your conversion ratio and the better it is for you.

Using the example above…

If you could sell one out of every ten prospects (a 10% conversion rate), you would need 1000 visitors each month to reach a monthly target of $9700. A conversion rate of 1%, would require 10,000 visitors, while a .2% response means you'd need 50,000 visitors to achieve the same result.

Now that you've decided the kind of results you want, it's time to get clear as to how you're going to achieve it. Consider the following question…

What's the one action you want readers to take after reading your letter?

Are you going for a direct sale… or merely asking prospects to raise their hands in an expression of interest? It's important to decide your strategy early on. You need to know the specific outcome you want.

Whether your letter is designed to generate leads or close sales, your objective should be to foster good vibrations and positive feelings. You want to create a comfortable, pleasurable environment where prospects take away nothing but good feelings about you, your product, and your company.

Since closing sales and building profits is ultimately what it's all about, this book will focus on sales letters that go for the sale every time.

Define Your Market

First, find a hungry market. Then, shape your offer to satisfy this already existing hunger. That's the logical way to do business. But unfortunately, most people get it all wrong. They find themselves in a particular industry out of habit. Or, they've acquired the rights to a product guaranteed to be the next "pet rock". Problem is… they've done so before clearly identifying a plentiful, hungry market that would do almost anything to get this hot new product into their own hands.

Identifying and fully understanding your target market is a crucial prerequisite to business success. Knowing the type of individual you're aiming for and understanding their habits, preferences, interests, and lifestyle, makes it much more likely that you'll be able to reach them with your message of importance.

Who exactly is your ideal customer? Can you describe this kind of individual? Start by listing some basic demographic information that typically defines your prospects and customers. Consider details such as age, geographic location, spoken language, occupation, association or group memberships, outside interests, income, hobbies, and preferred reading material. Try to get as realistic a picture of your typical prospective customer as you possibly can.

After you've compiled your basic demographic information, begin to develop a psychological profile. What thoughts, worries, anxieties, or problems, weigh heaviest on your prospect's mind? What does he want? Think in terms of having, doing, being, earning or acquiring and try to isolate the deepest desires of your prospective customer - desires that your product can fulfill. Look at how these people make purchases and consider the likelihood of them buying from your website.

Creating both a demographic and psychographic profile enables you to piece together an actual 'sketch' of your prospects and customers. Assembling basic information about those you wish to reach gives you a composite of the target - someone you've defined as being the right prospect for your offer.

When you can picture a living, breathing individual with problems to solve and desires to fulfill, it's much easier to craft a message that gets noticed -- and acted on.

"If you can't turn yourself into a customer, you probably shouldn't be in the ad writing business at all."

-- Leo Burnett

Identify Your Competitors Strengths and Weaknesses

The next step is to review current and potential competitors. Get to know the other players in the game. Anticipate the arrival of new competing forces as the web continues to grow and word of your success spreads.

Study known competitors - both online and offline. Visit their websites and observe their marketing material and processes. Look at what they offer now and compare current offers to previous proposals. How do competitors entice prospects? What special incentives do they use?

Take a good hard look at competing products. Dissect them - one by one. Take a look inside to see what makes them tick. Evaluate their strengths and identify potential weaknesses.

Examine the various guarantees offered by others. Do these guarantees help to encourage additional sales from unsure prospects? Does any guarantee stand out among the rest by completely favoring the prospect - in effect, making the proposal entirely risk free?

How are your competitors perceived in the marketplace? What reputation do they have? How deeply entrenched is their brand on the psyche of the prospective customer?

Assessing the competition gives you an understanding of your opponents before you step into the ring. Not only will you have a better idea of the challenges facing you, but you'll also be able to create a more appealing offer and a stronger guarantee, giving you an advantage right off the bat.

Get To Know Your Own Product Inside-Out

Become an expert on your own product. Chances are, you already have some in-depth knowledge… you may even have created it on your own. But now is the time to break it down and look at it with fresh eyes -- as any prospect would.

Write down every physical attribute -- every feature -- you can think of, anything that describes or defines the product itself.

"There's no secret formula for advertising success, other than to learn everything you can about the product. Most products have some unique characteristic, and the really great advertising comes right out of the product and says something about the product that no one else can say. Or at least no one else is saying."

-- Morris Hite

If your product was a book, your feature list might include things like:

    Number of pages
    Printing format - single sided or double sided
    Typeface style and size
    Width of columns
    Page layout
    Average number of words per page
    Type of cover
    Type of binding
    Size and shipping weight
    Publisher/ copyright holder
    Number of chapters or main sections
    Table of contents, index, and appendices
    Major topic and sub-topics covered
    Available formats - hard copy or digital

How product is shipped
Order packaging and fulfillment
Bonus items included with order
About the author
Recommended resources

In short, you want to write down every conceivable component or feature of your product. Don't overlook this step thinking you have all this information tucked away in the back of your mind. Get it down on paper or open up a new file on your computer.

The next step is to take each of the features listed and convert it into an appealing benefit to the buyer. One exercise I like to do when tackling a new sales letter project is to get out a fresh sheet of paper, and draw a line down the page from top to bottom. On the left side, write "FEATURES" - on the right, "BENEFITS". You can use the *Features and Benefits Chart* included at the end of this chapter as a template.

Features are all about products. It's all about the physical thing the customer gets in exchange for his money. A feature is any specific product detail.

Benefits, on the other hand, are about prospects and customers. Features are about products and benefits are about people. Therefore, benefits matter most. They represent the true value in the customer's eyes. Benefits are the primary reason prospects become buying customers. It's what having the product will do for them.

Now go through your list of product features and turn each into at least one benefit.

Continuing with our example above…

If your book was a lengthy tome of some, 300+ pages, you can transform that fact into an appealing benefit…

"You get 347 full-size pages jam-packed with hundreds of "secret" strategies, tips, and little-known tactics you can use today to shoot your web traffic through the roof!"

On the other hand, if your product was a short report or booklet that consisted of a mere 16 pages of information, you can still use size as a major benefit to your prospect.

> "You get no filler and no fluff - just 16 pages of hard-won, time-tested, extraordinarily-effective strategies you can put into action within minutes… and start reaping the rewards of an overflow of website traffic immediately."

Every feature has at least one inherent benefit. And it's up to you to find this benefit and bring it to the forefront. After all, if you don't uncover the benefit and make it obvious to your prospect… essentially, it doesn't exist. And it won't help you make the sale either. What you want to do is solve your prospect's problem and help him fulfill a dream. But he won't know your product is capable of helping if you don't bring it to his attention.

Okay… so now you have a long list of features and their accompanying benefits. Good. The next step is to prioritize your benefits. Rank them in order from most appealing to least - from your potential customer's point of view.

You want to deliver your biggest bang up front. It's this top benefit that's most important -- therefore, you need to unveil it first. Arrange your advantages in an inverted pyramid format - starting with the benefit that best fulfills a major desire. Find the benefit that almost instantly solves the prospect's problem -- the benefit that delivers a "magical" solution. That's your strongest marketing weapon - one that needs to be exposed with maximum power and enthusiasm.

Jotting down a full list of benefits makes the task of writing a compelling sales letter much less daunting. It gives you a great foundation from which to craft attention-grabbing headlines, compelling bullet points, and intriguing sub-headings.

Determine Your Strongest, Most Unique Selling Advantages

What sets you apart? Whatever it is that makes buying from you more advantageous - that's what you need to bring to the forefront. Distinct, highly valued advantages give you an edge over anyone else offering competing products.

Why should prospects do business with you? How are they greater advantaged in doing business with you vs. any other competitor?

These are key questions -- worthy of reflection. You want to uncover or create an overwhelming edge… something that will give you an almost unfair advantage over everyone else selling anything even remotely similar to your goods.

When you've articulated your main unique selling advantage, work at making it a foundational principle of your business - one that is talked about, or at least thought of, whenever your business or product category is mentioned. Consistently communicate what it is that makes your product a much better purchase for the buyer.

Your unique advantage is your most effective tool in drawing first-time customers to you. It establishes an original perspective and position in the minds of prospective customers.

Your unique selling advantages are what sets you apart from anyone else -- even those who happen to be marketing the exact same products to the exact same crowd. It gives your business distinction in any competitive marketplace. Your original and exclusive benefits help to position you favorably in the eyes of your market.

The key to capitalizing on a distinctive advantage is to make that advantage clearly and unmistakably known to your prospects. Make it easy for people to grasp your advantages. That's why free samples, test drives, and trial offers work so well -- they give the prospect a hands-on experience -- in effect, an actual demonstration of the advantages.

Think of your *Unique Selling Advantage* as a ten-second commercial for your business. What can you say in ten seconds that gives you superior positioning in the eyes of your target prospects?

Unique benefits are your strongest and most compelling sales statements because they separate you favorably from everyone else.

Actively promoting your distinct advantages, as opposed to your company name, (which everybody else does because they don't know any better) gives you the most valuable exposure of all. It actually means something to prospects and gives them a reason to respond to you, first. Prospects relate and respond because a strong benefit or advantage appeals specifically to the innermost wants of those prospects.

Your unique advantages tell the marketplace what you offer that others don't. It's about being different from everyone else. It's about clearly and succinctly communicating what you do for customers to make you the decisive choice over all other options -- including doing nothing.

Create An Irresistible Offer

An offer comprises much more than your main product. It's the full package including your product, multiple bonus items, and any extra premiums or incentives all rolled into one. It's everything your buyer gets in exchange for payment.

Your product may have dozens… even hundreds of positive attributes. It could be the hottest how-to program ever devised… or the greatest thing since the Internet. But, it's still just a product. You need to make it into something larger - something worth 5, 10, 20, - even 100 times more than the asking price.

An offer makes the product much more appealing. That's the key. You want to stack the positives on your side, making the decision to buy an easy one because of all the extra value the buyer gets. You want to encourage those people considering a purchase to decide in favor of action. To do otherwise would be to miss out on the glorious opportunity that's theirs for the taking right now.

Creating a powerful offer is about putting together a collection of value-added enhancements - additions to the main product that make it even more useful or valuable to own. It's also about minimizing the risks, making it easier for prospects to go ahead and buy because they have a safety valve in place, should they be dissatisfied for any reason.

Here's an example of an offer - one I've used for some time to sell my headlines package:

> Great Headlines Instantly Manual (Main Product)
> Best Headline Words And Phrases -- Reference Guide
> 7 Quick & Easy Headline Formulas - Special Report
> The Ultimate, Idea-Inducing Headline Collection - Special Report
> How To Get More Done In Less Time - Tips Booklet
> 2 Free 30-Minute Consultation Packages - Certificate

Add A Strong Guarantee

Your prospective customer is naturally hesitant about buying. He fears losing his hard-earned money. He's deathly afraid of being the victim of a scam… or being ripped off in some way. He worries about getting less than promised, less than he bargained for. Unscrupulous merchants are everywhere… and the Internet is no exception. Your prospect knows this. Cheats and con artists proliferate in cyberspace. You have to be cognizant of the added fear your potential customers might be feeling about buying on the net.

How will you alleviate these fears and assure prospects they have nothing to worry about? That's the challenge… and now is a good time to start thinking about it, while you're drafting your plan.

Review competing offers. See how others work to reduce fear and anxiety. Then, take what's already out there and make it better.

Your goal should be to make doing business with you as risk-free as possible. You can do so by extending the time period of your guarantee. Instead of offering a 30-day guarantee, make a radical extension to 120 days or more. Break the mold of the industry standard.

Be willing to go out on a limb. Assume the risk yourself so your prospects won't have to.

Another strategy is to simplify the process. Reduce the red tape. State your guarantee in the simplest, most-easily understood terms. Make it easy for any dissatisfied buyer to get their money back quickly and hassle-free. Don't make them jump through hoops to get what they want, for you'll rarely discover the real reasons anyway.

Extend the terms, simplify the process, and make your guarantee a major part of your letter and it will become a powerful and effective marketing tool. The secret to success with a guarantee is to make it as risk-free as possible.

Build A Case In Favor Of Your Product

It's never enough to express the benefits of your product. You also need to present as much credible proof as you can gather. After all… prospects know you're trying to sell them a product. They expect you to expand on the attributes and make it sound like your product leaves the competition in the dust. But they're also inclined to be skeptical of mere sales talk.

That's where 'proof' factors into the equation. Proof provides legitimacy to any sales argument. Proof is back up material that supports your claims and lends credibility to your presentation. Any proof you put forth should address prospect concerns and provide solid answers as to why they should listen carefully to what you have to say.

At this early planning stage, begin gathering anything that can help build your case in favor of a sale.

Look for…

> Success Stories
> Editorial Product Reviews
> Laboratory Tests
> Customer Testimonials
> Endorsements From Recognized Names In Your Field

Customer feedback is crucial. Get prospects to beta-test your new product for free in exchange for their honest opinions and reviews. Encourage responses from customers - particularly those early buyers. Place your product into the hands of experts (with their permission, of course) and ask them to offer any comments. When you do get feedback whether it's delivered via email, telephone, fax or in person - make sure you record it first. Then, always ask for permission to use all comments. Most will gladly oblige.

Outline The Order Process

Set up a flow chart that documents the entire process from attracting prospects to depositing the revenue into your account. It's a worthwhile exercise to chart the course of action, from beginning to end.

- Prospecting
- Attracting Attention
- Keeping Prospect Engaged
- Injecting 'Magic' into Your Proposition
- Proving Your Claims
- Leading Prospects to The Order Form
- Optional Ordering Procedures
- Shipping Options
- Receiving and Processing Order
- Notification and Shipment
- Depositing Your Revenues At The Bank

The Ultimate Sale Letter Plan Work Sheets

Identify Your Goal

Number Of Monthly Sales: _____

Conversion Ratio: _____

Define Your Target Market

Describe Your Typical Prospect:

_____
_____
_____

Understanding Your Competition

Competitor's Strengths:

_____
_____

Competitor's Weaknesses:

_____
_____

Features & Benefits

Prioritize Benefits From The Prospect's Point Of View - Starting With The Most Appealing, Unique & Valuable Benefit

Benefit #1:

_____

Benefit #2:

_____

Benefit #3:

_____

Benefit #4:

_____

Benefit #5:

_____

Benefit #6:

_____

Benefit #7:

_____

Benefit #8:

_____

Benefit #9:

_____

Benefit #10:

_____

Benefit #11:

_____

Identify The Major Emotional Motive(s) For Action In Your Specific Market

Love/ Romance
Gain/ Reward/ Greed
Duty/ Responsibility
Pride
Recognition
Self-Indulgence
Self-Preservation/ Immortality

Choose The Specific Pain/ Pleasure Reasons Why Anyone Would Be Interested In Buying Your Product

To make money

To save money
To achieve comfort
To enjoy health
To live longer
To be popular
To satisfy curiosity
To gain pleasure or enhance enjoyment
To feel clean
To be praised and admired
To be in style
To satisfy an appetite
To own beautiful possessions
To attract the opposite sex
To be an individual, independent
To emulate others
To take advantage of opportunities
To get a surprise
To be successful
To make work easier
To gain prestige
To be sociable
To express creativity
To be efficient or more efficient
To protect oneself and family
To protect the future of a family
To be a good parent
To be liked
To be loved
To express a personality
To be in fashion
To fulfill a fantasy
To be up-to-date with the latest trend
To own attractive things
To collect valuable things
To satisfy the ego
To be "first" at something
To enjoy exotic tastes
To live in a clean environment
To be strong and healthy
To renew vigor and energy

To find new and rare things
To be more beautiful or attractive
To win the affection of others
To satisfy sexual desires
To bring back pleasant memories
To be lucky
To feel important
To gain knowledge
To improve ones own appearance
To be recognized as an authority
To enhance leisure
To do things well
To get a better job
To be your own boss
To gain social acceptance
To keep up with others
To appreciate beauty
To be proud of possessions
To resist the domination of others
To relieve boredom
To gain self-respect
To win acclaim
To win advancement
To seek adventure
To satisfy ambition
To be among the leaders
To gain confidence
To get on the bandwagon
To get something for nothing
To gain self-assurance
To have safety in buying something else
To protect reputation
To "one-up" others
To relax
To replace the obsolete
To add fun or spice to life
To be in style
To conserve natural resources
To protect the environment
To make others happy

To find love
To feel intelligent
To be benevolent
To be part of a group
To prepare for the future
To feel wanted, appreciated and valuable
To work less
To save time
To have security in old age
To overcome obstacles
To avoid shortages
To avoid criticism
To avoid loneliness
To take their mind off their troubles
To avoid personal injury
To avoid damages
To avoid physical pain
To avoid loss of reputation
To avoid loss of money
To avoid trouble
To prevent unemployment
To avoid embarrassment
To get rid of aches and pains
To escape drudgery
To gain freedom from worry
To escape shame
To avoid effort
To protect possessions

Create An Offer

Main Product: _____

Potential Extra Bonus Products, Accessories, And Premiums That Add
Value:

_____

_____

_____

Piece Together A Guarantee

Guarantees Offered By Competitors:

_____

_____

Best Imaginable Guarantee From The Prospect's Point Of View:

_____

_____

Your Strongest, Most Appealing And Viable Guarantee:

Gather Support Materials

List Suppliers Of Key Endorsements And Testimonials (Establish a file
folder for the collection of actual user testimonials):

_____

_____

Identify Key Words From Testimonials:

_____

_____

Chart The Desired Course Of Action And The Tools/ Methods Used At Each Step:

Prospecting/ Getting Leads:

_____

Commanding Attention At Your Site:

_____

Keeping Prospect Engaged:

_____

Injecting Magical Appeal:

_____

Supporting Claims:

_____

Leading Prospect To The Order Form:

_____

Order Options:

_____

Shipping Options:

_____

Order Processing/ Fulfillment:

_____

Customer Notification:

_____

Sales Letter Planner Questionnaire

Following are questions I typically ask my clients at the beginning of a project. By thinking through and jotting down the answers, you'll have solid material from which to develop a powerful, compelling sales letter. Answering these questions alone will prepare you to proceed to the writing phase… but if you create your own plan, that's even better.

How would you describe the primary audience you plan to target?

For each target market… create a composite of the ideal buyer.

Demographics: Age, Gender, Interests by Association, Status, Education, Income, etc.

Psychographics: Mindset, Buying Habits, Preferences, etc.

What are they thinking about?

What are they looking for?

What is the compelling "want" they desire?

What solution does your special package offer?

What problem does it solve?

What are their inherent fears about buying this type of product?

What benefits does your product offer? What are the major advantages your customer gets from doing business with you as opposed to someone else selling apparently similar products?

What is one key reason prospects should respond to your lead-generating ad messages as a FIRST STEP? Why should they respond to your ad or listing vs. any other from alternate sources?

What are the main reasons for buying your product package? (Gift, self-learning, security, comfort, status, gain an important advantage, make more money, add to convenience, variety, healthy lifestyle change, etc.)

List the most important considerations (to your prospect) in choosing where they would make such a purchase worth the money? (Value, price, ease of purchase, risk factors, dependability, performance, believability, quality, level of comfort training, and support, right place/right time, something new and different, etc.)

How different is your product from what others offer? What makes it so?

List all the information that your audience would want to know before responding to your offer. For example: product details and features, refund policy, how to use the full package for maximum benefit, degree of simplicity, who has used it in the past and what do they have to say about it?

What are the main objections or obstacles that could be preventing prospects from ordering today? What could possibly be holding them back?

What are the top 3 competing products in each market niche? Who else is vying for the same customer?

What do you offer that competitors don't... or, which attributes can be emphasized that haven't been stressed by others? Why buy your package? Why now?

What is it specifically about competing propositions and products that seem to work for them in producing more sales?

What are the long-term benefits your product offers that may not seem obvious to new prospects? Any hidden benefits not yet un-veiled?

What special offer could you make to further improve response and attract new customers to you? List any additional incentives to make your sales proposition even more inviting and unique from others.

Complete these phrases: "This is the only _____ (identify niche) product that....

_____" (state what makes your product unique, special, or more valuable)

What is the most appealing point of differentiation - your most valuable (as perceived by prospects) unique advantage?

What is the goal of this sales letter? Six months from now... if this project could accomplish one major objective, what would it be?

OK... You have 2 minutes to recap your ADVANTAGES. SELL ME on your package as though I was a highly qualified prospect -- someone who could really benefit from what you offer. Jot down any ideas that could intensify interest and convince me to buy NOW.

At this point, you're ready to move on to the actual writing of your letter. You're better equipped than most others from the start -- because you took the time to do the grunt work first. Armed with this valuable material beforehand makes the task of writing a successful sales letter far easier.

Sales Letter Templates

Why Use a Sales Letter Template or Formula?

A formula is a general guideline - not a paint-by-numbers process to an instant sales letter. It's a blueprint designed to help you get to your desired destination in the most direct way possible. Formulas are established methods or formats that have worked for others to produce results.

Essentially, a formula is a way of organizing and presenting your material in a way that generates sales. Successful formulas are founded upon an understanding of human behavior. It's not merely a matter of extolling all the virtues of your product - it's about adapting a strategy that attracts an audience, addressing already existing *wants,* and then serving up an appealing offer that's crafted in a way to push the emotional hot buttons of targeted prospects.

Sound sales letter formulas work well on and off the Internet. It's a planned presentation, the same kind of sales pitch an effective salesperson would use to persuade interested prospects.

The A.I.D.A. Method For Writing Effective Ads

> Attention
> Interest
> Desire
> Action

Grab your prospect's ATTENTION. Expand his INTEREST. Build the DESIRE to a feverish pitch, and move your prospect along towards taking ACTION. Essentially, the AIDA Formula is about converting a passing interest into an intense desire for ownership to the point where action is taken immediately.

Attention - Every sales letter must command an audience - first and foremost. You simply have to catch surfers/readers/prospects INSTANTLY as they land at your site.

The attention-getting task is primarily left to your headline. You've got to hit their sweet spot - quickly and definitively -- with a headline that catches their attention and grabs their interest. The best headlines draw the eye and generate excitement. They mesmerize and captivate prospects, compelling them to read on.

Interest - You can't begin to build serious interest if you don't first have your prospect's undivided attention. With the prospect's attention, it's crucial that you fuel his interest. Intensify his interest and curiosity. Clearly the best way to do this is to pile on the benefits. Give him benefits of value and significance. Make it clear how your product will enhance his life in some way. Tailor your benefits to the audience.

Desire - Continually build prospect interest to the point where that interest gets converted into desire. Desires drive people - it's a force that comes from within. Once your prospect's interest becomes a desire to won, the sale is almost a sure thing. Make them an offer they can't refuse. Add irresistibility by providing far more value in terms of products, than you ask in price. Pile on helpful and in-demand bonus items, a strong guarantee and limit your offer.

Converting interest into desire is all about salesmanship. You want to make your offer sound so advantageous… so easy… so affordable… and the perfect solution to your prospect's problem.

Action - This is where you either close the sale or lose the prospect. You want positive action NOW. That's the target and that's the mindset you must adopt if you want to make your sales letter a direct-response tool. Close your letter by asking for action. It's an important final step in the process… but one that many seem to miss.

It's not enough to grab the attention of target prospects, stack multiple benefits sky-high, and generate a burning desire with a superb offer and guarantee - you also need to lead to buy. Make it easy to buy with multiple payment and ordering options. Make the action phase a logical and reasonable conclusion to your benefit-laden presentation.

That's it… short and sweet. Easy to learn and recall at will. The AIDA formula can be tremendously effective on it's own. You can also take its basic framework and adapt it into your own formula, method, or system.

The AIDA formula is the best known and probably the oldest advertising formula ever developed. This one is clearly time-tested and proven effective beyond any shadow of a doubt. With just 4 basic elements, it's also very easy to remember.

AIDA provides a solid foundation for any type of advertising - including sales letters. If you used nothing but the AIDA method, you could, with a little practice develop powerful, persuasive sales letters.

Alternate Sales Letter Formulas By Noted Copywriters

Victor Schwab

> *Get Attention*
> *Show People An Advantage*
> *Prove It*
> *Persuade People To Grasp This Advantage*
> *Ask For Action*

Robert Collier

> *Attention*
> *Interest*
> *Description*
> *Persuasion*
> *Proof*
> *Close*

Bob Stone

1. Promise your most important BENEFIT in the headline
2. Immediately ENLARGE your most important BENEFIT
3. Tell the reader specifically what he's going to get (WIIFM)
4. Back up your statement with PROOF and ENDORSEMENTS
5. WARN the reader what might be lost if he doesn't act
6. Rephrase your prominent BENEFITS in your closing
7. Incite action - NOW

Jay Abraham

Telegraph your message only to PRIME PROSPECTS
Attract the attention of your target audience in the headline or open
ing remarks
State your proposition or offer
Use the rest of the ad to DEVELOP, SUPPORT, and PRESENT
YOUR OFFER and the REASONS WHY the prospect should em-
brace it
Tell your prospect how to take ACTION

Henry Hoke

Picture
Promise
Prove
Push

Frank Dignan

Star -- An opening that quickly captures the readers imagination
Chain - A series of facts to change the reader's casual attention to a
real and sustained interest
Hook - Something to impel the desired action

Gary Halbert

1. Write a fact sheet about your product's FEATURES
2. Create a BENEFIT list - then prioritize it in order of
    importance to the prospect
3. Write out your OFFER
4. Craft a HEADLINE that reveals NEWS or the biggest or
    multiple BENEFITS
5. If more than 2 big benefits - use a sub-heading
6. Reveal who's writing the letter
7. Insert a salutation - "dear (target subject)" or "Dear Friend"

8. Use the first sentence to reveal what's in it for the prospect if he reads your letter
9. Elaborate specifically on promises
10. Tell why you're offering such a great deal
11. Enumerate facts that translate into benefits and list them - 1, 2, 3, 4.
12. Include all believable reasons why you're selling this product
13. Ask for response and urge hurrying
14. Sign off with "sincerely,"
15. Write a P.S. that gives the prospect a new little wrinkle on one of the hot reasons you've already given him as to why he should buy your product NOW

Earl Buckley

Interest
Desire
Conviction
Action

Here's my own simple adaptation of the AIDA Formula - called the "AHA" Formula

1. Attract ATTENTION and interest immediately
2. HOLD their attention and interest while continuously increasing the intensity of the positive feelings related to your solution
3. Present an irresistible offer and guide the prospect to ACTION

The 2 Most Important Steps Of Any Formula

Inevitably, you must first capture the ATTENTION of your prospect before you can even hope to impact him with your sales message. It all starts with winning an attentive and receptive ear.

But the ultimate objective is to not merely gain a reader of your letter -- it's to win action. You want your prospect to buy NOW. So every effective sales letter should conclude with a push for ACTION.

You grab the prospects attention with your headline and the first frame of your sales page. Action is obtained by advancing prospects through the letter from A - Z and on towards the order page. That's where prospects must land in order to buy. Between your headline and order form lies the bulk of your sales letter.

ATTENTION -- ACTION

There are several ways to nudge prospects from the attention phase into action. It's about converting the mildly interested prospect into an eager-to-buy new customer. To do so, you must maintain their interest and build it into a desire for whatever it is you're offering.

Make prospects feel that your product isn't just something they should get - but something they simply must own. Elevate their interest and desire to a level where prospects are convinced that taking action to acquire the product is the only sensible thing to do.

In essence, we're back to the AIDA formula again. Get attention. Arouse the prospect's interest in your proposition. Stimulate a desire to experience the perceived benefits. And finally, ask the prospect to take action by placing an order now.

It's crucial that you target your audience, base your message on benefits, and include an outstanding offer.

Additional Elements Of Power and Persuasion

Between ATTENTION and ACTION, you can employ various tools, techniques, and strategies - all culminating in a call for action.

Here are several proven effective elements to include somewhere between the attention-getting and action phases…

Proof - You need to add believability and credibility to your sales message. Proof adds realism and value, while strengthening your benefit-packed message. Show proof and your message gains much more interest and respect. Proof eliminates the 'fluff factor'. Testimonials, endorsements, and success stories offer credible proof that your advertising claims are true.

Tell A Success Story - Everybody loves a great story. Make it exciting, dramatic -- even shocking. A true story of how your product evolved, or how it helped one buyer change his life makes for intriguing copy.

Urgency - Experienced copywriters know that their moment of truth is NOW. If they don't win action while the prospect's mind is still filled with glorious images of life after a purchase, there's less chance of winning the sale at all. Everyone needs a push -some more than others. Add an element of scarcity to your offer .Let prospects know it won't last and that by failing to respond immediately, they'll lose out on this rare opportunity.

Damaging Admission - Admit a flaw and you gain respect. Everybody knows perfection doesn't exist. If you look closely enough, every product has some flaw - major or minor. But most marketers only address the positives. In fact, they overdo it. What happens is their message is perceived as sales hype and looked upon with heightened suspicion. When you admit to a shortcoming, you are in essence leveling with your prospect, as you would a friend.

Reasons Why - An exceptional offer needs some kind of explanation. Tell prospects why you're sweetening the deal and how they benefit from it. Providing a reason helps justify the deal without cheapening the product.

Reward For Reading - Establish value at the outset. Make it worth your prospect's time to read your letter and let him know why it's important to do so.

Consequences Of Inaction - A sobering reminder of all the prospect will lose out on by not responding can help sway them into action.

Establish Value - Give them much more in perceived benefits than you ask for in price. Add bulk to your offer with bonus items. Add security with a guarantee.

Supporting Facts - Reveal the key product features that make specific benefits possible. Facts (features) give your interpretations (benefits) solid legs to stand on. They justify the benefits and make your claims more believable.

Create An "After" - Establish a vivid image of life for your prospect after a purchase. Make it clearly advantageous - a stark contrast from where they are now. Place your prospect inside this image and allow him to feel what it's like to have what he wants. Let him fully grasp the advantages of owing your product.

Phase II

Start Your Sales Letter With Powerful Attention-Grabbing Headline

"If your advertising goes unnoticed, everything else is academic."

-- William Bernbach

Begin writing your sales letter with the most important and powerful weapon in the copywriter's arsenal - the headline. Your main headline is the first thing visitors see when they arrive at your sales page. It's your first and perhaps only opportunity to pull them into your copy -- where they can get the full story.

Headlines reveal what you have to offer. They represent the culmination of the finest, most attention-getting, interest-arousing arguments you can muster. It's your best attempt to grab your visitor's interest and get them to stick around awhile.

If your headline fails to magnetize prospects to your message, the rest of your sales effort is in vain. It really doesn't matter how stellar or persuasive the rest of your sales letter is. If the headline fails to draw an audience, the rest is irrelevant. Without an interested and attentive audience you can't deliver your pitch and you can't make sales.

With such a significant role assigned to your main headline, it stands to reason that this is one area that demands a significant amount of time and creative effort. But fear not… I'm going to give you the tools that will help you instantly create more riveting headlines than you can ever use in any one letter.

For now, just remember to launch your sales mission with a full-blown attack. Hold nothing back. You need to give it your absolute best shot in order to grab the attention of people and have them spend what precious few moments they have with you.

Since your headline is of primary importance, it only stands to reason that you should give it the visual prominence it deserves. You want your headline to jump out quickly as soon as the page loads on your visitor's screen.

Think of your headline as a marquee at the theatre… or a billboard on the highway. Place your headline in lights where it's sure to be seen by interested prospects as they speed down the highway of life.

The Purpose Of The Headline

Capturing attention, flagging targeted prospects and luring them inside are the main functions of the headline. To accomplish these tasks, your headline should be benefit-oriented… make complete sense instantly… and hint at that special something that follows, that's both interesting and promising.

Grabbing attention is step number one. As Maxwell Sackheim put it…

"People go through life with their minds only half turned on, except when they're promised an adequate reward for their full attention. Ordinarily their attitude toward nearly everything they see, read and experience is -- so what?"

You need to stop the swift-surfing prospect in his tracks and get him to raise an eyebrow. But the major challenge online is to thwart the prospect's temptation to click away. Surfers know that the instant they tire or grow bored of a site, all they have to do is click a button to redeem the feeling of instant gratification elsewhere. If that happens, you lose.

Stopping prospects is important. But just drawing attention from anyone will do you no good whatsoever. You want to capture the attention of interested, qualified, and preferably ready-to-buy prospects. That's why it's so important to target your message and identify early on, the kind of audience your words are intended to reach. Capturing the attention of non-prospects is of no direct cash value. Stick to those you can best serve. That's your target market. Flag them in your headline and they'll be sure to perk up and listen to what you have to say.

Simply identify the specific market you're addressing. Often a single word added to your headline does the job. It could be teachers, plumbers, Bayarea residents, seniors, home-based entrepreneurs - any one a million different possibilities. Add the appropriate label and it acts as a magnet in pulling in targeted prospects.

You might think that you don't need to flag your prospect. After all, your lead-generating marketing is only addressed towards prospective customers. But online, people will find you through various ways and means.

Search engines play a large role and the more you actively promote your site and your business, the more accessible your message becomes to the many millions online -- around the world. It makes good sense to let people know who you can help the most. To think that everyone is a potential candidate is simply ludicrous. Narrow your market and your message stands a far greater chance of getting noticed by that specific group.

Following are 3 examples of headlines that flag specific targets:

"Investors! Make More Money In The Next 45 Days With This New, Fast & Easy System For Organizing, Planning & Tracking All Your Investments In Just 27 Minutes A Day!"

"Attention entrepreneurs, small business owners and anyone who has ever dreamed of running their own successful business...New Surefire Business Success Library Reveals Breakthrough Tips, Techniques And Secrets For Boosting Sales... Cash Flow... And Profits... Starting Today! Satisfaction Guaranteed 100% -- Or Your Money Back!"

"300,000+ Houston Area Homeowners Want To Know More About Ozone Nursery... Here's How You Can Reach Your Ideal Target Market For Less... And Boost Your Sales, Your Cash Flow And Your Profits... Every Single Month!"

Grab attention, identify your audience and woo them inside. Temporarily stopping surfers in their tracks... and identifying ideal prospects are two crucial headline functions. But your headline only delivers when it pulls true prospects deep inside your sales copy.

What makes prospects read beyond the headline? It's the promise of a payoff… something of specific interest to that particular reader. It's a solution, a new or better way to accomplish a task, fulfill a dream, or to solve a worrisome problem. In short, it's about specific benefits to the precision target.

Why Headlines Are So Important Online

Headlines are perfect tools to capture the eyes of skimming readers. That's how most people get their information online these days; they click, arrive at a site, then quickly scan the page looking for items of specific interest and relevance. When they don't find what they're looking for, they click again and again, traveling through cyberspace as fast as they can.

"On the average, five times as many people read the headline as read the body copy. When you have written your headline, you have spent eighty cents out of your dollar."

-- David Ogilvy

For the surfer, headlines are a terrific deal. They reveal what a site or page is all about. Picture a page without a headline or title of any sort. How do you know the site's purpose and who they're addressing? You don't. At least, not without reading some of the body copy. But not many people are willing to take the time to do this. Not in this day and age where free time is a rare commodity, and something almost everyone would like to have in greater quantity.

Time is precious. Consumer choices are multiplying exponentially. There are multiple demands on personal time. It seems like there's so much to do… and precious little time to do it.

Placing a targeted headline at the top of your sales letter serves the busy reader. It catches eyeballs and reveals key information to skimming surfers. In fact, this principle can apply to any page on any website. With a strong, descriptive headline at the top of each page, you actually help visitors by saving them time. The headline tips them off. It tells them instantly whether the page is worthy of an investment in reading time, or at least justifies further consideration.

In the online world, people travel at record speed. Your headline serves the busy, speeding prospect by revealing -- at a glance -- what you have to offer and why they should stick around.

The Role Benefits Play In Headlines

Benefits are meaningful advantages to the prospect. They penetrate any filtering devices automatically programmed to deflect the "noise" of competing messages. Today, virtually everyone - your prospects included -- is subjected to a non-stop barrage of commercial messages, distractions, and demands all clamoring for attention on any given day. Most of it is simply ignored as a mechanism of efficiency and survival.

Just imagine what life would be like if you had to stop and listen to it all, knowing that the huge majority of messages are of no interest whatsoever. There would be no time to do anything else. In order to cope, we've learned to shut out 99.9% of the incoming chatter... and we do so automatically, often without any conscious thought at all.

Headlines are he best place to reveal your big idea or ultimate benefit. If your most appealing attribute fails to generate an enthusiastic reader, surely nothing else will do the job either.

"It takes a big idea to attract the attention of consumers and get them to buy your product. Unless your advertising contains a big idea, it will pass like a ship in the night. I doubt if more than one campaign in a hundred contains a big idea."

-- David Ogilvy

Headlines act as informative leads, helping prospects make the decision to stay or go. As the dominant lead to a page, the headline is a sign of what is to come. It enables the prospect to make an instant, gut-level decision as to what to do next. The only messages that get through are those that hit a nerve... and the surest way to do that is with a benefit that solves a specific problem that's troubling your prospect.

Benefits address the thought foremost on every prospects mind:
"What's In It For Me?"

If the promised benefit isn't in alignment with the prospects interests or thoughts, it makes no impact and is simply relegated to the noise category. But benefits that hit a nerve are right on target, and offer a timely answer, cut through the clutter and receive a welcome reception.

Specific benefits are meaningful to the right targets. Hence, they're given priority, as helpful advantages or benefits are what the prospect looks for. No one buys products -- they buy what the product does for them.

How To Get Started Writing A Great Headline

Research gives you a tremendous advantage. The time spent in this area furnishes everything you need to create a compelling, intriguing headline from scratch -- one that's sure to attract and interest far more prospects.

If you've followed this book in sequence, you might have already mined the ore… and now you're left with a wheelbarrow of gems, perfect for creating outstanding headlines.

Knowing you audience clues you in to their specific desires and aspirations… as well as their problems, frustrations, and anxieties. These are the things that your prospect is thinking about on a regular basis. It's these issues that occupy his or her mind. Therefore, it's no surprise that when you touch on these in your headline with a specific benefit, you win an eager and attentive audience.

Delivering a key benefit-oriented headline also means understanding the capabilities of your product and the unique advantages it gives others. Why would anyone be willing to listen to you if you don't have anything to say that's beneficial and worthy of their time and attention? Online prospects won't wait. If you don't provide a key benefit right up front - something that piques their interest and gets the blood rushing a little, you won't stand a chance. It's too easy to avoid the unexciting and unimportant.

Presenting a unique benefit means you're also intimately aware of what others are offering. Take the time to review your competitors. Know what they're doing and what sales tactics they've tried before. If you know your competitor's products thoroughly, you'll understand their strengths and weaknesses. This makes it easier to develop a strategy that positions you in the most favorable light.

The Most Effective Headline Formats For Website Sales Letters

Headlines with sub-headings, multiple benefits, and combination packages tend to work best. Longer, strongly worded headlines tend to pack more of a punch. Fit your combination headline into the first frame of your sales letter - that's how you maximize the use of your most valuable online real estate.

One great advantage of web site marketing is the dirt-cheap price of space. With virtually every other form of advertising, you have a finite amount of space and a set fee for the use of space. Exceed it and it costs you more money. Cost overruns could even be the undoing of a marginally profitable campaign.

But in the online world, these limitations fail to exist. You can, in effect, use as much space as you want. Obviously, your message must remain intensely interesting. Having usable space and making it captivating are two different things. The low cost of space is inviting… but the challenge is that online, attention spans are at an all-time low.

Space ads are costly. So you really need to maximize the value of every square inch you buy. Regardless of the size of your ad, the available space allotted the headline is somewhat limited.

In direct mail, you have weight restrictions to deal with. What this usually boils down to is a specific number of pages in which to get your message across. Make your headline any longer and suddenly your eight-page letter turns into a nine-pager. The added cost at the post office could be self-defeating to your advertising campaign.

In cyberspace, these restrictions are lifted, giving you much more freedom to use a longer headline and pack more power and punch into your prime property - the first frame.

Here are some examples of website headlines and sub-headings that work well:

Introducing… The All-Natural Bodybuilding System For Gaining MAS-SIVE SIZE, INCREDIBLE STRENGTH And AWESOME POWER!

…I'll Show You 67 Specific Insider Secrets For Transforming Your Body Into A Finely Sculpted Mass Of Huge, Rock-Solid Muscle --The 100% Safe And Natural Way

Fed up with all the deceptive "how-to make money online" garbage out there? Wish you could find just one REAL LEGITIMATE WAY to make REAL MONEY right from you kitchen table - starting today? Well… listen up -- in the next 4 minutes I'll show you...

How To Easily Get Full Cases Of Top Quality, Name-Brand Products At Half The Wholesale Price… And How To Quickly Sell Every Piece At A Huge Profit On EBAY - Hassle-Free And In Less Time Than You Think! My "Amazing" New Book Reveals The Simple Secrets Of How I Average $11,212.00 A Month -- 100% Online

Finally! Here's Your Direct Roadmap To The Exact Same Highly Profit-able -- Yet Exceptionally Easy -- Money Making Techniques I Use Every Day To Make Big Money While At Home With My Kids! I've Never Shared This Information With Anyone - Until Now! Read On And You'll See How My Story Could Just As Easily Be Your Story…

… Please Don't Spend Another Second, Or Invest Another Dime Trying To Make Serious Money From Home -- Until You Read This!

Ready to achieve true financial freedom? Here are the exact same methods experts use to build fortunes...

Discover How To Substantially Improve Your Investment Success, Elimi-nate Costly Commissions And Take Complete Control Of Your Financial Destiny - Starting Today

...Here are 37 closely-guarded investment secrets to creating your own personal fortune. Make more money and build lifelong wealth, with greater ease and more confidence than you ever thought possible.

If you like to call your own shots... If you want to build your own personal fortune quietly... methodically... systematically... if you want to take advantage of the incredible technology that's right at your fingertips, now... then, you must read this letter very carefully...

Ezine Publishers! Looking For A Reliable Way To Consistently Build Your Subscriber Base? Here's A Proven Program That Delivers Quality Subscribers Without Costing You A Dime! In Fact... We Pay You!

Introducing --Two Dollar Ads.... A Surefire Way To Automatically Attract New Subscribers... Increase The Value Of Your Publication... And Earn Additional Income At The Same Time!

Attention UK Entrepreneurs and Small Business Owners...

Stop Losing Sales and Profits Needlessly! Now You Too Can Substantially Boost Your Business Straight Away By Accepting Visa, MasterCard and American Express - Online, In Person, By Phone, or Mail

Are You Among The 94.7% Of Entrepreneurs To Instantly Qualify For A Merchant Account Of Your Own, This Month? Find Out NOW - It's 100% Risk Free

How To Create A Winning Headline In Just Minutes

Keywords that cut to the heart of your prospect's pleasure or pain zone are certain to capture the attention and interest of that specific group. Dynamite benefits, extra advantages and unique solutions all naturally draw attention and interest.

To the prospect suffering from a seemingly incurable case of Hay Fever, a headline such as *"Stop Hay Fever In Seconds With This Secret Ingredient Found In Every Refrigerator!"* is guaranteed to interrupt his online travels and the dozen or so thoughts swirling around in his mind and draw him towards your message.

The obvious keyword is "hay fever" -- this is what the prospect's radar is set to detect. More specifically, it's the cure, or the alleviation of pain and discomfort that the prospect seeks.

But it's the use of the term "hay fever" that identified the message as having importance, triggering the reaction and shift in focus.

Prospects are constantly on the lookout for new ideas, solutions, and upgrades -- hence the common practice among marketers to unveil "new and improved" versions of older products.

"New" implies an improvement over the old, established way. It hints at the promise of a greater benefit than what was previously available.

Promise a unique advantage in your headline and you'll pull eyeballs towards your proposition.

As humans, we're wired to be on the lookout for ways to get more living out of life. We want more… and we want it faster, and easier -- and preferably at a lower cost too. Headlines that scream such advantages reap the reward of higher readership.

Another strategy to create powerfully-effective headlines on demand is to employ proven, attention-getting words and phrases.

Following is an ongoing list of such headline words and phrases. Obviously you'll want to customize the collection of words you assemble to suit your own purposes. But stringing together a few from this list can often get you off to a solid start on a decent headline.

Powerful Headline Words & Phrases

Best Headline Words

You	Magic	Hot
You're	Seductive	Daring
Your	Important	Alluring
Secrets	Warning	Provocative
Now	Suddenly	Timely
New	Stop	Surging
Free	Urgent	Make
Proven	Vital	People
Money	Confidential	Money
Guaranteed	Explosive	Results
Magic	Thrilling	Sale
Energy	Electrifying	Better
Winning	Win	Discount
Introducing	Sex	Save
Announcing	Startling	Soar
Results	Stunning	Unlock
Facts	Crucial	Look
Easy	Bonanza	Formula
Instantly	Bravo	Blockbuster
Breakthrough	Insatiable	Revolutionary
Amazing	Remarkable	Unleash
Reveals	Beauty	Unlock
Yes	Beautiful	Earn
Here	Sizzling	Keep
Quick	Vivid	Look
Discover	Dynamite	Discover
Only	Heart-Wrenching	Find
How	Dazzling	Reap
Exciting	Mouth-Watering	Harvest
Discover	Delicious	Uncover
Secrets	Gift	Obtain
Amazing	Fun	Slash
Shocking	Potent	Secure
Revealing	Mind-Blowing	Protect
Surprising	Successful	Win

Get	Surefire	Unsurpassed
Use	Fascinating	Outstanding
Have	Startling	Exclusive
Own	Miracle	Lavishly
Effective	Fortune	Scarce
Daring	Profitable	Useful
Accomplish	Wealth	Rare
Achieve	Quick	Strange
Garner	Remarkable	Valuable
Compare	Unparalleled	Discount
Make	Suddenly	Reduced
Hurry	Excellent	Lowest
Boost	Tested	Popular
Burst	Proven	Special
Enjoy	Reliable	Wanted
Imagine	Sensational	Power
Explode	Improved	Who
Grasp	Direct	Want
Reach	Better	Why
Attain	Refundable	Which
Blast	Interesting	Hot
Profit	Challenge	Attractive
Benefit From	Profits	Famous
Profit From	Profitable	Successful
Powerful	Informative	Professional
Strong	Revealing	People
Health	Practical	Unusual
Unique	Bonus	Weird
Surprise	Plus	Highest
Odd	Gift	This
Quickly	Selected	Profusely
Limited	Instructive	Absolutely
Security	Valuable	Simplified
Safety	Sensational	Practical
Safely	Trusted	Colorful
Special	Genuine	Approved
Superior	Important	Delivered
Expert	Critical	Easily
Ultimate	Quality	Authentic
Increase	Sturdy	Bargain

Unlimited
Surprising
Beautiful
Big
Huge
Mammoth
Enormous
Gigantic
Colossal
Bargain
Complete
Full
Confidential
Greatest
Helpful
Immediately
Largest
Endorsed
Crammed
Latest
Noted
Personalized
Sizable
Terrific
Lifetime
Tremendous
Unconditional
Wonderful
Formula
Alternative
Truth
Flourish
Enterprising
Solution
Incredible
Crucial
Daring
Explosive
Floodgates
Lifeblood

Bonanza
Timely
Energy
Energizing
Surging
Wanted
Simplistic

"The secret of all effective originality in advertising is not the creation of new and tricky words and pictures, but one of putting familiar words and pictures into new relationships."

--Leo Burnett

Best Headline Phrases

How To…
How Would…
How Much…
Who Else Wants…
Inside Secrets Of…
Do You…
100%-Guaranteed!…
Little-Known Secrets…
Closely-Guarded Secrets…
How Would…
Advice To…
At Last…
Money-Making…
Special Offer…
Limited-Time Offer…
Act Now To Get This…
Money-Saving…
No-Risk…
Zero-Risk…
Must See…
Must Attend…
Late-Breaking…
The Shocking Truth About…
Do YOU…
What You Should Know About…
Complete Details, FREE…
Free Report (Course, Book, DVD, etc.) …
Call Now For …
Limited To The First _____ (quantity) To Reply…

Limited-Time Opportunity…
How You Can…
You Get…
You Have…
Facts You…
Profit From
Save Time…
Save Money…
If You're Serious About…
The Truth About…
Free Bonuses…
The Single Most-Important…
Let Me Show You…
Once In a Lifetime…
Learn To…
Make Money…
Secrets Of The Pro's…
Don't Spend Another…
Trade Secrets Of…
Key Secrets To…
Urgent Information…
Surprising New Discovery…
13 New Ways To…
Do You Feel…
Do You Have…
You Can Start With Less Than…
Starting Off With…
Yours Free…
Discover How To…
The 3 Secrets That Can…
If You Qualify, You Could…
Yes You Can…
Could This Be…
What Would You Do…
Are You…
If You Have…
If You Are…
No More…
When It Comes To…
Here, At Last…

For Preferred Customers Only...
Take Advantage Of...
Make The Most Of...
Reserve Your...
Act Fast And You'll Also Get...
Test Drive...
Are You Ready...
Nothing Else Compares To...
Our Best-Selling...
New Lower Price...
For Busy People...
If You're Worried About...
Top 10 Reasons To...
You're Invited To...
Prepare For...
The Ultimate In...
Makes Life...
Looking For...
The Perfect...
The Quickest Way To...
Individually Designed...
There's Nothing Quite Like...
Tax-Resistant...
One-Of A-Kind...
Personalized Service...
Starter Kit...
Starts Working Instantly...
The Intelligent Way To...
Inflation-Beating...
No-Nonsense Advice...
100% Pure...
Designed To...
Built To...
A Breakthrough System For...
A Breakthrough Formula...
It's So Easy, The Only Thing You Need Is...
Take One Moment...
Time-Tested...
Proven To...
Everything You've Ever Wanted From...

It Works …
You'll Never Have to Worry Again…
Simple But Powerful…
A Safe, Easy Way To…
The Safe Way To…
Worry-Free…
Pamper Yourself With…
Everything You Need To…
Isn't It Time…
A Simple Solution To…
Results In Just…
For The Serious…
You'd Never Guess…
Now It's Yours…
Last Chance For…
Last Chance To…
Absolutely Free…
For Less Than…
Get Ready To…
Join (Hundreds, Thousands, Millions) Of Others Who…
Used By…
Plus… You Get…
Get Ready For…
Take Advantage Of…
Your Chance To…
The Choice Of…
Knocks Your Socks Off…
Information-Packed…
More Powerful Than Ever…
Free Trial Size…
Yours Free If You Act Now…
Here's How…
Now Available…
Treat Yourself…
Thousands Have Been…
Which Of These…
Astounding New _____ Secrets…
7 Reasons To…
Best-Kept Secret…
12 Proven Steps To…

Reveals Powerful Secrets…
Now You Can…
Proven Steps To…
Gives You The Added Advantage Of…
Are You Still…
Say Goodbye To…
Closely-Guarded Secrets…
Reserve yours now…
A Breakthrough In…
The Choice Of…
In Test After Test…
Surprisingly Simple…
Remarkably Rugged…
As Easy As…
Easy To..
Hassle-Free…
Makes _____ Easier (Faster, Trouble-Free, More Convenient, Disappear, etc.)…
_____ Made Easy…
Easier Than Ever…
You'll Wonder Why…
One Call Away…
One Time Only…
_____ Without The Problems…
Your One-Stop Source For…
Cash In On…
Everything You Need For…
Professional Results With…
Instant Impact…
Helps You…
The Next Best Thing To…
Unlock The Hidden…
Perfect For Any…
Limited Edition…
Never Before Seen…
It's So Simple, Even…
Satisfaction Guaranteed…
At Last…
Advice To…
100%-Guaranteed…

Guaranteed To…
Unconditionally Guaranteed…
Money-Back Guarantee
No Questions Asked Guarantee…
Guarantees You…
Discover The Magic Of…
Get More…
If You're Looking For…
Learn To…
Last Minute…
Top Dog Secrets…
Hot Property…
Beyond Your Wildest Dreams (Fantasies, Expectations, etc.)…
For Fun And Profit…
Live Like…
Enjoy The Ultimate…
Experience The Thrill…
You've Never Seen…
For That Special…
What Better Way To…
Tired Of The Same Old…
Instant Results…
High Yield…

How To Make A Good Headline Even Stronger

Guarantees, added incentives and, definite deadlines give an added sense of urgency and importance to your headline. A guarantee offers immediate backup for any claim stated previously. You still need to prove it, but the fact that the promise is "guaranteed" adds power and significance to the message of the headline.

Picture your prospect reading your headline. You offer benefit 1, benefit 2, and benefit 3. Benefit #1 seemed impressive… benefit #2 astonishing. But Benefit #3 has never been offered before by anyone, as far as the prospect is concerned. It seems too good to be true… almost unbelievable. But then you follow this triple benefit headline with the statement *"Guaranteed 100% Or It Doesn't Cost You A Dime!"*

The guarantee by itself adds credibility to each of the benefits. The perception is that since it's guaranteed fully -- it must be true. Now, I'm not suggesting that you misrepresent your benefits. Not by a long shot. In fact, I implore you to tell the truth, the whole truth and nothing but the truth. But at the same time… it's your duty to make your offering as interesting and desirable as humanly possible. A guarantee helps you accomplish this by making your statement less of a stretch in the prospect's mind.

Added incentives compel readers because of the value they offer. When you can pack an appealing freebie into your headline, you attract more eyeballs. Free offers of specific importance tends to interest large numbers of people. The more lop-sided the value (in favor of the prospect) -- the more appealing it becomes.

A definitive deadline adds a precise timeline to the offer by introducing an element of urgency. It's a hot potato in your prospect's hands - something he must deal with immediately, rather than cast it aside for a later time. Adding a specific expiry date in your headline and combining it with a strong offer gets people interested and activated. They know the material is time-sensitive, so they check it out right away.

How To Write An Emotional Headline

Touch on the key issues in your prospect's life. Use picture words that trigger strong mental images and tug at your reader's desires. Add feeling to your message and give your audience the solutions they've long sought.

There is nothing more seductive and more appealing to your prospect than a few powerful words that immediately trigger positive, pleasurable feelings. Desire is a powerful force that can work in your favor. But it first needs to be unleashed. It's your challenge to awaken the sleeping giant and present a scenario of possibility. If your prospect can see it as a possibility, it creates a feeling of confidence that he can achieve it too. But you need to paint the picture first to offer hope and inspiration.

What are your prospect's hot buttons? What does he really desire? How does that make him feel? How can you ignite these happy feelings in your headline?

Using emotion in your headlines means painting a more provocative and appealing picture. Express your benefits in vivid color. Allow your prospect to experience temporary ownership of the actual benefits. Describe it clearly in graphic detail. Allow your prospect to instantly make the transition from where he is in reality, to wherever it is he'd prefer to be.

Here's an example of an everyday headline:

"Sport Fishing Made Easy"

Now here's a headline for what could actually be an identical product - but this one has been brought to life in Technicolor with an infusion of emotion:

"5-Time Derby Champ Reveals 7 Simple Secrets To Landing Huge 'Trophy' Fish And Big Cash Prizes In Any Contest!"

The best way to write powerful, emotionally charged headlines is to get yourself prepared mentally. Get psyched-up first. Know that you have something to offer that can change the prospect's life in some way. Get clear about the benefits in your own mind… and get passionate about your offer. Inject enthusiasm and drama into your word compilations. Write as though you have the ultimate answer to your prospect's plight. Do whatever it takes to get your prospect closer to the magical results he yearns for.

What Kind Of Things Do Successful Headlines Offer?

Strong headlines offer the promise of a benefit - not just any benefit, but one that is sure to delight the specific market to which it is presented. Compelling benefits are the heart and soul of headlines and all effective sales copy for that matter. But anytime you can offer a strongly desired benefit that's new… something that requires little effort and is sure to produce satisfaction, you've got more to offer.

Benefits need to offer unique solutions or unexploited angles, something that sets your offer apart from someone else selling the same kind of thing. If your product is truly unique, by all means promote this distinction and claim it as your own. But if you happen to be in a market that's filled with competing products all making similar claims, find a unique, underused advantage and base your headline on this particular point. Doing so gives you an authentic and original position in the minds of your consumers.

Simplify life by offering a solution that's both quick and easy to apply. With time being the most precious current resource, anytime you can offer a time saving bonus feature in your headline, you should do so. Your prospects and customers work long and hard. They're pulled this way and that way. By the end of the day, they're exhausted - physically and mentally.

Now imagine your prospect scouring the Internet for information on a particular topic. Various solutions are available but most require an investment of time and energy, something that's in short supply. Suddenly, your headline leaps off the screen, offering a near-instant solution that's virtually effort free. Your headline is too tempting to ignore. So your prospect is captivated from the start… giving you a much better chance of making the sale.

Now if you can guarantee a particular result, that's even better. But if you're going to mention your guarantee in the headline, it should be a powerful, 'no holds barred' type of guarantee -- a guarantee with teeth.

In short…

The most important thing a headline delivers is a relevant benefit -- preferably a benefit no one else can match. Add fast action, convenience and a guarantee.

Big New Benefit + Quick & Easy Solution + Guaranteed Results =

Powerful and Appealing Headline

Here are a few examples of strong headlines with a combination of appeals:

"How To Create Your Own Hot, Best-Selling Information Product On Your Favorite Subject In Less Than 3 Hours - Guaranteed 100%!"

"Want To Write Copy That Can Make You Rich? Here's My GUARAN-TEED, Market-Tested, A-Z Formula For Writing Words That SELL -- Plus $979 Worth Of FREE BONUSES -- If You're One Of The First 47 People To Respond To This One-Time-Only Offer!"

"Sell More Suits At Full Price TODAY Than You've Ever Sold In A Single Day Before! Remarkable Quick New ABC Technique Fills Your Store With Customers Eager To Buy More Suits, Shirts, Dress Pants, and Ties Than Ever… And At Full Price - Guaranteed!"

Where Else Do These Headline Ideas Apply?

Headlines are the most important component of any ad or marketing piece - in both the real and virtual worlds. You can apply many of these ideas to any promotional material including brochures, print sales letters, display ads, classified ads, yellow pages ads, flyers, card deck ads, package inserts and the like.

Online, headline opportunities abound. Consider discussion forum postings, web page title tags viewed by search engines, directory listings, article titles, ezine ads, squeeze pages, promotional videos, lead-generation product names, and the subject headers of both newsletters and individual email messages.

Whenever you get the opportunity to attract the interest and attention of your target audience, employ your best, most effective tool. Without a doubt, your headline is the key to getting your message noticed in virtually any arena.

Key Points To Keep In Mind When Creating Website Sales Letter Headlines

Targeting your ideal prospect with a compelling and concise statement designed to arrest attention and interest is what a headline is all about. It's your first and only chance to woo them in… and getting them there is crucial to your success.

Use your best, most alluring appeal to capture the attention and interest of your niche audience. Never hold back something that could help at the get-go. Avoid saving the best for last. If you don't use your most powerful advantage upfront, prospects will never take the time to go beyond your headline.

Keep in mind the simple fact that online prospects are busy people. They won't give you a second chance in their search for information and resources that will move them closer to their goals.

In order to grab attention, you've got to be different. Using the same words… making the same promises as everyone else will not help you. Your prospective customer sees such an approach as simply more of the same. It's "blah… blah… blah…" to them. You need something different… something more. You need a headline that's riveting… one that demonstrates a clear understanding of your market and the unmet want it's had to endure - until now.

Employ your greatest advantages in your headline. If your offer can't be beat - say so. If your benefits are unmatched through traditional means - by all means, vault that message to the top of your page.

Whatever advantages you use, remember, the task of the headline is to capture the attention of your target audience and deliver enough enticement to lure them deep inside your sales copy where you can gently persuade and lead prospects to the order form.

Make it captivating, compelling, and concise. Be different. Do the unexpected. Refine your biggest bang down to a handful of words that are sure to arrest attention, arouse curiosity and ignite desire.

Simple Enhancements To Make Your Headline Impossible To Miss

Drawing the prospect's attention to your headline is job one. To accomplish this task, place your headline where people expect to find it - right at the top of your page. Create an obvious visual contrast between your headline and body copy.

Make your headline big and bold. If your body copy is set in 12-point type, place your headline in 18-point or 20-point type. Make the difference clearly distinguishing. Avoid the look that's virtually the same -- such as 11-point body copy with a 12-point headline. It's a minor difference that's barely distinguishable.

Experiment with the type size and style of your headline. One key point to remember is to get your main headline to appear in its entirety, within the first frame of your sales letter. That means to assume your prospect is viewing your page through a distorted, 14-inch monitor. Make your headline fit the first frame and be legible enough to be easily read and instantly understood. After all, it's the headline that's the key to any future action.

Try setting your headline in bold type. Does it still fit the frame? Is it clearly readable? If so, use it. Bold text establishes a position of prominence and importance. It signals to the reader that this particular segment is something of significance -- something that must be seen. Headlines set in large, bold type attract attention first, as the eye is naturally drawn towards large, dark objects. Anything that stands out… anything different from the typical text on a page tends to pull the eye toward it. It's a natural reaction and one that's difficult to avoid even with a concentrated effort.

How To Be Sure Your Headline Is Effective

The only measure of success in any marketing endeavor is the result it produces. You can have the best headline, sales letter, presentation, product, price, etc… but all that is academic. You can follow guidelines and still come up short. There is no panacea; no one-size-fits-all answer that will ensure your success.

Follow these ideas. Apply them. Take action and get your headlines out there in front of the marketplace where response reveals true effectiveness. The main thing is you've got to test and test again. That's the only way to accurately determine your most effective headlines. By the way, this principle applies to all elements of your sales letter, not just to headlines. By following these techniques, you'll easily triple your chances of success.

The best way to create one strong headline is to write several. Start by jotting down a few headline ideas. You can always add to your list later. If you can write a dozen different headlines, chances are that somewhere within your list of twelve, there lies a gem of a headline waiting to be brought forth and used for maximum impact.

Finding a winner can be challenging. The best thing to do is to become your own prospect. Slip into the role of the individual you're trying to reach. Examine each headline through your prospect's eyes. What grabs you? What catches your eye and pushes your hot buttons?

Often the best headline evolves from a combination of several elements from various headline ideas you've jotted down. When writing headlines, just let the ideas flow. Don't try to craft the perfect headline at once. Instead, write compelling words and phrases that best describe what you have to offer. String a few of these words and phrases together into a potential headline. When you get a bunch of these, single out the most alluring variations. Then take the various elements that make the most dramatic impact and reshape, repackage or recast them into a new version - a hybrid. That's an important secret to creating a headline with massive pulling power.

Here's how I developed a headline for a client's sales letter I was working on...

Rough Draft Headlines

End Your Money Worries Forever With Your Own Successful Home-Based Business

No More Struggling Just To Earn A Paycheck - Here's A Quick And Easy Way To Cash In From Home With Your Own Money Machine!

How To Quickly Make $400 A Day From Home In Your Own Carefree, Cash-Generating Business!

Enjoy More Freedom, Peace Of Mind, Even Financial Independence With Your Own Home-Based Direct Marketing Business

Imagine You... A Successful Home-Based Business Owner -- You're Your Own Automatic $400 A Day Cash Stream!

Looking For An Easier Way To Earn A Comfortable Living? Here's A

Time-Tested, Proven System For Earning $10,000 A Month In Your Own Home Business

27 Proven Ways To Quickly And Easily Build An Automatic Income Stream Of $10,000 or More

If You're Looking For An Honest Way To Make More Money Than You Ever Have Before - Here's A Guaranteed System And A Step By Step Plan For Earning $10,000 A Month Or More From Home

Discover How To Make $10,000 A Month With Your Own Home-Based Business. It's Easier Than You Think With Step-By-Step Instructions Anyone Can Follow To Make Good Money - Starting Today!

Just Released… The Ultimate Business-In-A-Box - It's Everything You Need And A Step-By-Step System To Generate A Cool $10,000 A Month From Home

Discover The Secrets Of Earning A Comfortable Income While Enjoying A Carefree Lifestyle

New Business-In-A-Box Gives You Absolutely Everything You Need To Make At Least $7275.00 In The Next 30 Days! Introducing A Turnkey Home-Based Business That Runs Like Clockwork - Giving You A Consistent Stream Of Huge Cash Profits!

Discover The Little-Known Secrets For Launching Your Own $10,000 A Month Home-Based Business From Some Of The Worlds Finest And Most Successful Mail Order Experts! Your Satisfaction Is Guaranteed 100% With This Easy-As-Pie, Step-By-Step System

This list gave me plenty of ideas to work with. Ultimately, I chose the following headline and sub-heading combination:

How You Too Can Earn $112,794.00 A Year From Home, In Your "Free" Time... And Escape The Payday-To-Payday Rat Race Forever! (While Everyone Else Is Busy Working Longer Hours, Just To Earn A Living!)

Just Released... The Ultimate Business-In-A-Box: Everything You Need To Make More Money With Far Less Effort, Anytime -- Anywhere Using A Time-Tested, Automatic Cash Flow System!

Discover Surefire Secrets To Launching Your Own $10,000 A Month Home-Based Business From America's Most Successful Direct Marketing Millionaires! Your Satisfaction is Guaranteed - 100% PLUS... You Get The Unlimited Resale Rights To The Entire Package - ABSOLUTELY FREE!

When you've got a main headline you think will work for your sales letter, test it with a classified ad in a magazine or newsletter that reaches your audience. Run your classified ad using nothing more than your best, most promising headline and your site address or URL.

If your headline alone draws clicks from a tiny classified ad in a targeted print publication, chances are you've got a winner. The reason? You're relying solely on the headline to stimulate enough interest so prospects make a note of your URL and take the time to visit your site. Even news-paper classifieds can worthwhile places to test headlines - though I gener-ally don't suggest them as good choices for direct-response, lead genera-tion classified ads.

Another way to test headlines is to set up two identical pages with the exact same content, except for the headline. Run two different versions and split test your ads 50/50 so you get virtually the same exposure to each unique URL. Since traffic will vary, pay particular attention to conversion rates. Measure the response. You may be surprised by what you discover. The only way to know with absolute certainty is to test your marketing and the first and often most revealing test is the headline variety.

How Long Should A Sales Letter Headline Be?

Make your main headline long enough to deliver a compelling message. Limit it to something that can be digested in a single gulp… or read with-out the need to come up for air.

Your headline should be a bite-size morsel that tempts, teases, and tantalizes enough to win over more of the prospect's time. You want to stimulate emotional desire. Get the greed glands working, or the mind thinking about new promises and possibilities.

Deliver a complete benefit-laden message and take as much space as you need to do this. If you try to tease prospects by short-changing them on information in your headline hoping they'll read your body copy, you're only fooling yourself.

With so many choices, today's website visitor won't spend extra time trying to figure out if what you're offering is worth the time and effort. A better strategy is to be explicit in the beginning - starting with your headline.

Unleash your ultimate benefit or advantage and make it as interesting and appealing as you can. The purpose of your headline is to get them to pay attention and to focus on your sales copy. Give yourself enough space to accomplish your goal. If you need more room to fully deliver the ultimate refinement of what you offer, add a sub-head... or use a super-headline to set up your main headline.

Make it short enough to be understood at a glance by the skimming reader and long enough to make it absolutely compelling and magnetic.

How To Create a Riveting Opening That Intrigues, Invites and Compels Prospects To Read On

"You can't expect them to read your story unless it's more important than whatever it is they are doing or thinking about at the moment."

-- Maxwell Sackheim

What Makes The Opening So Important?

Transitioning your prospect from the headline to the body copy itself is the job of the opening few paragraphs. The headline may be the single most important component of your sales letter, but the opening paragraphs rank right up there too. Here's why...

Your successful headline has already sparked some interest in your proposition. That's the first hurdle you had to clear. If your headline doesn't work, it doesn't really matter what you do the rest of the way.

Having consumed your headline, the typical prospect now either begins reading your story, or continues scanning through your message looking for key bits of information.

Essentially what the skimming prospect does throughout the process of reviewing your letter -- whether an initial scan or a more detailed reading -- is this: he looks for reasons to click away. He seeks reasons to justify leaving... and so looks for holes in your sales argument. If your prospect finds nothing while scanning sub-heads, bullet points, the P.S. and other highlighted areas -- chances are he'll go back to the beginning of the letter. That is of course, as long as his interest is sustained throughout the skimming process. In other words, if he likes what he sees and the desire is still brewing, there's a good chance your prospect will go back to get the full and complete details.

Your opening needs to be friendly and inviting. It should beckon the prospect inside and with the promise of transforming a new find (your website) into a burning desire to experience the benefits by owning the product. Your opening takes him from an initial state of surprise and delight into one of *"Yes this is real and yes I really can, do, have, or achieve the same thing."*

The opening is where you get up close and personal. It's where you launch your sales pitch. It's your introduction to the story of your magical product. It's what separates the sales letter from virtually every other kind of advertising and what makes this sales tool the ultimate marketing weapon available to online entrepreneurs and home-based businesses.

"People screen out a lot of commercial messages because they open with something dull. When you advertise fire extinguishers, open with the fire."

-- David Ogilvy

Why Are Openings So Difficult To Write?

Confusion about how to best tell your story is a common problem. Most people can handle headline creation. Stringing a few words together into a powerful and provocative statement can be accomplished with a little direction and effort. But writing effective body copy -- particularly the opening paragraphs -- is where many people simply drop the ball.

One of the most common frustrations I hear is *"I've studied the basics of writing advertising copy. But the problem I have is getting started with the actual sales letter. How and where do I begin?"*

Crafting an interesting opening is definitely a challenge. Personally, I spend a lot of time on the lead, particularly the first paragraph. Why? The headline did its job by dangling a big, juicy carrot. Now the opening must get prospects to bite on it -- so they too can get the full benefit themselves.

You've already commanded the attention of your reader/prospect. You did so by crafting a headline that dealt a specific message to a specific reader in a way that aroused personal interest and curiosity. Your opening should then feed off the material that captured the prospect's attention in the first place. It's like having a big fish following your line in the water. If the bait doesn't encourage a bite - you lose.

How would you begin your pitch if you were selling your product face to face? Imagine that you're selling a specific type of furniture and your prospect shows up at your store as a result of your lead-generating advertising. The prospect is interested, qualified and capable of buying. But he's far from being *sold* on your product. What would make him want to know more?

The best advice I can offer is to simply dive right in. Continue painting a picture of what you have to offer prospects. Don't try to "write" a brilliant opening - simply communicate with enthusiasm what you have to offer and why your prospect should listen to your message now. When you attempt to write something... you often end up with a page or two of material that's less than compelling. But if you simply speak it and record your thoughts, results improve because you communicate as you would in a personal conversation. There's no wind-up. No concern over formalities. No *correct* way to get you point across. You simply transcend those limitations and your enthusiasm becomes infectious, compelling, and motivating.

Many people struggle with the opening simply because they don't know where to start. It can seem confusing - particularly at the beginning. But if you'll take each component of your sales letter and follow the ideas presented in this text, you'll find it gets much easier.

The Best Way To Get Started

As with all components of the letter, you'll want to begin to take note of the various approaches used as leads in sales letters. Keep your eyes and ears open. Become aware of the tools and techniques writers and marketers use to pull you in to the heart of their messages.

For a quick start method to writing openings, see the various samples I've provided later in this chapter. Go through the list. Take any opening line that could fit your scenario and apply it to your sales proposition... and do so with enthusiasm.

Take a few examples that seem to fit and tweak them a bit. Word for word duplication may or may not work for you. But often a slight variation is all the creative inspiration you need to get your mind moving in a fresh, new direction. This is exactly what you want to happen. You don't want your message to sound the same as any other.

You'll know when you've found a great opening because it will inspire you to continue on the same wavelength. Once you've got an opening that works - you're off and running.

After seeing an identical opening a few times, its effectiveness starts to wear off. The first time you see *"I've got to get this off my chest before I explode!"* -- it makes an impact. But after a while, you realize that this once unique gem has simply been lifted from one letter and inserted into another.

If your prospects suspect that your words have merely been taken from another sales letter -- you're in big trouble. You lose the appearance of sincerity. They'll automatically begin making assumptions and may liken your product to another -- whether it's true or not. You lose any perception of originality and uniqueness.

In marketing, perception is everything. You don't want to be seen as a copycat. Use the samples presented here and those you accumulate in your swipe file as idea generators only. You can always adjust them ever so slightly to make them appear more original.

Do Salutations Help?

A salutation can make your sales letter appear more of a personal, one-on-one communication. It addresses the reader in general terms and provides further clues as to the value and relevance of the message.

Specifically targeting your audience is a good way to shape a salutation. *"Dear writer in search of more magazine article assignments"* targets a specific audience. *"Dear frustrated dieter in search of a permanent solution for weight loss"* targets another. This approach can be helpful when your audience hasn't been specifically identified somewhere in your headline. In other words… you wouldn't want to use a headline/ salutation combination like this…

Headline -- "Introducing The Ultimate Weight Loss Solution For Frustrated Dieter's Desperate To Shed Excess Pounds -- And Keep Them Off For Good!"

Salutation - "Dear frustrated dieter in search of a permanent solution to weight loss…"

When you look at it this way, the mistake is obvious. If you've already targeted your audience, there's no sense repeating yourself - that would only insult your reader's intelligence.

One common technique is the "Dear Friend" approach. It's hardly personal with such widespread use. But it does signify the opening of a letter… and a letter is traditionally perceived as a one-on-one communication between writer and reader. No one is fooled into thinking the letter is actually a letter from a "friend" - this is particularly true online. Though these words are largely invisible… they do help to set the stage and tone for what follows.

I've seen other successful online marketers use salutations like these:

> Dear subscriber
> Hi…
> Dear Internet Friend
> Hello
> Dear Entrepreneur
> Dear computer user in search of extra income
> My dear business friend
> Dear professional

Some writers prefer to omit the salutation altogether. In my experience, it usually doesn't make a whole lot of difference which option is used. But testing is the only way to find the best option for you.

Another technique is to identify the supposed writer of the letter, the time the letter was written and occasionally the place (usually the hometown of the writer). Usually this is done to make the letter seem more authentic or timely. Similarly, a subject title could be included - as though it were an important memo or note. It's another opportunity to deliver a mini- headline. The challenge is to do so without it appearing phony or insincere.

Here are some examples…

From: Bill Smith
Thursday, 8:43AM
Rolling Hills, California

From: Cory Rudl
10:33 a.m.

Re: How To Skyrocket Your Profits Online
Wednesday -- 1:07 p.m.

From: Jonathan Mizel
Boulder. CO

Tried and True Techniques For Creating Riveting Openings

Connect with your prospect and build rapport. Present a statement from a recognized authority. Open with a punchy direct statement, or a provocative question. Paint a picture of a brilliant future and allow your prospect to feel the associated pleasure. All these are proven approaches that have worked for others and can just as easily work for you.

Whatever style of opening you choose, you must use it to help establish a friendly basis for a relationship.

Build a bond with your prospect and he's much more likely to accept what you have to say. Your headline captured attention and aroused interest. Now it's up to you to sustain this interest and transform it into a burning desire for your product.

Establishing rapport is a good way to start. It happens when you demonstrate a genuine interest and understanding of the prospect and his concerns. It's all about empathy - being able to put yourself in your prospect's shoes and see things from that side of the fence. When you do so and you speak with this kind of understanding, your words have much more importance and cut a path straight to the heart of the reader. After all, you're just like him. With that established, you're on a solid footing to progress with the rest of your story.

Kicking off with a quote from a name your prospect knows, respects, and admires can instantly ensure continued readership. It's a form of qualification for any statements you've made previously. It's an endorsement -- whether direct or implied. The name itself of an expert or celebrity will generate interest and the statement will lend credence to your entire message.

Packing a direct hit with a punchy statement is another way to pull readers inside. It's like a mini headline that further incites interest and stimulates the desire to find out more.

Questions can also be used at the outset. Just make sure your question can really only be answered one way. Don't give prospects the opportunity to disqualify themselves before you get a chance to make your full presentation. Proceed with caution when using the question approach.

How Opening Paragraphs Encourage Further Reading

Set the stage and create an easy-to-read, non-intimidating opening that encourages readers inside. What got the reader to this stage were the words contained in your headline, sub-heads, highlighted areas and the P.S. It only stands to reason that you continue along the same theme, expanding on the benefits and painting a rosy picture of what life can be like at the other side of a purchase.

When the prospect realizes the headline wasn't fluff designed to merely grab attention, he begins to take your message more seriously. The continued discussion of the promised payoff is confirmation to the prospect - it's the validation that what he seeks might just be available right here, right now.

A strong opening compels prospects to read on. It could be intriguing, compelling, or curiosity arousing. Either way, it's interruptive and attracts the prospect's focus away and causes him to give more time to hear what you have to say.

One of the most important functions of the opening - and something many people get wrong - is to ease your prospect into your full, multi-page message. How? By using an opening that's easy to read in a flash - something that's not the least bit intimidating to the most remedial reader in your prospect pool.

Short paragraphs are the best way to start a letter. Concise paragraphs of one line - even the odd paragraph of a single word or phrase can be very effective. Why? They're so easy to read, they seem so inviting -- that almost everyone reads them.

Get your prospect to read the opening and you've got a good chance he'll read on. In fact, that's something you need to be aware of at all times. Each paragraph needs to move the reader on to the next.

How The Headline and Opening Work Together

Set the stage with your headline and you'll have an attentive audience anxious to hear your story. Headlines interrupt the dizzying array of thoughts percolating in the busy prospect's mind. They temporarily at least, capture attention and control the focus of the prospect's thoughts.

It's the kind of attention a school principal gets after sounding the tone over the public address system. Suddenly ears perk up anticipating the delivery of an important message. For the moment, the audience is receptive. Another analogy is to imagine a flagman frantically waving a warning sign at the side of the highway. Instantly all vehicles slow to a crawl, as drivers look for clues as to what's going on down the road. Headlines work the same way. They arrest attention and interrupt the thought processes of your prospects -- leaving their minds completely open to suggestion.

Strong headlines work in a similar fashion. They grab the reader and catapult them straight into your opening paragraphs. The headline has caught their attention and caused them to channel their focus in a single direction. It's a glorious opportunity to deliver a compelling message. After all, the first, and most difficult challenge - getting attention - has already been accomplished. Now it's a matter of sustaining that attention and interest long enough to move them to the order information. That's why it's crucial to have compatibility between the headline and the lead of the letter.

State your biggest, most attractive benefit in the headline. Then, launch right into your body copy with an expansion of the benefits already revealed. For the moment, you have a captive audience. These prospects are interested, excited, curious, and attentive. They want to know more and are listening with both ears. It's the perfect set up -- enabling you to present your case to an eager audience.

How Long Should The Opening Be?

One line or multiple paragraphs -- the actual lead can vary in length considerably. It's your introduction, an opportunity to transport the prospect from a state of simple awareness, mild interest and curiosity to intense interest and a driving desire to learn more.

Opening paragraphs are essential links that connect the headline to the rich array of detailed benefits revealed in the body copy.

In reality, there's no distinctive line of demarcation separating one element from the next. You don't want to break up your copy into separate pieces. Instead, you want your prospect to easily process it all.

Your letter may be made up of various components, but you always want to move the reader along from one line to the next, in an uninterrupted, continuous flow. Any break is a disruption and another opportunity for your prospect to flee.

A good lead or opening is a connecting link designed to bridge the gap from the beginning (the headline) to the heart of your sales message (the body copy).

Use only the space and words you need to make for a smooth, logical, and interesting transition. If this mission can be accomplished in a line or two, by all means go for it. If more space is required to introduce your offer, use it. The key is to make it interesting so your prospect will want to read on.

The 3 Crucial Tasks Successful Openings Complete

The first couple of paragraphs of your sales letter should:

1. Build Rapport
2. Rekindle Interest
3. Pull Prospects Inside

Building rapport is all about connecting with others. It's about being accepted and respected by an audience because they sense your deep understanding of their plight or circumstance. Make a connection with your prospect by revealing your knowledge of, or connection to his position, problem, or primary desire. Demonstrate empathy and understanding and you'll open up the eyes, ears, and minds of your target market.

Spark your prospect's interest and fuel his desire to get the complete details. Dangle the biggest, brightest, juiciest carrot you know you're prospect wants. Ease them into your body copy by making it an effortless read - particularly at the beginning.

Magnetize your message by giving the reader a taste of what's to come. Use your opening to pull prospects inside with an interesting, enthusiastic, and compelling introduction. Activate their emotions so they're literally driven to read on.

The Quickest Way To Create A Magnetic Opening

As with any other sales letter component, adapting the ideas others have successfully used is the easiest way to get started writing your lead. Review various sales letters from other successful online marketers. Pay particular attention to the opening 2 or 3 paragraphs of any sales letter that catches your attention.

Start your own "swipe file" by gathering specific samples from other ads, sales letters, brochures, postcards, websites, infomercials, etc. Notice how other marketers grab the attention and interest of their respective target markets.

Note the various approaches used. Observe how smooth the transition is from headline to lead -- and from lead through to the closing copy. Jot down any leads that seem to be particularly interesting or useful and set up a separate file for these. You can also use the samples I provide later in this chapter as an idea starter to help get you going.

If you really want to write a powerful opening, get enthusiastic about it! Communicating with enthusiasm makes an impact. It's exciting and infectious. Enthusiasm and passion fuels more of the same among the audience. When you can't wait to share your story and present your offer because it truly is life changing, that kind of feeling bubbles over and your opening becomes irresistible to true prospects.

Where Most Openings Go Wrong

Long, drawn out introductions that get into detailed explanations are far too common. Excessive wordiness crammed into a single paragraph is enough to discourage anyone.

The worst thing you can do is lose your otherwise interested prospect with your opening because you've made it uninviting. Long sentences and paragraphs require too much mental effort. They force people to expend time and energy before they're really sure they want to.

If it looks daunting, chances are your prospect will flee by clicking away. Long paragraphs equal effort. It's easier to flee than to burn valuable time and energy trying to wade through a message that seems challenging, uninviting and may not even be the ultimate solution the reader is seeking.

Lengthy openings are a definite no-no. I strongly advise you to keep your opening paragraph as short as possible. Don't set up any unnecessary roadblocks -- it's challenging enough dealing with the inevitable difficulties of a competitive marketplace.

Leads that confuse readers are another problem. Stick to the theme introduced in your headline. It there's no obvious connection between your headline and your lead paragraph, you'll only confuse readers and confused readers never stay around. Remember, your opening is a tool of transition. Your readers are already hooked on the promise and they want more. Give them what they want and they'll have no reason to leave.

Avoid overused openings. An easy way to do this is to craft your own by modeling others -- rather than by copying them, word for word. Use other leads as inspiration, but inject your own brand of passion and personality.

Make it inviting and enticing to prospects. Woo them inside your message where they can get complete details about how to enjoy all the benefits themselves. Keep the sentences and paragraphs short, providing little tidbits that are quick and easy to process, while encouraging the reader to delve deeper. Don't waste your efforts and opportunity by giving prospective buyers an easy reason to leave.

Examples Of Effective Opening Lines

The following leads are taken from actual online sales letters written for clients. These are the first few words or sentences that immediately followed the salutation. Use them as idea starters to help you create your own powerful openings. The only modifications are the combinations of sentences into single paragraphs. In most cases, I use the first segment or sentence as a stand-alone paragraph for the sole purpose of getting more prospects to read beyond that first line.

Do you have what it takes to earn $10,000+ a month from home? Here's your chance to grab hold of unlimited success, freedom and independence...

Just suppose... that five short years ago you started a simple "investment plan" with a little spare change. Think how different your life could be today...

Let's face it. If you want to make money in business... you need to reach people.

Sometimes in our hectic lives, important things are missed.

Get ready... You're about to discover the secrets behind a fun, exciting, and very different way for you to automatically make big money from home!

And yes… this "secret" system is guaranteed - 100%!

- If you like to discover new ways to make more money… you'll love this!

- It's true. This information can completely transform your body and your life!

- How long has it been since you took a good, hard look at your child's schoolwork?

- It doesn't matter if you have 500 subscribers… or 5000. The fact is… Your ezine is more than just an asset - it's a potential goldmine… and it's all yours!

- Imagine YOU at your ideal weight… for the rest of your life!

- Okay, so you're interested in having more money. Lots more money. Terrific! Now… here's how my Secret Income System guaranteed to help you escape the payday-to-payday rat race - fast and forever. The amazing thing is…

- It's absolutely true. There's no more cost-effective business tool than a great website. A well-designed site pays an exceptionally high return… on a comparatively tiny investment.

- Here's a rare opportunity to put more money in your pocket.

- Here's the key to surefire business success…

- Sometimes it's a little thing that make the biggest difference - in life and in business.

- I'd like to send you a valuable marketing success checklist. It's yours without obligation and will be sent to immediately by mail.

- When you're looking for the right cleaning company, it can be a little confusing.

- Let's face it. If you want to make money in business… you need to reach people.

- This FREE program that can start making you money - almost immediately!

- If you prefer reliability to uncertainty... simplicity over chaos... and true value rather than the "cheapest" price -- you're going to love this…

- Would you like to earn an easy $400-$800 a day?

- If you're looking for new ways to attract more customers, you're going to love this…

- Would you like to skyrocket your income up to $5,000 per week?

- I have a picture of you in my mind's eye.

- Imagine 40 to 50 hot, qualified leads delivered to you, every month.

- Did you know that for less than the cost of dinner for 2, you could protect your family and property for a full 120 days -- with no risk whatsoever?

- If you're interested in creating a huge and continuous cash flow for yourself, than this message is for you.

- If you've ever tried _____ before... you know how difficult it can be.

- Sounds crazy, doesn't it? Making money without having to "work" for it.

- Have you settled for making just a few extra dollars… when in fact, you could be making as much money as you want - whenever you want it?

- If you've put off living your dreams… now is the time for you.

- There are only 3 things you need to build your own personal fortune:

- Imagine the feeling of total well-being. Vibrant health. Joy. Energy and vitality.

- Would a regular second income make life better for you and your family?

- There's nothing more important to your future success than the use of your time.

- There are only 3 things you need to build your own personal fortune…

- Are you tired of settling for a few crumbs… when what you really want is a lavish feast?

- Here's a powerful marketing tool for financial planners -- guaranteed to put more money in your pocket -- every 30 days…

- Would you like to earn $500 per day from home? Thousands already are. Now you can too!

- Shopping around for a merchant account? Get low prices, quality service and genuine value. Now you can profit from your own merchant account with no headaches, no hassles, and no unpleasant surprises!

Successful Sales Copy Is All About Buyer Benefits

"It may be said of men in general that they are ungrateful and fickle, dissemblers, avoiders of danger, and greedy of gain. So long as you shower benefits upon them, they are all yours..."

-- Niccolo Machiavelli

What Exactly Are Benefits Anyway?

Think of benefits as advantages to the customer. It's what your product *does* for buyers... rather than what it *is*. Benefits give value to a product -- value that exceeds the cost of the product itself. Benefits make your product appealing, causing others to willingly shell out their hard earned cash in order to get the perceived benefits. Benefits are the real reason your product exists and has a chance in the marketplace. Without major benefits, you have nothing to sell.

Benefits are what prospects get as a result of buying your product. They're all about prospects and answer the foremost question on every visitor's mind "What's in it for me?" Benefits give meaning, significance, and value to a feature and make the product more appealing in the prospect's eyes. For example, a desktop widget that's available in 43 different colors enables buyers to suit any imaginable office design and decor.

What About Features?

Features on the other hand, are actual product details. It's all about your product and what it is and may include details about the product color, size, shape, and materials used among many other things. Features are facts and characteristics. Used alone, they offer little in terms of selling power. But when employed as the reasoning behind a benefit, features can act as effective supplemental sales tools.

The most effective way to use a feature is to align it with a compelling benefit where the exclusive feature creates in essence, an exclusive benefit. Make the feature a valuable characteristic because of what it does.

Always use benefits first and foremost. Benefits influence, persuade, and sell prospects on your product or offer. Features play a secondary role, if they play one at all in your sales letter.

Turning features into benefits is about collecting facts, figures, product history, customer comments, and experience… then repackaging or recasting them in a way that addresses the *wants* of your target market. Turn straightforward, factual product information and data into compelling advantages that appeal to prospective buyers. Powerful sales copy is primarily about benefits because that's what prospects are interested in.

Every feature has at least one corresponding benefit and it's up to you as marketer to uncover it, dust it off, and present it in a way that gives the product added value. The idea is to build a credible and realistic bridge from a product's feature to an appealing benefit.

The following example comes from an instructional ad created many years ago. It shows how one copywriter espoused the benefits of your basic wooden pencil. This excerpt appeared in Entrepreneur Magazine.

How to sell a secondhand pencil that has no eraser

Forget laundry bills forever! This pre-tested, chrome yellow, hard-finished writing instrument positively will not leak and keeps your hands free of ink and your clothes safe and spotless.

Fabricated from the finest second-growth hickory, it is graphite-filled with fine-grained, jet-black carbon that cannot snag or catch on any paper surface. Oven-baked enamel coating, with die-stamped copper in two-toned filagree. Removal of the erasure guarantees pencil to be 100 percent latex-free.

No push-pull, no click-click. The point is always there, ready to write. Free from unsightly pocket clip, it writes in any weather. Funnel-shaped point is handsomely decorated with scalloped edge. Refilling unnecessary; can be discarded when finished. Fits any standard sharpener. Send for free information today!

Now… if something as simple and basic as an ordinary pencil can be presented in such an appealing way, creating compelling sales copy for your great new product should be a breeze!

"You must make the product interesting, not just make the ad different. And that's what too many (copywriters) today don't yet understand."

-- Rosser Reeves

Which Benefits Should Be Included?

Everything that represents a genuine helpful advantage or benefit to your prospect should be included in your sales letter. List every conceivable benefit. Prioritize and deliver your benefits in the order from the most relevant and important to the least. Omit any single benefit and you might be leaving out the one advantage that could sway an undecided shopper.

The more benefits you stress in your copy, the more opportunities you have to sell others and the better will be your response. In fact, your sales letter should consist of one benefit on top of another.

Launch your sales letter with a big benefit in your headline. Expand on this major benefit in your subheading. Continue along with a string of benefits throughout the body copy of your message. Repeat your main benefit in your close or on the order form. The more benefits you present, the more convincing, persuasive and effective your sales copy is as a decision-making tool in the hands of prospects.

The Easiest Way To Turn Features Into Benefits

Simply take any feature and ask yourself what it means to customers or prospects. Since features are about products, you need to give it a new twist, making it about the prospect.

Here's an easy way to convert any fact about your product into a prospect benefit. Simply take a feature and add the words "You get". When you think in terms of "You get" -- you're thinking about how the prospect/

customer is greater advantaged by having or using the product.

Here's an example…

Fact or Feature: Fax machine prints on regular paper

Benefit: As a result, you get clearer printouts on standard paper. No need to buy costly fax rolls again like you had to a few years ago. In addition, there's no cutting required. Plus, never again will you ever have to deal with unsightly over-sized pages that jam your filing cabinet and make a mess of your files.

Another way to phrase it is... "so that you get". State the feature and follow it up with "So that you get…"

"How To Get More Done In Less Time is a concise, 21-page tips booklet so that you get only the most crucial, hard-hitting, time saving information -- without any filler. Read it all in a single sitting and put these time saving ideas into practice immediately. No need to read hundreds or thousands of pages to uncover the key ideas - you get it all in just minutes!"

Think the answer through from your prospect's point of view. See it how he's likely to see it. What's the advantage from their perspective? What is it about that particular feature that makes it valuable and advantageous to the audience? That's what you need to think about… and that's what you need to communicate to your prospect.

Why Benefits Are So Important

Meaningful advantages sustain and build reader interest. Lose interest and you've lost any chance for a sale. Benefits focus on prospects and address human wants, so they naturally attract and hold the interest of readers.

Your prospect has a problem he'd dearly like to solve, or a goal he desperately wants to reach. He wants less pain in his life and more pleasure. Suddenly, he discovers your product. But it's not the product itself he's most interested in; it's the perceived benefit he'll get to experience as a result of buying.

But how does your prospect know if your product is the ideal answer he's been searching for?

If you merely reveal descriptive details about your product in your sales copy, it won't have much appeal. You can't simply present your goods in a "here it is" approach and expect prospects to figure out the advantages for themselves. That's lunacy. Yet, many do try this approach.

A much more effective strategy is to paint a glorious picture of the kind of results that are possible with your product. Make it absolutely clear and utterly obvious. If you don't unveil all the benefits, they'll never figure it out for themselves, nor will they waste a minute of their precious time in trying to do so. If your message doesn't reach out and grab them because of its magical appeal - due to the benefits expressed - you don't stand much of a chance in an increasingly competitive online marketplace.

Benefits tell prospects where to go in search of the answers. They have magical, emotional appeal and offer hope and promise to those in want and need. Benefits are solutions to problems, cures to symptoms. Few purchases are made without a strong reason. The reason prospects are even remotely interested in your sales message is because they have a problem they'd like to solve, a symptom they'd like to cure, or a desire they'd like to attain. When you communicate benefit on top of benefit, your words cut through the noise and directly trigger your prospect's hot buttons.

Features are about things - specifically your product. Benefits are about feelings -- and it's these feelings that control human actions. If you want to communicate effectively, you've got to arouse feelings consistently throughout your body copy. Emotions give life and passion to your words.

Since benefits are explained in self-serving terms (self-serving to the prospective customer, not the marketer) they immediately strike a chord with the audience. To prospects, perceived benefits are reasons for paying attention ultimately buying.

Without appealing benefits your product or offer has little value in the minds of consumers. They haven't yet been sold. But stack up a huge list of benefits and suddenly the perceived value of the same product goes sky high.

It's the relative value that ultimately determines the prospects decision to buy. Benefits build value and make the purchase decision an easier one. Prospects add up the perceived value of your offer - the sum total of all the benefits. Mentally, either consciously or subconsciously, they attach a figure to the list. At the same time, they look at the real cost - the actual dollars and cents required to purchase.

Value of Benefits = $X
Cost of Product = $Y

The benefits and the implied value must clearly outweigh the cost to the buyer. The more lopsided the comparison in favor of the prospect, the more likely it is you'll make the sale. If you can pack a boatload of value into your offer and clearly drive home the benefits to your prospect, you increase your chance of success by a considerable margin.

How To Reveal Your Product's Benefits For Maximum Impact

Paragraph copy, bullet points, numbered lists, headlines and sub-headings can all be used to deliver benefits. You'll want to get right to it with your presentation of benefits.

Use your main headline to introduce your biggest benefit. Can't decide on one that stands out among the rest? Use a multiple benefit headline, or a benefit, offer, and guarantee combination.

Another approach is to use the *Ultimate Benefit* in your headline. The ultimate benefit is the culmination of all the other minor benefits combined. A health book might contain hundreds of specific benefits for getting more sleep, losing weight, overcoming mild depression, feeling energized, etc. But the ultimate benefit is… how to look good and feel great about yourself.

Continue unveiling more benefits throughout. Paragraph copy is great for telling your story and keeping the reader moving along. Bulleted and numbered lists are powerful tools for drawing attention visually and hammering home specific benefits in headline-like fashion. Sub-heads draw the eye too, so they're another effective method of expressing benefits in a sure to be seen way.

The most effective method I've used is a combination of all of the above. Headline at the top of the page, usually followed by a sub-head. Then I begin the body copy with paragraph copy before unveiling a series of bulleted lists. After writing the body copy, I like to add sub-headings throughout -- to emphasize the key benefits and draw attention to the major letter components like the guarantee and special offer.

In What Order Should Benefits Be Presented?

Drive home your strongest, most enticing, and unique benefit first. Don't hold back in hopes of building interest first before unleashing your greatest attribute. In marketing, you've got to come out of the gate with your most effective artillery. To do otherwise is foolhardy.

Look, if your strongest, most amazing benefit fails to pull readers in and get them enthused about your message, nothing else would work either. If that's the case, I'd seriously reconsider the product and the market. A bad match simply will not work, no matter how smooth and influential the copy.

Always start with your best. Consider this your one chance to impact prospects and help them out by making your product available. They'll never get to the order page if they're not compelled to absorb your message. Fail to grab their attention at the beginning and they'll be long gone before you know it.

It's also crucial that you structure your benefits list to suit the specific target. Not all buyers are interested in the same things. If you're approaching two or more different groups, tailor your benefit presentation for maximum impact on that one specific group you're targeting.

Stress your best attribute first, followed by the next in line. Get them interested first… then sustain that interest and enthusiasm. Another powerful technique is to reveal an additional major benefit in the close or P.S. It can be the clincher to the sale. It's not a matter of holding back or saving a big benefit for later. It's more a matter of introducing an extra incentive, or recasting the same benefit in a new light right at the moment of truth -

when the as yet undecided prospect must make a decision. The added benefit is thrown in a matter-of-fact manner.

Should The Benefits Of Bonus Material Be Unveiled Too?

Writing sales copy is all about delivering powerful benefits and creating enticing offers. Bonus material plays a big role in boosting the perceived value of your product. That's the beauty of marketing with offers as opposed to products.

Offer-based marketing takes you out of the competitive area and positions you in exclusive territory. It's all the add-on value and extra incentives that make your offer more appealing. But merely listing additional products usually isn't enough. You've got to make each bonus item worth solid value to your audience. Again… if the benefits aren't clear to prospects, they don't really exist.

One way to get benefit copy into your bonus items without taking much space is give them appealing titles. Use the concepts revealed in the sections on headlines and bullets to create provocative and highly desirable bonus items. This is the way to go with booklets, special reports, audio-tapes, CD's and the like… but you can also do it with virtually any add-on product in your offer.

Create sizzling titles that imply benefits. Another technique is to follow each title with a testimonial excerpt about that specific bonus item. You'll need lots of testimonials to draw from, so make the acquisitions of such, part of your regular marketing routine. The more resources you have to tap, the easier it is to craft compelling, got-to-have-it sales copy.

How To Make Writing Body Copy Easier

The more you have to work with, the easier the task. That goes for any writing project… and it's especially true for writing sales letters. With plenty of resources and reference material at hand, writing copy is a breeze. The trick is to spend the time and effort digging up the gems before you begin. Again, by this stage, you should already be well equipped.

When I take on a new project, the first thing I ask clients for is all the background material they currently have, or have access to. I want everything - laboratory tests results, customer testimonials, press releases and media kits, old sale copy, brochures, product development plans, drawings, photographs. Often much of the material never gets used again but it does provide me with a quick education and a selection of resource material from which to get ideas and inspiration.

In addition to my request for all such material, I also prepare a customized version of my basic questionnaire (see earlier material). The responses I get back from clients give me more ammunition to use and greater insights as to where they are and where they want to go. Do your homework and your letter will come together much easier.

A big part of your background planning should be your features and benefits list. Examining the features of your product will give you a better understanding of it. Converting those features into customer benefits will put you in tune with the desires of the marketplace.

Body copy consists of three major elements:

1.   Benefit Copy
2.   Appealing Offer
3.   Risk-Free Guarantee

Benefits expose all the great advantages you provide. The offer makes it exceptionally good value and the guarantee removes any risk to the prospect. When you look at the body copy of your sales letter this way, it's easier to identify the key elements and shape it into a coherent and compelling message.

Think of it this way...

You could probably state your guarantee in a single sentence or paragraph. Your offer is nothing more than a list that consists of your product and the package of bonus materials you include to make it a powerful and exclusive offer. So most of the remaining body copy can be created from your benefits list. Just describe benefit after benefit - everything the buyer gets and why he should jump at the opportunity now.

Okay, let's briefly review...

Benefits are:

- Helpful advantages
- Answers to problems... steps towards fulfillment of a desire... and cures for symptoms
- Interesting information that makes a feature or product significant and valuable
- About prospects - not products

To make your benefits more powerful and irresistible, shape them to suit your audience. Know your target market and word your benefit copy to hit the relevant hot buttons.

Know what it is your customer is looking for. Hit their hot buttons and you'll trigger emotional interest.

For example...

If you market nutritional supplements, you need to know that customers aren't buying blends of *Bee Pollen, Ginseng, Ginkgo Biloba, Wheat Grass,* and assorted other extracts. They're actually buying a healthier lifestyle, an extended life, and a slimmed down, more attractive look -- something others will notice and admire... making them feel even better about themselves.

Identify the feelings and wants your prospect desires to experience. Keep those feelings in mind as you shape your benefits. Present your benefits as interesting information your audience will want to know about.

Emphasize the benefits prospects cannot get elsewhere. The more exclusive your offer and the more in tune it is with the desires of the marketplace, the greater the demand.

Speak openly about your product's attributes. Stress the value and sell the sizzle. Bring out all the goodness, all the positive qualities. But avoid the excessive hype that turns off many would-be buyers. Simply tell it like it is with passion, enthusiasm, and confidence.

Make your benefits more impressive by adding simplicity while reducing the time requirement. Any promise that can be obtained quickly and easily is sure to appeal more to today's harried, time-poor prospect. Simplify life for your audience. Make it easier to get what they want in less time then ever. Then, add this fact to your benefit copy.

Add specific facts and figures to your claims and you make them appear more real to prospects. Real numbers, actual results achieved, the average time taken to reach a particular level - this is the kind of quantitative information that helps prospects grasp your benefits instantly. It's the kind of data they can easily digest.

> *"Read books 10 times faster."*
> *"Master driving in one quarter the time."*
> *"Save 87% every time you need ink for any office printer."*

Specific, impressive results put your claims into perspective, making them appealing, understandable, and easy to compare/contrast with other marketplace options.

Guarantees built into benefit statements provide additional marketing firepower. When added to specific benefits, guarantees add emphasis. They underscore the benefit with an expressed promise - something that makes the benefit appear foolproof.

Employ words that bring benefits to life. Use visual words that release strong mental images. Add color and vividness to your descriptions and your benefits will leap off the page and not only be seen, but felt on an emotional level.

How To Uncover Features That Can Be Converted Into Benefits

Dissect your product. Place it in front of you and take it apart if possible. Look at every aspect -- size, materials, function, speed, sound -- whatever applies to your particular product.

If you were selling binders, you'd examine the cover, pockets, shape of the rings, the number of rings, anodizing process used on the rings and inside spine, thickness, size, capacity, materials used in the cover, coating, clear vinyl cover pockets, available colors and sizes, etc.

The idea is to really get inside your product and gain as complete an understanding as possible of what it is and what makes it tick. Take each singular element and examine it under a virtual microscope. Virtually every element can be translated into a benefit, but your prospect will never know or appreciate a particular benefit if you don't bring it to his attention in vivid and exciting detail.

Some benefits will rank high in terms of value to typical prospects. Others will play a lesser role. But every benefit must be genuine, or it doesn't belong.

"No matter how skillful you are, you can't invent a product advantage that doesn't exist. And if you do, and it's just a gimmick, it's going to fall apart anyway."

-- William Bernbach

Is It Ever Acceptable To Stretch The Truth?

You know when you're pushing the limits… and so does your prospect.

If you stretch the truth, sooner or later it will come back to haunt you. Once word gets out that your product doesn't quite live up to the promises of your copy, you're in trouble. If prospects think you've been deceptive, they'll never trust you again. That's a hefty price to pay and one that's guaranteed to be fatal to your long-term business success.

No one appreciates being taken advantage of. It's why most people tend to be suspicious of advertising as a rule. They want to believe you but… they've been burned before and they're not about to go there again. Your prospects enter your website with a degree of suspicion and trepidation. They have high hopes… but they don't want to get hurt. It takes a strong sales effort to overcome these negative feelings and get first-time prospects to buy.

With that kind of effort involved, once you've gained the prospect's trust, you should do everything in your power to keep it. The more they trust you, the easier it is to serve (and sell) them again. Online, your reputation can spread quickly. Short-change your customers and you'll pay the price as word spreads like wildfire. Stick to the truth. Make your claims real and present them in a way that's enticing - but also real and credible. Never fabricate a claim. If you do it once, you'll do it again. Prospects and customers instinctively know this and will avoid doing business with you ever again.

Benefits are the heart and soul of good sales copy. Without clearly defined, compelling benefits, you don't really have much to offer. You're just another merchant with another product. Benefits inform, intrigue, and arouse interest in prospects. It's the benefits that bring your product to life and make it a desirable acquisition.

When considering your sales proposition, prospects weigh costs against benefits received. Benefits build value and the more benefits you unwrap - - the more favorable your proposition becomes and the more you tilt the scale towards a sale.

Load your entire site with benefits. Start by placing benefits on each page of your site. Higher ticket items means prospects are more likely to read every page available to them before making a purchase. So you want to have benefits everywhere.

Use benefit-oriented headlines, sub-heads, and captions as frequently as possible. Don't describe the product… convey the benefit and align it to a predominant "want" that already exists deep in the recesses of the prospects mind.

The more benefits you can unleash, the more effective the overall message. Overwhelm them with benefits and never worry about overdoing it. As long as it's a benefit to your prospect, it deserves honorable mention.

Make it exceptionally easy for prospects to see the benefits for themselves.

Spell it out in clear, coherent, everyday English. Highlight the most important benefits. Allow them to get it all at-a-glance by using visual contrasts to highlight benefits in headlines bullet points and other key areas like your guarantee. Provide for easy absorption, understanding, and assimilation of your main benefits, without the careful reading of each and every word.

Using Bullet Points To Present Your Benefits

Why use bullet points and not just straightforward paragraph copy?

Bullets are eye-stoppers. They leap off the page like miniature headlines when surrounded by the plain text look of paragraph copy.

What sets the bullet point apart is that it always begins with a visual symbol - an asterisk, check mark, square dot, round dot, or some other type of character. Bullets are usually indented - separating them from the rest of the text.

The content of a bullet point reads like that of a headline - it's hard-hitting, direct, provocative, and compelling. It summarizes the benefit in an interesting and enticing way.

Here are several sample bullet points extracted from actual online sales letters:

* An inside source you can visit online to discover in advance what hundreds of publications are planning to publish - and how to use this information to get a ton of free publicity for your products...

* How to give your tiny little ad the moneymaking power of a gigan tic display ad - this secret alone can put thousands of dollars in your pocket...

* How to use a tiny piece of paper worth about a penny to drive interested, qualified and eager-to-spend prospects to your website...

* How to replace fat with solid muscle mass giving you superb definition and a physique others can only admire (or envy)...

* The single most important tool for taking you from where you are now to where you want to go (and it's dirt-cheap for anyone)...

* What to buy, when to buy it, how much you should pay and… how to know when it's time to sell!

* The #1 rule of successful investing (this one may surprise you)...

* 3 incredibly easy ways to uncover the huge (but hidden) profit potential of quality stocks and how to spot them before everyone else!

* 13 common investment mistakes made by "novice" investors and how to avoid making the costly blunders that could wipe you out before you get to the really big cash returns that are yours for the taking…

* Revealed: The guilt-free way to enjoy all your favorite foods and still lose those extra pounds automatically - 24 hours a day. Melt away FAT like magic… without ever feeling deprived!

* Discover the time-tested way to lose 30 pounds in 30 days… eating the foods you love!

* 7 simple secrets to having the body you've only dreamed about… until now…

* Get wholesale prices for life on an exclusive line of superb-quality health products that customers continually order again and again, earning you impressive commissions on every order…

* The "Magic Number" Surefire Formula that quickly tells you whether a potential 'buy' is really a bargain

* How to make one simple transaction that can put $2000 to $3000 in your pocket in just days…

* How to build a network of cash-ready buyers that makes the whole process even easier

* The 3 magic words that hold the key to runaway profits in buying and selling…

You may have noticed a lack of punctuation at the end of most of the above bullet points. While exclamation points can help underscore an important point, periods act as natural stop signs -- and every stoppage is another opportunity for prospects to flee. I want prospects to get the gist of the benefit and to hunger for more information, more details, and more juicy benefits. For that reason, I favor ellipses, exclamation points for emphasis, or no punctuation at all. The period serves no useful benefit here, in my opinion.

Concise, powerful benefit copy designed to give prospects a taste so they'll yearn for more - that's essentially the task of the bullet point. Like headlines and sub-heads, bullets have the opportunity to take any product feature and transform it into a statement that makes true prospects salivate and crave more of the same.

Most successful sales letters are loaded with bullet points. Look at the online portfolio of any prominent copywriter and you're sure to find bullets used frequently.

Some letters, like those created by Frank Cawood for the alternative health market, make use of bullet copy almost exclusively. Every point is directed at the specific target reader and loaded with power, passion, and intrigue. Each and every bullet touches a hot button and works at pulling the prospect in deeper.

Carefully crafted bullet points arouse interest and desire and make prospects want to learn more about the offer. Bullets afford quick delivery of powerful and alluring advantages. They stand out on the page and quickly pull in eyeballs. Bullets allow the writer to tempt, tease, and tantalize prospects headline style -- using just a handful of words each time. But that one bundle of words packs a punch that captivates the prospect's imagination, creates intrigue, and literally compels genuine prospects to read on.

Keys To Successful Bullets

Start with an understanding of what it is your prospect desires most. Then, simply tap into that hunger. Give him a nibble. Allow your prospect to sample your wares enough to make him want more. It's kind of like eating potato chips. A single chip tempts your taste buds. Once you've had a taste… the craving kicks in. That small sample soon has you reaching for more of the same. That's the same reaction your bullets should trigger. Let your buyers reach further and further into your bag of goodies. You want to stimulate the desire for more - a desire that can only be fulfilled to the fullest degree with the purchase of your product.

Employ bullets to tap into the existing "wants" of your target market. Don't try to create desire or establish a market. Fulfill the hunger that already exists - it's an easier, more logical approach that expedites your success.

How To Write Provocative, Interest-Arousing Bullets

Create explosive bullets by taking specific facts and product features and reshaping them into powerful, irresistible and intriguing statements.

Deliver facts in a way that gives meaning to the prospect. Keep it 100% accurate… but make it as alluring as you can.

If you're marketing a book, you could easily create an appealing bullet point for each chapter or section. In fact, if you were to go through the book page by page, you could quite handily write solid bullet points for each and every paragraph.

The more bullets you write, the more skill you develop.

Writing bullet copy is a lot like writing headlines. But instead of an all-encompassing power-packed statement designed to interest readers in your letter, your bullet copy simply takes one small aspect and turns it into something huge with massive appeal.

Bullets allow you to present benefits with a twist. It's an opportunity to reveal a secret or an unexpected benefit or advantage.

Bullets can stop prospects cold - in a mesmerizing, captivating or curiosity-arousing manner. Plus, you can pack more explosive power per square inch using bullets than you can with standard text.

More Examples Of Effective Bullet Copy

Gary Halbert

* A dirty little secret many real estate brokers hope you never find out!

* Something crucial (and unusual) you must do to every closet in your house before you show it to a would-be buyer!

* The single best investment you can make when selling your home!

* What you should do to the light bulbs in your house that can dramatically help you sell it!

* A brand new discovery (just approved by the FDA on February 28, 2000) that any man can use to instantly (and safely) boost his testo sterone level. Note: This will not only improve his sex life... but also... his overall health!

* The single most important thing a woman can do to make herself more attractive to the opposite sex!

* A special place (and a special way) to touch a woman to guarantee mind-altering sex! (This technique is so simple... and... so little-known... even 75% of all women don't know about it.)

* One very common (so-called "safe") surgery that increases the chance of getting prostate cancer by 300%!

* Why the "by-pass surgery industry" would shut down tomorrow... if... everybody knew the truth!

* Why staying out of the sun... increases your risk of getting skin cancer!

* A secret your doctor will never tell you that... guarantees... you will recover as fast as possible after any surgery!

* How to "signal" your fat cells to shed excess weight!

* A non-prescription antidote for anxiety that would put Prozac out of business... if... the American public ever found out about it!

* What word one company used to double their sales! (This one will blow your mind.)

* 3 little-known reasons why people don't buy from you! (Once you discover these reasons, you will be able be able to sell virtually every prospect you see.)

* Two "magic words" that will put you light years ahead of your competition!

* The single biggest mistake most people make when writing copy... and... how to avoid it!

Anthony Blake

* How To Launch Your Product Effectively And Immediately Generate At Least 100 Money-Carrying Customers!

* How To Beat The Search Engine Merry-Go-Round - Simple "Power" Techniques That'll Let You Beat Everyone Else Playing The Search Engine Game And Leave Them In The Dust!

* The Secret To Using An Easy To Employ Follow-Up System To Create A Sales Explosion - Here's How To Increase Your Sales Rates By Using An Almost Automatic Strategy Aimed At Putting More Money In Your Pocket!

* How To Land "Trophy" Fish From Cashflow River - Discover The Secrets To Generating Multiple Income Streams From One Web Page!

* How to stack the deck so virtually any expert will see the advantages of working with you... even if you're just beginning the business

* Five techniques to keeping your interviews focused and on track, to get the answers your customers need and the best-selling tape you want

* How, with one inexpensive extra step, you can double the perceived value of your tape and increase your selling price… and your profits!

* How to literally force your expert to dig deeper than "yes" or "no" answers, to get your listeners the specific details they want to hear

John Carlton

* A truly "no-brainer" (yet usually overlooked) way to bump the amount of your average order by 100% or more… automatically! The absolutely essential First 3 Things you must do before you attempt to sell anything to anyone!

* 20 Guaranteed Ways to increase readership and response to your sales letters and ads… without touching your current copy!

* "Insider" tips from the world's savviest (and richest) businessmen on how to shortcut your way to obscene riches and success!

* The 58 most important questions you need to ask yourself before you can really start to pile up the profits in your business!

* How the 3 Basic Elements found in every single successful (multi-million dollar) television infomercial can also be used to boost the profitability of your newspaper ads!

* How to "read" the signals of women who are dying to date you right now! (They think they're being obvious, but I'll bet you're blind to these signals. Just learning this one secret - how to "read" women - will boost your "romance potential" through the roof!)

* Why having money or a nice car is 100% irrelevant to having a great love-life! (And the 3 "basics" that are relevant, but ignored by

nearly every lonely guy!)

* How to easily "position" yourself so women actually compete for your attention!

* Why your weight, strength, speed and agility are the least important parts of winning a street altercation! (And why the one simple secret that is important will give you an immediate and enormous advantage over any other fighter you meet!)

* How to turn everyday items in your pocket (or your wife's purse) into vicious weapons that will (1) show you mean business, (2) instantly frighten anyone with an ounce of common sense, and (3) allow you to dominate any situation with a single blow!

* Simple fight-ending moves that require no strength whatsoever! (I know of arthritic 80-year-old grandmothers who have knocked young male attackers senseless!)

* What women really want from a man! (Nine times out of ten men are absolutely floored by this secret!)

Where To Find Rich Sources Of Bullet Point Material

Look at your list of unused headlines. If you followed the ideas presented earlier, you already have some solid raw material to work with. Take each discarded headline and convert it into a bullet point.

You can do the same with your benefits list. Take each individual benefit and craft it into a mini headline that possesses power and punch. Consider how your product helps buyers avoid pain and gain pleasure. Use a magnetic appeal by tying one element of your product to a condition, feeling, or result your prospect really wants to acquire.

Take any feature and convert it into a benefit. Now add a little magic, suspense, intrigue, and interest to the benefit by converting it into a powerful bullet point.

Great Lead-Ins For Powerful Bullets

The first few words of bullet copy are key - it's what makes the point powerful, provocative and interesting. Simply take the list of sample leads below, insert your own product benefits and you'll instantly create bullet points with 'magical' appeal.

Another technique is to use these leads as idea generators that spark your own compilations. Either way… these openers will get you thinking in the right way. Simply fill-in-the-blanks with your own benefit teasers and you'll soon have a sizable list of powerful bullets you can use in your next sales letter.

Here are several effective leads to help you get started writing powerful bullets:

> How To…
> Why…
> Advice Doctors (Mechanics, Accountants, Attorneys,
> Chiropractors, Guidance Counsellors, etc.) Give To…
> The Shocking Truth About…
> 17 Easiest Ways To…
> The One Thing You Must Do If…
> Shockingly Simple Methods For…
> 3-Step Formula For…
> 7 Guaranteed Ways To…
> The Dirty Little Secret…
> 11 No-Brainer Ways To…
> Crucial Tips From…
> The 4.5-Minute Solution For…
> 13 Deadly Mistakes…
> 7 Time-Tested Techniques Guaranteed To…
> The Number One Reason Why…

Numbers are great ways to begin bullet points. "The 5-Minute Solution For…" or "7 Guaranteed Ways To…" immediately gives readers a frame of reference. The "3-Step Formula For…" suggests a precise, step-by-step method.

Use the exact number of "Ways To", "High-Profit Techniques", "Time-Saving Strategies" that apply and you'll heighten interest and desire -- driving prospects to want to know more.

The idea here is to write one or two line headers that highlight the key attributes of your product in a riveting way. Knowing that you have a maximum of a couple of lines to use forces you to create enticing benefits succinctly.

Play around with these samples and see what kind of bullets you can create for your sales letter. Try different variations. Write pages full of bullets. If you do just that, I guarantee you'll have at least a handful of powerful, provocative bullets that will help grab prospects and keep them glued to your sales message.

Look at bullet points used by others. How do they stack up? Unfortunately, many lack power, clarity, and intrigue. You can avoid this kind of mistake by writing bullets the same way you'd write headlines - lean, mean, direct, and benefit oriented. Make every word justify itself. Delete any word that isn't absolutely necessary. Use powerful attention-grabbing words like shocking, surprising and advice.

Review sales letters created by experienced copywriters and you'll find the kind of benefit-oriented bullets that grab the prospects attention and practically force him to read more with an increased sense of interest, enthusiasm, and desire.

Take a trip to your local bookstore and scan the covers of magazines. Do this as well whenever you find yourself visiting the pharmacy, convenience, or grocery store. Why? Because people buy magazines right off the rack for one reason -- the headlines. More specifically, it's the short, bullet-like copy that graces the cover page. These covers consist exclusively of short, bullet-point headline copy. Publishers are well aware of the power of these provocative, interest-arousing shopper-stoppers. That's why issues of *Men's Health* feature headlines like…

Build This Body - Our Cover Guys Show You How
15-Minute Fat Burners

Incredible Arms In Just 3 Weeks
10 Greatest AB Exercises Ever!
Are You Too Stressed? Take Our Test, P. 73

Take a look around your home. Gather past issues of any magazines that depend largely on newsstand sales to keep them publishing. Start a notebook or open up a file on your computer where you collect as many of these sample bullet points as you can. Then, the next time you set out to write a powerful sales letter, you have a vast resource of headline, subhead, and bullet point "idea-starters".

Essentially, these headlines are more like sub-heads or bullet points. They're precisely targeted, provocative, and deal with one specific benefit rather than the merits of reading the entire publication.

Build Your Case With Solid Proof

"The head certainly can't go along and concur with the heart without some reasons. Now all this process is one of rationalization. To rationalize is to bring props of reason to support decisions arrived at emotionally. The skilled copywriter attempts to provide the reader of advertising with a basis for rationalization. In short, the real advertising writer who is after results makes the reader want something - and then provides what the reader will consider a good excuse for buying it."

-- Clyde Bedell

Why Proof Is Such An Important Element

Proof reassures prospects by backing up your claims. It makes your statements more believable by presenting evidence that reinforces your benefits.

Prospects have learned to become suspect of sales claims in general. They question everything. After all... they don't know you or your product. You could be thousands of miles away in a distant land far beyond the scrutiny of local lawmakers. This apparent immunity presents an opportunity for the hucksters and scam artists to thrive online. Prospects are aware of these thieve and scam artists and as a result, they're on guard more than ever. In the world of online marketing, the marketer is considered guilty until proven innocent -- rather than the other way around.

Proof goes a long way to alleviate your prospect's doubts and fears. It makes the questionable seem much more believable and gives an unknown marketer a higher ranking in the minds of consumers.

The lesser known you are, the more significant role proof plays in presenting your case for a sale. And the best back-up proof you can have are the actual words, feelings and experiences of previous customers who were delighted with their purchases. Anyone can make claims. But the smart marketer finds ways to back them up.

How Other People's Experiences Help Influence New Customers

Prospects have a natural distrust of merchants. They know your principle motivation is to make money... and you do that by selling your goods. Some vendors will go to any length to make the sale, including crossing the line of ethics, morals and even legalities. Therein lies the problem. Prospects dislike questionable claims and naturally doubt anything that seems even remotely inaccurate. They're skeptical of all advertisers and have experienced misrepresentations on numerous occasions.

But *proof* helps change all that. Proof makes your benefit message appear much more credible... and the best form of proof is the real world customer testimonial.

Testimonials are seemingly objective, third party endorsements. It's someone else conveying their thoughts and experiences of using your product and doing business with you. Prospects relate well to testimonials from customers - people who were once in their shoes, considering whether or not they should buy. It's someone they can easily identify with.

It's comforting to prospective customers to hear the actual words of those who risked their money and blazed a trail before them. The perception is that these people are merely expressing their heartfelt thoughts in an honest and objective manner. After all, the prospect reasons, if these buyers weren't absolutely delighted with their purchase, why would they take the time to convey their experiences and willingly allow marketers to use their comments for promotional purposes?

While all testimonials are not of the same origin or quality, the good feelings they generate can make or break your sales letter.

It seems much more convincing coming from someone else... particularly someone who earlier had the same doubts and concerns, but still went ahead and ordered the product on faith. It's comforting to prospects to see that others have received their shipments in a timely manner and are thrilled enough with the purchase to make a public declaration expressing their level of satisfaction.

Additional Ways To Build Credibility

Endorsements from recognized experts or institutions immediately inject credibility into your sales letter. Direct endorsements are best... but implied endorsements can also help enhance your credibility.

A direct endorsement is the expressed approval of a well-known individual in your respective field. The best endorsements read like convincing testimonials... plus, they have the added impact of coming form a voice of authority. After all, what expert would risk their reputation to endorse a product for nothing... unless they really had no qualms about doing so because they absolutely loved the product!

Endorsements and testimonials are the top two credibility-boosting tools. Good endorsements are typically toughest of all to collect. Why? Well... there are only so many experts in any given field... and these people aren't just sitting around waiting for product developers to get in touch and send them review copies or trial editions.

It never hurts to contact these experts and ask if you could send your product along. The worst they can do is refuse. But chances are, if you show some respect and knowledge of your topic, even busy experts will give your product a shot. But keep in mind that sending a sample copy does not guarantee any response. If you do get favorable feedback that you can use in your sales letter, follow-up with a thank you note and consider yourself fortunate.

Testimonials, on the other hand are much easier to acquire.

Follow-up with customers after each sale -- particularly in the early days of your product launch -- and respectfully ask for feedback. Many customers will happily oblige. With their permission you can record these comments and use them as you would any testimonial.

Offer a limited number of free sample products to qualified prospects in exchange for their feedback. Ask respected names in your industry if you could send along a sample for their review. Follow-up later and solicit their candid feedback.

Collecting testimonials should be an on-going part of your marketing. Nothing is more effective in convincing unsure prospects than hearing glowing words from others who were once unsure prospects themselves.

Genuine commentary -- the type of raw, unedited, spontaneous text conveyed by real, live customers -- is fresh and original. It's unlike the slick, well-planned communications of a corporation seeking to sell more of its wares.

It's this unpolished look that adds to the credibility and believability of your customer's words. That's the reason why you should never edit or rephrase their verbal expressions. Present them verbatim. Take them exactly as they're offered and they'll convey energy, enthusiasm, and a sincere voice of appreciation.

How Perception Affects Your Results

Positioning is key and perception determines where prospects 'place' you in the market. You need to look the part. If you're selling business advice from a free, advertising-supported web site, you're fighting an uphill battle. If you don't appear professional, prospects will quickly lose confidence in you and they certainly won't buy.

Perceptions are powerful and often determined by first impressions. If your site looks unorganized and amateurish, visitors naturally assume you are too.

Present an image of competence, expertise and professionalism. Don't jump all over your visitors with pop-up windows immediately upon their arrival, like an overly aggressive salesman. It's not exactly an inviting approach.

Avoid tired old phrases, flashing images and an excessive use of bright colors. Instead, focus on an organized presentation that pulls prospects inside due to its meaningful, interesting and fresh new content. Concentrate on your biggest, most unique benefit. That's how you can impact your prospects perception of you from the get go. And oh yes… insist on your own domain name and professional hosting service. Avoid those free offers with blatant pop-up windows, flashing banner ads and lengthy domain name extensions. With today's options and accessibility, there's really no reason to go that route.

* While reviewing this section, I was reminded about an order received a week erarlier from a free site I set up as a test several years ago. Seems I forgot about it completely. Well, lo and behold, there I was holding a cheque from someone a few thousand miles away who stumbled upon this advertising-supported site -- complete with moving banners and pop-up window supplied by the hosting company.

Other Factors That Come Into Play

Building credibility has a lot to do with how you conduct your business. Sincerity, responsiveness, and an intimate knowledge of the issues of concern to prospects and customers are all vitally important.

Think of your marketing message as a personal conversation between two friends. Make a sincere effort to help your new friend. Speak in your own voice and inject your own individual personality. Use a conversational tone -- rather than trying to write the perfectly formulated message.

Follow up on all inquiries promptly, as any caring friend would. Follow through on every promise. Maintain a presence online and keep your site active with regular updates and new material. Show that your business is active and thriving.

Be willing to share information. After all, information is the most highly sought commodity in the online marketplace. Share more and you benefit more. The implication is that the more you share, the more you have available and the more people will seek out your expertise and your product recommendations.

Develop a mindset of service. Be service oriented. Make delivering top quality service a huge priority of your business. Remember this… your prospect has doubts about you. After all, he doesn't know you, your product, or your organization. But you have a chance to win points and influence their opinion in a positive way by delivering prompt service on all fronts. As you develop such a reputation, word spreads and making sales gets a whole lot easier when fast, efficient service becomes a part of your business culture.

The Kind Of Proof That Matters Most To Prospects

The best proof or evidence you can provide in your sales copy is quantitative in nature. It's measurable and achievable. Thus, the best testimonials are those that state actual results in detail such as skills learned in little time, dollars made or saved, number of customers acquired, the hours saved by new automation, etc. But just because somebody claims a particular result doesn't mean you should use it.

It could be an issue of time, money, or skill... or a specific result that was previously unattainable by your prospect through any other means available.

Here are a few examples of "quantitative" proof...

> *"I was shocked to see how well I was typing after just 3 days!"*
> *"I now see why over 85% return here after the first visit."*
> *"The food is in a class by itself... but the extraordinary service made it an experience to remember."*

Prospects want to know what they can reasonably expect to accomplish, acquire, or achieve too. By sharing the actual experiences of others in precise detail, it becomes instantly processed by prospects, giving them a better understanding and appreciation of your product.

Quantifying results adds to the believability of your message. Precise, documented figures tend to ring true - more so than a general claim.

How Your Reputation Serves You Online

In any business, reputation is important - and it always precedes you.

If your company is a known name in the industry, prospects already have determined how they feel about you. If you're unknown, your market will have its doubts as to whether you can deliver quality product in a timely manner. Clients for whom I write online copy who are already established as credible businesspeople, tend to enjoy better results right off the bat.

For others, it takes time to establish a reputation that pulls prospects in by itself.

Like it or not, we're all judged in advance as people, business entities, products, and services. It's the same way opinions are formed of books based solely on the appearance of the cover.

Prospects remember past experiences. They'll recognize your name and form an opinion of you based on an article you wrote, or a discussion board post you made several months earlier. This could be a good thing or a bad thing - it all depends on how you project and present yourself. That's why it's so important to always put your best foot forward. Never let down your guard or get careless. Your future market is paying attention and will not forget.

The impression you've created and the reputation you've established can help you tremendously by "pre-selling" your product to some degree. When prospects are sent to your sales letter, they carry with them a snap-shot of all past experiences, opinions and impressions. If history left a favorable impression, you've got a head start in the race to win the sale. The higher your ranking from the prospect's point of view, the greater the chances of converting him to a customer.

"Top of mind" is the ideal spot to occupy in any marketplace. You want prospects to think of you and your product first, as perhaps the best solution to their problem. That can only happen when you establish a solid presence first.

What Makes Some Testimonials Better Than Others

Compatibility and resonance are the keys to a quality testimonial. The most effective testimonials connect with the prospect's state of mind and place at the time. Great testimonials grab the prospect's interest because it resonates with his current thoughts and feelings.

Here's someone who has purchased a particular product in hopes of solving a problem… and solve the problem, it did. Prospects can relate to this kind of a message, especially when they share similar traits or qualities such as being members of the same association, industry, or hobby group.

Testimonials increase confidence. The best testimonial stimulates this kind of thinking in the prospects mind...

"If this person who seems to be just like me can do it, surely I can do it too. Heck, even if I get only half the results, I'm still way ahead of the game."

Strong testimonials paint this kind of scenario for prospects...

*"Like you, I once had this problem and didn't know where to turn.
I heard about (name of product) but since it was new to me, I figured it was all smoke and mirrors. But I was desperate to find a solution that worked. It seemed I tried everything before and nothing really solved the problem -- long term. So I took a chance on (name of product) and haven't looked back since. Am I ever glad I was willing to give it a shot! Not only did it solve my huge painful problem... it also changed my life! I'm happier now than I've been in years."*

The more testimonials you can gather, the better. It gives you more options to draw from.

> * A word of warning: Be sure to comply with the most updated policies of govern ing bodies (like the FTC) in your jurisdiction. Recent changes in howtestimonials can be used could effect your marketing strategy.

What you don't want is multiple testimonials that all sound alike. Variety is the key and some testimonials are much more powerful than others. The more you have in your collection, the greater the chances are that you have some real gems worth highlighting.

Use whatever tools you have available. If you're just starting out, you may want to use any legitimate testimonial you can get your hands on. Even a lukewarm testimonial like this... "I read your book and I think it's great." can be helpful in persuading a prospect to go ahead and buy.

The better quality testimonials come across as being totally honest expressions of gratitude at the new, improved result obtained. They tend to come from people speaking in simple conversational language -- complete with spelling errors and grammatical inconsistencies. It's raw, unedited and seemingly truthful commentary relating their level of satisfaction in purchasing the product.

The most effective testimonials often feature specific amounts of money made… precise number of hours, days, or weeks saved… or any measurable result achieved enhances believability. These specifics tend to grab interest and arouse curiosity to a greater degree.

Dramatic "before and after" results make for a powerful testimonial. The classic "rags to riches" story has long been used in the business opportunity market… but the principles can be applied anywhere. The keys are the striking differences between the customer's life BP (Before Product) and AP (After Product).

Where To Best Place Your Customer Testimonials

Testimonials are effective anywhere in your sales letter. But since they're such important tools of persuasion - they deserve to be highlighted. Headlines, sub-heads, lead paragraphs, body copy or the P.S. -- can all be excellent locations to deliver a riveting testimonial.

It's best to have plenty of testimonials in your arsenal to create a strong, leak-proof case in favor of the sale. You want to present overwhelming evidence that the product lives up to your benefit claims. Since testimonials come from others, specifically people who have purchased your product, they tend to be more readily accepted -- without deliberation -- than any sales point you make. After all, prospects know that generally speaking, no one would bother to voice their support and put their name to it if they weren't thrilled with their purchase.

Testimonials could be scattered throughout your sales copy and set apart from the regular text by indenting, italicizing, or by using a simple text box. Many copywriters use this approach because it's very effective in drawing attention to each highlighted testimonial.

Another method, and one I generally prefer when I have lots of testimonials I want to use is to bundle them together - one right after the other. The effect of this grouped presentation is quite dramatic. It's one voice of delight after another. This stacking effect creates a compounded result on the psyche of the prospect. It's not just the voice of one happy customer… it's 7, 10, or 12 different people - real people from recognizable cities and states and web locations - and each one is willing to go on record to declare their thoughts about you and your product.

Got an exceptional testimonial - one that's strikingly original? Consider such a testimonial, or a segment of it for your headline. Another great location is the P.S. With such a high readership, it's a natural place to unveil an exceptionally strong and persuasive comment.

You can also use testimonials on your order form. It's another chance to drive home your message and further solidify the purchase in the buyer's mind. Be careful not to introduce any new thoughts at this stage, however. You've got them there because they want what you're selling. Reinforce the key benefits only -- don't provide and opportunity to redirect their thinking. Make the sale first.

How To Overcome The Fears That Concern Prospects

The best way to alleviate fear among prospects is to take the time and space to give them the whole story. After all, they don't know you from Jack… or your product from any other. Tell them all they're going to get out of the deal. Give prospective customers your full benefit story and provide every ounce of proof you can muster.

Concerns can only be addressed by facing each one head on. Answer every objection honestly. Don't hide from the issues - tackle them full out.

Be willing to admit your shortcomings - it shows integrity, openness, and honesty. No product is perfect and your prospect knows it. Prospects expect you to rave about your product and describe it in the most glowing of terms. That's fine for the most part. But admit a flaw or weakness and you've added credibility to your attribute-laden message. Prospects are much more likely to buy into your beliefs when you level with them and admit your product isn't the perfect answer for everyone.

Joe Karbo demonstrated this concept beautifully in *The Lazy Man's Way*

To Riches...

> "I have a new Cadillac that I've got to sell because I'm leaving for the Service next week. It cost me $8,000 and only has 732 miles on it. Rather than sell it to some thief of a car dealer or going to the trouble of advertising, I'll let you have it for $4,000.
>
> If you don't have the cash, don't worry about it because I only owe the $4,000, and you can take over my payments (which are about$75 a month).
>
> You know I drive careful, but I'd feel better if you'd have your mechanic check it out before you buy. In fact, if you'd like to drive it for a couple of days, I'll be glad to deliver it to you with a full tank of gas. And if you don't like the car, I'll take it back and you've had a free ride. No obligation.
>
> One thing - it's an awful green color (but you could have it painted).
>
> If you're interested, call me at (714) 111-1111 between 7 and 9 tonight."

The more you tell the more you sell. This isn't simply a cliché, it's a fact. Don't you want to know everything about a product before buying -- particularly if it means spending more than mere pocket change? Of course you do. Now, picture your prospect arriving at your website for the first time. He doesn't know you, or your company or product... but your headline has captured his attention and lured him inside.

"What really decides consumers to buy or not to buy is the content of your advertising, not its form."

-- David Ogilvy

Should you tell him a few things that'll tickle his fancy... or do you go all out and give him every bit of information he could ever need or want? The choice is yours... but I suggest giving all you've got and letting the chips fall where they may.

Don't forget, your prospect is constantly assessing your credibility from the very beginning. Every detail, every image, and every word is a cause and for every cause, there's an effect. That's why details are so important -- everything counts. Your best bet is to tell all. Paint a vivid, benefit-laden image of all your product offers to buyers.

Another technique is to introduce yourself to your prospect by attaching a small image to the headline. Allow readers to see with whom they are having this personal conversation. Give benefits and solid proof that you deliver. Let them hear from other people about their experiences with both your company and your product. Answer every question, concern and objection. Take away their fears with an ironclad guarantee. The more benefit information and credible proof you provide, the better your results.

Why Testimonials Are Such Valuable Marketing Tools

Third party endorsements are seen as more believable to prospects than straight sales copy. It's almost like comparing a friend's recommendation to a salesperson's pitch. The salesperson is there with one purpose in mind -- to get the sale. It's the same with your sales copy. Your message is there to convince prospects to buy and they know it. They also have a tendency to liken any sales method to that of a pushy salesperson.

Prospects expect to be told what they want to hear - whatever it takes to make the sale. So they very naturally have their guard up. They're weary of being sold something that may not be in their best interest.

But along comes testimonial after testimonial providing realistic accolades and comments of total satisfaction. It's not from a personal friend… but an ally. As such, they're welcome words. Suddenly, your message is seen in a different light. Maybe what you said earlier is true after all.

The realism of quality customer testimonials cuts through the sales talk and hits home as a more objective assessment of the product. The prospect wants to buy. He wants to believe your claims. And a good arrangement of testimonials provides the validation needed to move forward in confidence.

For testimonials to appear credible, you must include a full name as well as the city or town of residence and the state, province, or region. The more information you can provide - the better. It's additional proof that this is a real person who actually expressed these very sentiments.

Everyone is suspect of the testimonial signed with nothing but initials. The validity of such a testimonial immediately comes into question and the impact of the words is severely weakened. If you don't use a full name it raises a red flag. Such action suggests you never got permission to use the testimonial, or it's a total fabrication. These assumptions may be completely false… but that doesn't matter to the prospect. Perception equals reality. If it looks suspicious, it will never fly, especially online where prospects are more savvy and hip to deceptive practices.

Online, there's another way to enhance the credibility of your testimonials. Add an email address or website URL to the author's contact information. Get permission first, of course. Many people will gladly grant you this wish. Some only ask that you make theirs a "live" link, so they can benefit from the added traffic. The additional information gives prospects an extra opportunity to look for validation and to learn a little more about the people making claims about your product.

Premium Quality Testimonials

The very best testimonials are those that show up unexpectedly. When buyers take the time to craft a note of appreciation and send it to you without any provocation, you usually end up with an original treasure that's worth its weight in gold. The only problem is that this kind of testimonial takes time to acquire.

When you're just getting started, ask customers for their feedback. Conduct online surveys and encourage participation by offering a small thank-you gift. Allow participants to comment freely on any aspect of your product or business, or their experience in dealing with you.

Send review copies of books and software to review editors of magazines and ezines. Ask them to write a brief review of your product. Ask industry leaders and known experts if you can forward your product to them. Most who accept, will gladly offer a little feedback, some of which can be powerful testimony for your product.

Other Methods For Building Credibility

Become known to your audience online. Take part in discussion forums. Write articles and publish a regular newsletter. Become recognized for all the right reasons - quality information, prompt service, professional presence, delivering reliability and expert answers.

Be courteous and friendly - the kind of person you'd like to do business with. As your reputation for sharing information grows, so does your position in the minds of your target consumer group.

Keep your site focused and directed towards one result. Organize your information so prospects can get what they want, when they want it. Funnel prospects from each page of your site to your sales letter and then on to the order form.

Display consistency in your communications and your marketing efforts. Always stay focussed on getting your prospect closer to what he wants.

Use the same layout and design on each page to maintain visual congruency. Keep it simple and direct. If you vary design element between pages, you'll soon confuse prospects. They'll wonder where they went astray.

The more credible your message, the less skepticism you'll face. Back everything you say with real proof. At the same time, be aware of your prospect's natural distaste for questionable advertising claims.

Go the extra mile to clearly and logically justify the promises you make and you'll reap the rewards in terms of increased response.

Creating Irresistible Offers

"Your offer can make a hero or a bum out of the finest, slickest string of words you ever turned out."

-- Maxwell Sackheim

Offers Defined

The *offer* is the package deal -- "the whole shebang". The offer is a combination of your basic product, bonuses, plus any other special inducements that increase the perceived value of the whole package. It's not just another product you're making available to the marketplace - it's a bundle of extra goodies all rolled into and available at one low price.

Offers are based on a main product. But the product itself is not an offer -- despite your personal feelings towards your invention, creation, or acquisition. The reason for establishing an offer is to increase response. It's a matter of creating a proposition that offers such incredible value… that prospects would have to be crazy not to jump on it at once!

The Kinds Of Items To Include In Your Offers

Each offer is different from the next. But the most important single ingredient is the free extras -- bonuses, gifts and premiums. In fact, the more 'extras' you can include, the better.

But keep in mind the most effective extra bonus items are those…

1. In High Demand
2. In Short Supply… and
3. Exclusive to the package being offered.

Other possible offer elements include:

Guarantees
Payments On An Installment Plan

Deferred Payment
Price Discounts
Free Shipping
Priority Shipping
Rebates
Flexible Payment Plans
Additional Bonus Gifts
Early Bird Bonus or Special Discount
Beat Price Increase
Limited Availability

Why A Summarized Offer Is So Important

Simplify your presentation and you make it easier for prospects to under-stand. Lengthy offers can be confusing. A short summary, on the other hand, confirms exactly what it is the buyer gets in exchange for his cash. A concise checklist of each component provided makes for a quick review at the moment of truth, just as the prospect makes the decision to buy.

Seeing all the components listed - one after another - provides a dramatic presentation where the payoff looks considerable, yet the price does not. Such a list may contain 10 or 12 items in all.

Now… compare the value of this mega-package to the perceived value of the product alone. When you look at it this way, you'll have to agree that an attractive offer looks far more enticing than the product does as a solo package. That's the magic of a strong offer.

This summarized list can also have multiple applications. Not only does it give you a succinct description of each bonus and element of your offer, but it also gives something to use in the close, the P.S., or on the order form. Repeating the offer is particularly important when it appears so appealing that it's almost "too good to be true".

Key Points To Remember When Compiling An Offer

Value is the primary key. Your offer must be valuable in the eyes of pros-pects. The perceived value of your offer -- as assessed by the marketplace -

- is what matters most. If you want to gain an advantage in the market-place, make a better offer than they could ever imagine getting at twice the price from any other supplier - anywhere, anytime.

You need to monitor your competitors to keep one step ahead. Keep an eye out for competitors to respond to your offer with one of their own. This usually happens as soon as your offer gains new popularity and competitors start to lose market share.

Bonus items alone can be the deciding factor. Add bonuses that buyers simply cannot get anywhere else - bonuses that enhance the main product featured in the offer.

Another vital key is to shape your offer to fit the prospect. Make your solution tailor made - one that fits like a glove. The closer the match between your prospect's problem and your optimum solution (as presented in your offer) the more interest and positive response you'll generate.

Knowing Your Market Is Crucial

Imagine a doctor being asked to prescribe a treatment for an unknown ailment. Where would she even begin? Without knowledge of the nature of an injury or illness, even the most skilled physician would be at a loss. But deliver an accurate diagnosis and the chances of providing a remedy that solves the problem quickly and effectively are much more likely.

Your offer is in essence, a prescription. It's a packaged solution to a problem experienced by your prospects.

To create the best offer, examine your prospects and customers. What else could you provide (in addition to your main product) that would be helpful? Perhaps it's a special report showing specifically the many ways your new gizmo could be used around the house or cottage. Maybe it's a video offering tips and recipes for a new kitchen appliance. Think in terms of adding extra value to your primary product. What would make it last longer... be more versatile... or do the job faster, or easier?

Take your product and figure out how to add magic to it. What would make your already impressive product, much more useful, profitable, or functional to the buyer? Figure out a way to add tons more value and you've got the recipe for an irresistible offer.

Perceived value is what's most important here. The additional bonuses and incentives you bundle into the package must be held in high regard by prospects. It means little what they actually cost to produce in terms of dollars and cents. That's the beauty of information products. Targeted, relevant, and rare information enjoys a prominent place on the value scale. Yet it can cost you nothing in terms of out of pocket expenses. With such an exceptional advantage, no product should ever be sold from a sales letter -- online or offline -- without the added bonus of additional in-demand information products. These extras add value, making the whole package appear more desirable to buyers and worth a lot more money than the price would indicate.

What Makes An Offer Totally Irresistible?

Exclusive offers that provide exceptionally good value and represent little or no risk, are the most effective offers. When you have an exclusive package - something no one else offers - prospects have to come to you to get it. Give them outstanding value, far beyond what they could reasonably expect to get anywhere else. Make it as risk-free as possible and you've got a winning combination.

Key offer elements include:

- Exclusive Package of products (main product plus bonuses)
- Outstanding Value (5-100 times more in use value than you ask in cash value)
- 100% Risk-Free Opportunity to acquire the entire package

Bundle up a whole slew of nuggets that when combined, make for a powerhouse package. Create a package of products and bonuses that is so appealing, no sane prospect can refuse. Overwhelm them with value. Give them what they want. Make it absolutely painless to acquire without risk. Great value at a low cost is a surefire formula with universal application and appeal.

How To Convert Your Offer Into Direct Sales

Establish a sense of urgency. Introduce an element of scarcity into your offer. Don't simply create a great offer and put it out in the marketplace without limitations of any kind -- that's only self-defeating.

Creating an outstanding offer usually isn't enough on its own. You also need to move prospects into action now. Fail to get them to respond immediately and you risk losing them forever.

The trick is to introduce a limitation of some kind and to make it authentic. Too many online marketers create limited offers, only to change them repeatedly as the expiry date arrives. They obviously don't understand the principle of credibility.

Offer limited numbers of packages available at a certain price. Give an extra special bonus to those who order immediately. Change your bonus items to accurately reflect a loss of availability -- beyond the stated deadlines. If you fake it even once, you lose some of your lustre and credibility.

I know of some marketers who refuse to change their ways, despite having been called on their fictitious deadlines. Such is the power of a limited offer. Sure you can get sales by fabricating it... but you'll lose lots more in the process.

For one thing, you're lying to your prospects and customers. Should the marketplace notice, you'll immediately come under closer scrutiny. They'll question every one of your claims even more so than before and they're perfectly justified in doing so. Lie to them once and they'll be suspicious of you forever.

Set real deadlines. When the date of expiry appears, pull the offer and repackage it so new buyers aren't getting the exact same package of goodies beyond the stale date. Let them know you mean business. They'll respect you for it... and respond in greater numbers.

Genuine deadlines and limited offers do work well to motivate prospects stuck in limbo, sitting on the fence, unable to decide. When they know they need to act fast, or lose out on your special deal - something they're truly enthusiastic about - they often swing into gear. The fear of loss is a powerful force.

How To Improve A Good Offer To Make It A Great Offer

Test variables. Make it easier to get your product into the hands of interested consumers. Create a list of possible reasons why prospects may be resisting your offer -- then address each obstacle, one-by-one.

Try different bonus items. Vary your lineup of free gifts. Consider different bundles of premiums and always measure the results you get from each package offered. One combination will likely dominate your results and get more people ordering immediately. You can and should try to guess at the combination that will give you the best results in the beginning. But the truth is, the only way to be sure is to let the market decide. Let your prospects cast their votes with their wallets and that's always the most definitive measurement, one that discounts all theories.

Look at your offer as it stands. How can you make it easier for prospects to say yes? Maybe your product is revolutionary, unlike anything the marketplace has seen before. This newness might actually be hampering your marketing efforts simply because it is so different, prospects are reluctant to change their ways from the tried and true methods they're most comfortable with. In this scenario, you want to do whatever it takes to get prospects to sample your wares. This strategy might include a sample version, where they can put your product through the paces without any commitment. Or it could mean a delayed billing arrangement, giving them an opportunity to get comfortable with your new approach.

Identify the obstacles that might be getting in the way of sales. Anticipate the root causes that could be preventing prospects from going ahead with their orders.

What Is It About Offers That Make Them So Important?

The offer includes every component of your package - it's everything the customer receives from the transaction. Your offer enables the prospect to see and evaluate exactly what he's getting for the money. A strong offer is an enticing carrot dangling before the prospect -- designed to stimulate an immediate response.

Offers are the real deal. Stripped of all the other sales copy, the offer should stand out on its own as a superb value - an outstanding deal. Without a strong offer, you're hampering your marketing efforts from the start. No amount of brilliant writing can rescue a weak offer. On a ranking indicating the importance of offer, I'd place the offer among the most important factors of success.

1. Target Your Audience
2. Create A Great Offer
3. Craft Compelling Sales Copy
4. Design Your Sales Page

Without the first two primary steps taken care off, writing a compelling sales letter is a struggle in futility. But with a targeted approach and a perfectly matched offer, writing copy that sells is a whole lot easier.

Offers are about getting new customers to come on-board - a crucial component of success. But to maximize profits, you need to welcome them into the fold and then continue to provide outstanding service and additional products for years to come.

Success in business is not about making the sale one time and then going on in search of the next new customer. That's a recipe for failure. Real profits aren't made on the initial sale - they're made on follow-up sales, repeats, and referrals.

The toughest sale you'll ever make is to the first-time customer. Converting prospects who've never heard about you or your product before is a difficult challenge. The most effective way to answer the challenge is with an offer that's so overwhelmingly in their favor, that no sane prospect could walk away and feel good about their choice to do so.

An offer to a first-time customer is a way to baby-step them into your family of satisfied customers. If they never make the leap from prospect to customer, you've wasted your time, money, and effort. That's why it's so important to come out with the most alluring offer you can envision. You want the prospect to feel that he simply cannot lose by buying now.

Background Information For Building A Stronger Offer

You could spend hours stuffing extra goodies into your package. You could bundle a whack of bonus products and incentives into the offer. From your perspective, it might represent unheard of value. But what does your pool of prospects think about your proposition? That's all that matters. If prospects aren't buzzing about your offer and eagerly snapping up all available packages -- maybe it's time to reconsider. The trick is to know what your market wants.

Each individual element has to have merit and value. Don't just jam extra 'stuff' inside your offer in an attempt to inflate the value. Make sure that each and every component is something prospects can use and something they want.

Wants are the key. The fundamental concept to creating a great offer is providing items that are wanted. Hopefully your main product evolved from a dominant want among your target group. Now expand on the idea to make your main product more useful and valuable. Get creative and prepare a series of special reports, articles, lessons, videos, CD's or booklets.

Give your bonus products powerful titles like…

13 Ways Women In Business Can Get All The Credit They Need
Secrets To Choosing Vending Products That Deliver Maximum Profits
10 Decorative Ways To Use Your Wreaths After The Holidays
7 Trade Secrets To Keeping Your Carpets Looking New All Year Long
How To Sleep Like A Baby Through The Next Stock Market Crash
How To Find, Steal Or Create Million-Dollar Ideas Every 60 Seconds!
Secrets and Software That Will At Least Double Your Profits Guaranteed!

The title alone can be enough to get prospects salivating for more. E. Haldeman-Julius proved this more than 50 years ago when he sold millions of his "Little Blue Books". All that was listed in the Haldeman-Julius ads were the book titles. In other words, he relied solely on the power of the title or headline -- and it worked fabulously well.

The title of your bonus items alone can increase desire, arouse curiosity and create an overwhelming, got-to-have-it feeling that can boost sales immediately. And with your compelling offer, you can include several of these provocative and desirable titles.

Addressing the desires of your market is crucial. So too is presenting viable, workable solutions for whatever ails your prospects. Make it definite and tangible - something they can easily grasp and conceptualize. That's why special reports and other information products work so well in offers. They're real products and can be shown as such with a simple visual within your sales letter. The more tangible incentives you include, the more real value you inject.

What About Free Offers?

Free offers can get your name out in the marketplace and help you build your own mailing list of prospects. Free introductory offers get your product into the hands of the target consumers you want to sell to. Software developers use this method often and it works exceptionally well.

But in the online world, there seems to be a disproportionate number of "freebie seekers" - people willing to take anything that's given to them, but they rarely, if ever buy. Perhaps this prevalence stems from the roots of the Internet and the free exchange of information. Or perhaps it's due to the sheer volume of information that abounds in the virtual world. With so much information, there's always plenty to be had -- without spending a penny. The trick is to make your information special, valuable and exclusive.

Freebie seekers aren't exactly top quality prospects. But they do exist in large numbers. Just be aware of it. The more you invest (by offering freebies) in acquiring a name for your list, the lower the grade of prospect you'll tend to attract.

Make your most alluring bonuses part of the package you're selling. Present your strongest bonuses as part of your product offer, rather than as an enticement to subscribe. Save your best for buyers and give them so much more that they'll be completely overjoyed with their purchase.

Additional Factors To Keep In Mind

Make it safe and easy for prospects to act. Present an element of scarcity to hurry them up a little and give them a reason to get into gear. Deliver your package promptly and demonstrate your level of service.

Prospects are universally suspicious of vendors until they get to know you. Online, this mindset is even more common as your 'store' exists only in cyberspace, with little evidence that you'll even be there next week or next month, should the buyer need to contact you.

The more stories revealed in the news media about fraudulent business activity online, the more reluctant people are to place their trust in you. A few years ago, numerous stories appeared about credit card fraud online. Specifically, these reports focused on credit card information reportedly stolen online. Word soon spread and severely hampered sales for many Internet merchants. People were scared silly. But as consumers learned that the threat was no greater than using a credit card to buy from a local restaurant or gas station, sales improved.

Unfortunately, many first time customers are reluctant to buy out of fear. But as word gets out about more people doing business online successfully with reputable people, those fears tend to lose their power.

Your prospects want what you have to offer… they really do. And they want to trust you. But they're fearful of being ripped off in this new, un-known world of cyber-shopping. Anything you can do to dissolve these fears and give them a safe, secure feeling will certainly enhance your sales.

Provide a street address - it's a little more reassuring. Offer different ways to get in touch and to order from you. Give them options so they can choose whatever method provides the greatest ease, convenience and security for them personally.

Online buyers tend to favor secure order pages where credit card information is encrypted. Others prefer to fax their orders. Some enjoy the accessibility and low cost of email.

Surprisingly, with all these quick, high-tech opportunities, I still receive a sizable percentage of online sales through regular mail. Not having that option available might have cost me plenty in lost sales. It's all about choices and allowing the buyer to choose a method of ordering that's most comfortable for them personally.

No matter how magically enticing your offer is -- if it's an open offer without an impending deadline, there's no real reason to act now. As far as the prospect is concerned, he can buy now or buy later. What's the rush? Besides… having extra time to think it over sounds good too. This reaction is a death rattle to your business. You've got to do everything in your power to get prospects to act with urgency. If you don't, they likely won't act at all. Why? Even an outstanding offer loaded with value and appeal won't move prospects out of their 'comfort zone' thinking without a strong motivation for doing so.

Humans resist change naturally. Even the bleakest of conditions and circumstances provide some level of comfort to those who are used to it. Your solution isn't likely to move them to take immediate action. Unless… if they don't act now, they risk losing out on your exceptional offer altogether. That's the key. Let them know this fantastic deal ends soon.

Place an expiry or limit on your offer and you'll compel prospects to act. It's the fear of losing out that causes the deliberating prospect to get on with it and make a decision.

Following are a few different ways you could add scarcity to your offers. Just make sure you're not constantly extending the stated limitation and cutting off its strength at the source.

 - Order by midnight on January 30, 2010 and you get it all delivered in one huge, almost 10-pound box shipped by Priority Mail. At 12:01am this never before/ never again special is gone for good! Don't miss it! Call Now!

 - Only 75 seats are available for this special event and the last time we offered this -- it sold out in less than a week! It's first come - first served. Reserve your seat now so you won't be disappointed. Last time in Toronto!

 - This exclusive 2 for 1 introductory offer is available to the first 150 members only. This offer ends the minute our 150th membership is claimed... and that could happen at any time. Don't miss out! Act now and get all 7 BONUS GIFTS immediately! They're yours to keep no matter what!

Why Bother With An Offer Anyway?

Offers help to establish exclusivity and create a strong demand for your product. It gives you an opportunity to stand out and gain a unique advantage from all other entrants in the field.

Offers create interest and compel action. Unless your prospect arrives at your site pre-sold, you need to create some excitement and enticement about your wares. Otherwise, yours is just another product on the shelf. Benefits bring life to your product and appealing offers tempt prospects into buying.

Without an appealing offer, there's no stimulus to action. Special offers give prospects real reasons for considering a purchase - something they may have had no intention of when they first arrived at your sales page.

There's little you can do to easily modify products without spending a lot of time, money, and effort in the re-engineering process. But it takes comparatively little investment to add interesting bonus items to your product and create an offer that's worth many times the price of the product alone.

What Incentives Should Your Offer Include?

Offers establish a strong incentive to action. Tangible bonus gifts are a sure bet - particularly those with emotionally charged titles. But an offer can include other elements too.

Your offer is everything the buyer gets when he orders. It's the main product, bonus items, premiums, and lifetime service. That's how your market evaluates the appeal of your offer. Are they getting far more in perceived *use value* than they're being asked to pay in *cash value*? That's the key to a successful offer - give them far more than the product alone.

Consider all the positive factors your package offers and evaluate it as your prospect would. Look at everything, including: main product benefits, guarantee, how this package best solves a specific problem, major benefit of each bonus gift, ease of buying, methods of payment, methods of delivery, and the level of after sales -- service and support.

All aspects can be used as attributes and presented in a way that moves prospects closer to a buying decision.

How To Take A Basic Product And Create An Irresistible Offer

Start with your product and the benefits it provides. Survey prospects and customers. Solicit feedback on what it would take to provide a near 'perfect' product and buying experience. Find out what would make buyers happier. Then turn the most promising ideas into bonus items and include them in your offer.

Brainstorm ideas for bonus products. You can do this alone or in a small group. Allow for a set period of creative time where you simply let the ideas come to mind and you capture them on tape or paper. It's important to silence the editor within and just let the miracle of your innate creativity do its work. Let the ideas flow fast and furious for 5 minutes. Afterwards you can go back and rework the most promising possibilities and polish them up into complete titles. This is a great way to come up with riveting, emotionally appealing titles for special reports, booklets or other bonus items.

Think about all the incentives you're going to include and how you can make each truly irresistible. Extend your guarantee and make redemption absolutely hassle-free, should the buyer need to exercise this option for whatever reason. Simplify your ordering procedures. Improve your price. Provide easy options and make it less tiring to complete the order.

Great offers provide:

> Low cost - but great high-priced merchandise (Great Value)
> So appealing that prospect would be foolish to refuse
> A package of numerous items in addition to the main product
> Extra bonuses like gift certificates or free shipping

The key to a great offer is to deliver solid value - more value than any sane prospect could reasonably expect to get - and to do so without it costing you excessively. A package that's perceived to offer outstanding value while containing evocative *must have* elements obtained at a low production cost -- is a surefire formula for a winning offer.

Following is a sample of a powerful offer...

"Here's what's included in your huge -- 5½ pound *Blueprint To Profits* package:

What You Get:	Actual Market Value:
1. How To Get Rich With Your Website (8 tapes & manual)	$247.00
2. Unlimited Duplication/Marketing License to: How To Get Rich With Your Website	$2,500.00
3. How To Get A Million Dollars In Free Advertising On The Internet (8 tapes & manual)	$195.00
4. Unlimited Duplication/Marketing License to: How To Get A Million Dollars In Free Advertising On The Internet	$2,500.00
5. 42 Ultimate Secrets To Making Money Online (8 tapes & manual)	$195.00
6. Unlimited Duplication/Marketing License to: the complete 42 Ultimate Secrets To Making Money Online program	$2500.00
7. Surefire Success Marketing Tool Kit	$997.00
8. Turn-Key Websites For Items #1, #3, & #5	$1,997.00

9. Guaranteed Merchant Account Package $195.00

Special BONUS Product - Internet Wealth Secrets
CD Rom -- Complete with Unlimited Duplication/
Marketing License $997.00

TOTAL PACKAGE VALUE: $12,323.00

But with this special offer, you don't have to pay $12,323.00... not $10,000.00... not even $5,000.00, either! Though... at $5,000.00 you'd be getting an awesome deal - considering the incredible profit-pulling power of this full package!

Are you ready for this?

Order today and you get the full *Blueprint To Profits* package for only -- $1,497!

I think you'll agree - this is an unbeatable value! It's a whopping discount of almost 88%! Put another way, you save over $10,000. And you still get everything you could possibly need to launch your own multiple streams of Internet income - within just hours.

But wait... there's even more... I wanted to go one step further.

And that's how the Internet Millionaire's Library came about. Order today and you get the complete multiple-volume library -- FREE as an extra bonus! This rich resource of wealth ideas has a value of $997 - but it's all yours - absolutely FREE!

Your Internet Millionaire's Library contains a boatload of valuable books, manuals, and software package from other highly successful Internet marketers! Many of these products come with reprint or resell rights as well! This means that you can turn each of these bonus products into an additional cash flow - if you so desire!

There you have it -- the whole enchilada. And I'm sure you'll agree -- it's one heck of a deal!"

How To Craft A Powerful Guarantee

"Consumers are hesitant towards purchasing any product or service (especially major purchases) - and don't want to make the wrong decisions. If you can overcome that hesitation to take action by offering to guarantee their purchase and reverse the risk of buying, you'll get a lot more business. That's a given."

-- Jay Abraham

Why Having A Guarantee Is Important

Remove the risk to buying by providing an 'out' and you've effectively knocked down a major hurdle that often stands in the way of sales. That's the value of a guarantee. It makes the prospect feel a greater sense of safety and security in doing business with you. Don't forget… the prospect doesn't know you, and so he's naturally apprehensive. He's wary of the hucksters and doesn't want to get burned.

Your guarantee encourages prospects to go ahead and take a leap of faith. Often it's the final obstacle to overcome in the sales game. Make them feel as though they've got absolutely nothing to be afraid of and nothing to lose… and you'll increase your closing rate substantially.

Guarantees tell prospects how you feel about your product and its ability to deliver on the claims you've made. If your guarantee is filled with "fine print" forcing anyone who chooses to make a claim to jump through numerous hoops, your guarantee is of questionable value.

If it's short in duration, like 10 days, prospects will get an uneasy feeling. It's as though they're being rushed to confirm ownership, so the merchant can go ahead and chalk up another sale. These things are warning signs to prospective customers. It tells them to proceed with caution. And a short guarantee redemption period suggests a lack of confidence in your own product… a definite red flag for consumers considering opening up their wallets to buy.

Prospects need reassurance. They want to know that if the product doesn't live up to your claims... or if for any reason they are unsatisfied with their purchase, they have some recourse. Nobody likes the feeling of being 'locked-in' to any ownership situation, until they're e satisfaction is assured. They need to know that they have a way out. They want to trust you... they want to acquire all your promised benefits. But there's a little voice inside that warns of potential danger ahead.

What A Strong Guarantee Tells Prospects About You

A risk-free guarantee signifies quality and reliability. If as a merchant, you offer both quality and reliability, chances are you'll have no problem in providing a strong guarantee. A solid guarantee implies that your product offers quality and reliability, just as a weak guarantee suggests that there may be problems.

Strong guarantees show that you're willing to stand behind your product - 100%. The stronger your guarantee and the more it's emphasized as a major component of your package, the more believability and trust it promotes. And the more believability and trust your prospect places upon your messages, the more likely he is to buy.

First, create a quality product. Support it with as powerful a guarantee as you can muster. Confidently state your guarantee and give it a prominent place in your sales letter. You'll soon find that confidence is infectious. The more confidence you have in your product -- the more confident prospects feel about it too.

There's no more effective confidence builder that a risk-free guarantee. It's you putting your product on the line... and being willing to back it up to the fullest degree. This is much more effective than expecting others to place their blind faith in you by putting their money on the line. Assume the risk -- so your prospects don't have to.

Is A Standard Guarantee Okay... Or Do You Need More?

Double or triple the length of the guarantees offered by your competitors and you automatically gain a competitive edge. Try harder to outperform guarantees that are common in your market. Make it a lot less risky for prospects to go ahead and order from you.

What have you got to lose? No matter how good your product is -- you're going to get some returns. That's the nature of business. For whatever reason, a small percentage will ask for their money back. Understand this before you step up to the plate and you'll spare yourself the grief later.

If you've ever sold products before, chances are you've experienced refund requests. So knowing that it's virtually impossible to eliminate refunds 100%, why not do everything in your power to get more people to proceed with their order? Makes sense to me. Boost your sales with a stellar guarantee and don't worry about the few who want refunds. Accept those and move on. But the upside is that you'll produce a lot more sales with a foolproof guarantee.

Avoid the same guarantees your competitors are using - that only places you on par with them. Just as unique benefits and advantages have more appeal, so too does a guarantee that stands head and shoulders above every other guarantee in the field. Those are the guarantees that people take notice of. The implication is that if you have that much confidence in your product… it must be truly exceptional. Be bold. Make your guarantee as impressive to prospects as you can.

If your competitors offer a 30-day, money back guarantee - make your guarantee good for 90 or 120 days. Prospects will expect at least a 30-day guarantee anyway - even if you don't offer it, since that's what others do. Offering to match competitors doesn't make your guarantee anything special. It's just the same as the others. No big deal. But triple or quadruple the industry standard, and you'll get people paying attention to your guarantee. After all, it's three or four times less risky to buy from you this way. The prospect isn't rushed into an evaluation. He can take his time. The implication is that if you can afford to do this -- your product must be worth the investment.

The Most Appealing Types Of Guarantees

Make it hassle-free, lengthy, and leave even those that do want refunds with some kind of parting gift. Keep it simple and straightforward - in plain language. If you can't explain everything about your guarantee in a paragraph or two, re-write it. Refine your message as clearly and succinctly as you possibly can.

Avoid the fine print. Have you ever seen those ads offering great lease rates on new cars? The ad catches your attention with huge promises such as no down payment, low monthly rates, special option packages, etc. But then you get to the fine print buried at the bottom in type so small, you need a magnifying glass just to read it. And when you see all the limitations and conditions, it sucks the enthusiasm right out of you. It's enough to make you want to check with your attorney before you buy anything. That's exactly the kind of thing you don't want to do.

Keep it simple. Explain your guarantee and eliminate all the special qualifiers and conditions. Take out the fine print. That stuff doesn't serve anybody anyway. It builds walls instead of bridges. And your mission is to establish a lifelong relationship with satisfied customers. People are wary of any 'fine print' and will favor simpler, more straightforward options. Unfortunately, the automotive sales industry is one that hasn't adapted this concept.

The best guarantee is an absolute guarantee of satisfaction.

> *"If you're not 100% delighted with your purchase, simply let me know and I'll refund every penny you paid -- immediately."*

Now let's take this guarantee and go one step further…

"If you're not 100% delighted with your purchase, simply let me know and I'll refund every penny you paid -- immediately. Not only that but you can keep the 3 special reports as my gift to you just for trying out Willy Widget."

The ultimate guarantee doesn't just make the customer feel he cannot lose. It goes further than that. It makes him feel like a winner just for giving the product a try.

What this tells the prospect is that you're willing to go out on a limb just to place your product in his hands. You're taking all the risk, instead of asking the customer to do so. In essence, it's a 100% risk-reversal.

Here's an example…

"Join us and use as many of our key resources as you like.

Read the articles and special reports. Visit the discussion board and tap into the knowledge base you'll find there. Follow the Daily Marketing planner and glean every nugget -- every profit-building idea and strategy you can find.

Then, take these ideas and put them to work for you.

Take a full 60 days to decide if my "Blueprint System" and The Affiliate Club is right for you.

If at any time during those 60 days you feel the resources of the club aren't useful to you and your business -- just say so. I'll gladly refund every penny of your membership. No questions asked… and no hard feelings either.

But here's the best part:

Even if you choose not to stay with us as a member, you still get to keep all 5 bonus packages FREE.

It's my way of saying thank you, for giving the Affiliate Club an honest try. If you can't truly benefit from all we have to offer… well, you shouldn't have to pay for it. That's how I see it, anyway.

But how will you truly know until you try?

That's why I want to give you a full 60 days to discover for yourself how The Affiliate Club helps you make more money by working smarter - not harder.

If by any chance it doesn't… it absolutely won't cost you a dime. And you get to keep a fabulous bonus package --worth hundreds of dollars-- just for trying the club on for size.

Fair enough?"

How To Draw Attention To Your Guarantee

Set your guarantee apart from the rest of your text by creating a visual frame. Make it clear to readers that this is something of importance - something they will want to pay attention to very closely. Use tools of emphasis to highlight your guarantee and make it something no prospect can miss.

Create a simple text box to surround your guarantee. Anything that breaks up the normal flow of text gets attention -- and a framed box can certainly do the trick. Stick to simple, clear lines of one to three points in thickness for the frame. Avoid using a line that's excessively heavy. Your intention is to draw attention to the information within the frame - not the frame itself. The same can be said about any design enhancement used in your website sales letters. Let your words do the selling and employ any design tools as accent pieces to underscore or emphasize your message.

Another technique is to frame your guarantee with "white space". This is where you leave extra space before and after your guarantee... and you indent this section both on the left and right side, effectively centering your guarantee and setting it apart visually from the rest of your left-aligned text.

A strong guarantee is a valuable marketing tool. But it's only valuable to the extent that its inherent power is unleashed in full view for the prospect to see and instantly comprehend. When you set it apart, your guarantee has distinction and is more likely to be one the highlights that captures the skimming prospect's eye.

Repetition ensures your prospect gets the message that your guarantee is something worth noting. Get it into your headline or sub-heading. Spell it out in full detail after you've unveiled your offer. And by all means, repeat it on the order form.

If your guarantee is a major part of your proposition - it's worth repeating. Why? It's the guarantee that provides comfort and reassurance. Repetition ensures the validity of your guarantee and reaffirms prospects that there is indeed a safety value in place, should they need it after they've put their money on the table. The more you use it, the safer prospects feel. Your emphasis of the guarantee reinforces the fact that the prospect shouldn't have a worry in the world about your proposition or product.

Mention your guarantee in the headline and it's sure to get noticed early in your sales presentation. Highlight the full guarantee visually, by setting it apart from the rest of the body copy. As a highlighted section or sub-heading it's more likely to be seen again as the prospect takes his initial scan of your sales letter. Then, when he clicks on the link and gets trans-ported to your order form, once again your money back guarantee message is there to be absorbed. That's three times your guarantee has hit home, and he hasn't even read your entire sales letter yet. It's not about repeating yourself unnecessarily - it's about emphasis and creating reassurance.

When your guarantee is a major focal point of your offer - and it should be in most cases - you want to be absolutely sure your reader gets the mes-sage. It's one element that's worth repeating because it's often the final barrier prospects cross before deciding to buy.

Make An Impact With An Elaborate Promise

Summarize your guarantee as you would your offer. Refine and rewrite it until you have it down to a single sentence or paragraph. Make it empow-ering, easy to understand and hassle-free to put forward a claim. Focus on the strengths of your guarantee and how effective it is as a safety net for prospects.

Add credibility to your proposition by revealing how few have actually requested refunds - *"Over 2700 copies have been sold with only 6 refund requests to date"*. This kind of specific statement gives prospects a new frame of reference - one that's sure to impact their level of comfort in buying from you. Once again, specifics add realism to the overall picture.

Serious prospects don't want to exercise their option for refunds - they would much rather be totally satisfied with the package they get from you. Knowing that the overwhelming majority of buyers before them have been totally satisfied with the product makes them less worried about doing business with you the first time.

How To Make Your Guarantee Seem Like An Ironclad Promise -- Without Sounding Like A Legal Document

Add a personal touch to your guarantee. Use everyday language - the kind you'd use in a conversation with a friend. Avoid formalities and legal jargon, as that will turn prospects off quicker than just about anything else.

Be friendly and personable. Inject your own personality into your guarantee. Explain your philosophy. Let your audience know that you're interested in attracting happy customers only. Speak one-on-one and let them know you're the living, breathing individual who stands firmly behind your product with a simple "you must be satisfied" guarantee.

Guarantees are designed to protect customers and to successfully address any reason why the prospect might be hesitant to buy. The best guarantees are all encompassing. They're wide open and tend to establish a higher level of confidence among prospects.

They might have chosen the wrong size or color. Perhaps your package is not exactly what the customer had in mind. Maybe your product didn't work the way it was expected to. Regardless, the most highly esteemed vendors issue complete and immediate returns -- without dickering. It doesn't matter what the real reason is for the return, it's graciously accepted and the money returned swiftly. You don't want anyone to harbor ill feelings towards you. Online, words spread quickly and a disappointed customer can cause serious damage in no time at all. Treat everyone with courtesy and respect and most people will respond in kind.

Think about your guarantee from your prospect's point of view. He's considering buying… but he's a little worried. After all, your business is new to him and he hasn't done business with you before. Perhaps buying online is a new experience altogether for your prospect. Yet, you're proposing that he buy your product, sight unseen. You're asking him to trust you with his money. Without the advantages of a strong guarantee and market recognition, you're running an uphill race.

But a strong guarantee assures the buyer of total satisfaction. It makes buying a less risky venture by providing a safe outlet. And the more unconditional the guarantee, the lower the perceived risk and the greater the likelihood the interested prospect will proceed with an order.

Here are a few sample guarantees:

YOUR 13 WEEK UNLIMITED MONEY-BACK GUARANTEE!

Try the Chattel Report -- The Sprint To Freedom… and put the 12-week plan to $5000 into action. If after trying out the report and following this remarkable moneymaking system, you're not delighted with your results, simply return the package for an immediate, 100% refund.

155% Rock Solid Money-Back Guarantee!

Here's Your 155%, NO FUDGING AROUND, FULL MONEY-BACK PERSONAL PROMISE...

This is the "real deal." In fact, I'm so confident that my Home Study Course and Quick Start Guide will help you make money, I'm going to give you the whole farm just to get you to give it a try. So, here's what I'll do…

Test-drive my entire package RISK-FREE for a full 90 days. If you're not happy for any reason, return the course for a full refund! No questions asked.

Try it first -- then decide. Read through it. Try my techniques. Receive all the personal consulting you want.

If you decide to cancel for any reason, you not only get 100% of your money back but you also get to keep all the extra bonuses for FREE... Forever!

In other words, you can walk away with all the bonus materials, all the skills and techniques you learned, all the personal, one-on-one consulting you received and all the breakthroughs and updates you got during that time...

... And you NEVER have to give them back or owe me a single penny! Now, how's that for a deal? And if do you send it back, I won't even ask you why and my feelings won't be hurt either.

And to ensure that we live up to all this, we've put ourselves on the spot with this triple guarantee:

VITAMIN GUARANTEE. We guarantee the safe delivery of every package and your complete satisfaction with every vitamin purchase. If for any reason, you're not totally satisfied, simply mail in your empty vitamin box and we will instantly refund every penny.

DEPOSIT GUARANTEE. Every dollar deposited into members "Burst Accounts" is fully insured and completely redeemable at any time. We guarantee that your money is never touched by anyone but you.

EARNINGS GUARANTEE. We guarantee that you'll attain your chosen monthly income within one year of beginning your membership and that we will begin building your business and income stream within 90 days. We also guarantee that we'll do all the work to build your monthly income to the level you've selected.

There's nothing left to chance. Nothing to guess at. Nothing to risk.

Your Complete, 100% Satisfaction Is Absolutely Guaranteed For One Full Year!

Take my Pure Profit Business Toolkit and put it to the test for up to 12 full months.

If you're not absolutely delighted by the wealth of money-making information and practical, marketing tools contained therein, simply return your kit for a prompt refund of the full purchase price! No questions asked!

Plus, keep the Info-Max CD-Rom as my free gift to you. (This product sells well by itself for $189)

You simply cannot lose with my bullet-proof, full-year total satisfaction guarantee!

YOUR UNCONDITIONAL MONEY-BACK GUARANTEE OF SATIS-FACTION

I offer a simple, straightforward and absolutely unconditional guarantee:

Try my course, *Great Headlines Instantly... How To Write Powerful, Attention-Grabbing Headlines That Pull In More Prospects, More Customers and More Profits NOW!* If you're not completely delighted... if you're not totally blown away by the wealth of key copy writing information inside, just return the manual within 90 days. That's it.

I'll refund your money completely, cheerfully and promptly - no questions asked!

And I guarantee to rush your refund the same day it's received.

And here's more good news...

I'll give you a FREE copy of my new Special Report - *113 Ways To Get Twice As Much Done In Half The Time.* That's a $39.00 Value - Yours FREE!

I know I'm taking a risk here.

But I sincerely believe you'll find *Great Headlines Instantly* the most effective course on creating moneymaking headlines ever created!

You cannot lose. There's absolutely no risk. You must be completely delighted with the entire manual package within 90 days - or you get every penny back with a smile!

Closing The Sale

"Getting your prospect agreeing with you and saying 'yes' throughout your ad or sales letter will make it easier for them to say the big 'yes' when you ask for their money."

-- Brian Keith Voiles

How To Go For The Sale Every Time

The *close* is where you bring your presentation in for a landing and hope that the prospect decides to buy your product. It represents a shift in your presentation in two ways:

1) You lead the prospect to a decisive action and...
2) You introduce logic into your sales presentation.

For the most part, your benefit-oriented sales copy is full of emotion. You need to stir the feelings inside prospects by solving their anxieties and igniting desires -- and you can't do that without emotion. By the time you get to the close, you want your prospect to be fully engaged and totally consumed by the promises of your offer. You've got them reeling with desire from all the fabulous benefits... interesting customer comments... and irresistible offer. Emotionally, they've already said 'yes' to your proposition.

Getting the prospect emotionally charged is fundamental to achieving a positive response. But adding the reassurance of a logical argument into the equation can work like magic.

The reason?

You want your prospect to feel good about his decision to purchase after he cools off and the excitement fades a little. You don't want him second-guessing himself. That would only encourage product returns. A sound, logical argument following an emotion-evoking sales story introduces a new perspective. It gives the buyer the justification he needs to go ahead with the purchase. It provides comfort, reassurance, safety and security. It gives him the confidence to say "yes" to your sales offer for logical reasons as well.

Close your letter by summarizing the key benefits and reminding the prospect of all the great advantages just waiting to be claimed. Allow him to engage in the sensations -- to feel all the positive feelings again. Then, simply make a clear, coherent and well-reasoned statement about why buying this product is a sound and logical thing to do.

One method I often use for getting prospects to logically justify their purchase is to compare their current situation with the result they'd prefer to have in their experience. It could be anything. The more dramatic or expansive the difference between where the prospect is and the point he desperately desires, the better. Then... simply relate the two.

In other words... allow your prospect to feel the loss as a result of inaction. Let him know what he's missing out on. If he doesn't take charge and make the change he so desperately desires... than he'll just keep experiencing more of the same misery.

What you're offering in essence is the opportunity to attain the result your prospect wants (major reality shift) at an exceptionally low cost (small investment, low risk).

Proportionally, the potential payoff is many times greater than the relatively insignificant cost. You want him to feel that even if he only got a tiny fraction of the potential result, he's still way ahead in the game.

Some other logical reasons to buy include:

> Tax deductible expense
> Investment proven to appreciate in value
> Huge savings or discount... a rare opportunity
> Saves time and money running all over town
> Risk-Free Trial... cheque won't be cashed for 60 days
> Price increase pending... acting now saves money

The key to introducing logic in the close is to make the buyer feel that the decision to buy is definitely the right one.

Use logic to arm the prospect with sound, solid explanations. You want your buyers to feel intelligent and comfortable with their purchase decisions. A logical argument makes them feel good about finding a better way. It gives them logical reasons for telling others ... without revealing the driving force reasons, which are always emotional in nature.

How To Win New Customers Without Being Pushy

Customers control the buying experience and will resist if you push too hard for the sale. It's better to beckon them in with appealing benefits. Allow prospects to whip themselves into frenzy where they simply must have whatever you're selling. But never try to push it on them. You'll only push them away.

The purpose of the close is to guide your prospect to positive action - not to push him into spending money. By all means, use every alluring attribute you have to sell prospects on your offer. But respect them as individuals and know that they are ultimately in control of their own experience.

Lay your cards on the table. Unveil every powerful benefit and present an appealing offer. Then...let the prospect decide.

Make your case as convincingly as you can. Prove your claims and address every conceivable objection to eliminate buyer resistance. Allow your prospect to convince himself.

If you push too hard, you create an uncomfortable buying environment. The prospect feels less in control as the pressure to buy is coming from an external source. Contrast this with the internal pressure that triggers buying on one's own volition.

With a combined approach of emotional and logical reasons, the prospect is self-driven.

Now... the decision to buy comes from the heart and has the sound support of the mind. The customer feels good about the decision and the fact that it was his decision to make.

What Action Do You Want Prospects To Take?

It's critical to determine the specific action you want prospects to take before you begin writing. All your efforts from the headline to the P.S. are directed towards that specific result. If you're wishy-washy about the desired action, your copy will be wishy-washy too. Decide on a specific path for your sales letter. Make it singular in direction.

In other words, don't offer your prospect a free subscription to your newsletter as well as trying to sell him on your product. That only causes confusion and a confused prospect never buys and seldom responds in any fashion.

Maintain the destination in your mind at all times. You want to move your prospect through your sales copy and carry them through to the order page. The close is where you pull it all together and gently guide your prospect into action.

Every page of your site… Every element of your sales copy must ultimately steer prospects to your order form. If you don't get them there, they cannot respond. But you want to send them to your order page with bells on in anxious anticipation of all the benefits, advantages and associated good feelings that's soon to be theirs. And that's the job of your closing copy.

Summarize the benefits, repeat the offer, mention the guarantee and possibly deliver an additional, unexpected benefit. Then ask them to take action so they can get everything you've suggested. Tell them specifically what to do and how to do it. A simple, straightforward directive such as, *"To Order NOW, Click Here"* is the most effective way to encourage a click through to your order page. An *"Add To Cart"* order button can work well too.

What Else Can Be Done To Convert Prospects Into Customers?

Think of all the reasons your prospect could possibly entertain for not taking action immediately, to get what you know he or she wants.

A lack of disposable cash could be one major impediment to sales. Maybe the prospect isn't sure that this purchase is the right thing to do at this point in his life situation. Perhaps the prospect isn't quite convinced that your offer is truly an exceptional deal. Or... it could be that he wants it badly... but he also wants many other things too and can't decide what to buy and what to pass on, in light of his limited number of spendable dollars.

Whatever the major obstacle -- create an ideal antidote. If cash is a problem... offer three equal monthly payments billed to the customer's credit card. Three simple payments of $39.95... is less taxing on a limited budget, than paying the full price in one shot. And it's something that most people can easily afford.

Just look at the infomercials running today. Any product offered over $30, comes complete with a simple multiple payment plan. If such plans didn't increase sales substantially, they wouldn't be allotted such valuable airtime. Bite-size payments work because they take the sting out of the price. It's a deferred cost in exchange for immediate pleasure - a naturally appealing proposition for many people.

If you sense that your prospect might not be quite convinced on the value/price ratio, add an extra bonus product to boost the value of your entire offer. Adding another bonus incentive to your close is like having "found money" - it's a nice bonus that didn't cost a thing.

Give more and you'll get more sales. Maximize the value your buyer gets. Make it so much more advantageous than anything else he is considering... than let him know about the limited availability of this exceptional offer and why it's so important that he respond now.

Give your prospect so much value and such an easy way to acquire the promised benefits that it actually pains him to not order. Place the onus on him to respond in kind... but only after unleashing an outstanding and irresistible offer. Sum it all up in the close.

How To Reassure Cautious Prospects

Reiterate your main advantage. Remind your reader that his annoying problem won't go away by itself. Refresh his memory about how your solution is the most appropriate fix. Summarize your whole letter in a few paragraphs and make it even more appealing by tossing in an additional motivation for immediate action.

Repeat your guarantee. Convey your deep understanding of the issues facing your prospect and your willingness to help. Remind him of his current reality and mention the likeliness of more of the same without action of some kind. Remind him of his pain… and how close he is to being "pain-free".

Take a team approach to solving the customer's problem. Show your genuine concern by being every bit as enthused about the solution you have to offer as your prospect is about acquiring it. Convince your prospect that you're knowledgeable and quite capable of solving his problem -- by way of your product.

Reinforce your credibility by mentioning the number of people you've already helped… or what a recognized expert said about you. Use every power tool in the box to move even the coldest prospect towards the order page. If you can get him there… you've got a much better chance to close the sale.

The Best Methods To Sustain Interest Through To The Order Form

Your mission is to turn attention into interest… and interest into desire. Use active words and short sentences. Make your message one that's easy to consume while creating a strong desire for more.

It's important to emphasize the major advantages the buyer gets and allow him to experience the feeling of ownership of the benefits. Promise something your prospect wants… then continue to make it bigger, brighter and even more appealing by piling on benefit after benefit. The more they feel it, the more they'll want to experience it again and again. And the close is designed to direct prospects to this place of self-gratification and fulfillment. You've got them interested with your benefit-laden copy and an intense desire has taken hold.

Now it's up to your close to guide the prospect to the order page and seal the deal.

This is where your presentation shifts from a sensory experience to one of physical action. You've got to be clear and direct about what the prospect needs to do. And you've got to make it exceptionally easy to accomplish. This is where you're asking the prospect for a decision. For some, it's an automatic "yes". You've sold them on the merits and they cannot wait to whip out their credit card. But for others, a careful assessment needs to be made before they proceed.

Here, your quick summary comes into play. It takes your multiple pages of benefits, bullets, the offer and guarantee… and packages it into a succinct and powerful shortened version.

Think of it as your final opportunity to list everything the buyer gets in exchange for the stated price. Your sales letter went into great detail already - no need to repeat that here.

What you want is a few paragraphs, a bulleted or numbered list that sums up the major points in as few words as possible. Simply remind the reader of all he gets with your offer and then tell him how to obtain it. Think in terms of MAJOR BENEFITS, SPECIAL OFFER & GUARANTEE plus perhaps a BONUS INCENTIVE for immediate action.

Additional Closing Techniques

Sell first… then ask for the money. Make your best case. Put your incredible offer on the table… promise a risk-free guarantee… and then make it exceptionally easy to get it all.

Give your prospect 10 to 100 times more than what he could expect to get for the same money. Let him know what he'll miss out on by not ordering today.

Pull out all the stops to get prospects hot for your product package, before asking them to buy. Load on the advantages first. Let prospects realize just how special your proposed solution is… then tell them what they need to do to get it.

Make it simple for anyone to order. Create a straightforward path - an expressway instead of a maze - directly to your order form. Be explicit in your directions. If you don't give clear, easy-to-follow directions, you'll lose sales. It's that simple.

Agitate your prospect's pain ever so slightly by reminding him about the cost of inaction. Use fear to activate anxiety just enough to trigger a positive action and get him to buy. Warn him about missing out on a golden opportunity - something that could really make a difference. Let him know just how close he is to the desire that lies deep within. Mention the extra bonus item (worth $X) that he'll lose forever if he doesn't respond within a specified time-frame.

Be absolutely truthful about your prospect's situation. If he does nothing - his life certainly won't change for the better. In fact, it may very well get worse. That's a hefty price for anyone to pay. Is your prospect willing to pass on the very solution that can get him closer to his goal? These are the kinds of thoughts you want swirling through the minds of deliberating prospects - those still sitting on the fence, undecided about buying. Get him to question his own thought processes and resulting actions.

Be gentle as a friend… and blunt as an objective advisor. Let your prospect know that his moment of power is NOW. Explain that this very minute can be a turning point in his life. He can take control… Gain better health… Make more money… Learn a new skill… whatever the case may be. And your offer can fast track his progress.

But the decision he makes now will have a direct effect on his "tomorrows". The only point in time that really matters is NOW. So the opportunity to make lasting change is before him - but only temporarily. Lose it and it may be gone forever. Take action and his life can change forever. It all comes down to a decision made in the moment.

How To Avoid Losing The Sale

Address every issue that could be a concern. Begin with a list of every reason why a prospect doesn't buy. He may want it, need it, even crave it -- and be quite capable of paying your price. Yet still, he doesn't buy. So you need to go deeper to discover all possible obstacles that may be preventing sales.

Anticipate those objections and create a way to address each. You can get into some depth here, and provide complete answers without adding excessive words to the sales letter. Simply create a Question and Answer (Q&A) or Frequently Asked Questions (FAQ) page and make it available by a separate link from your home page. This is an effective way to provide additional information - key details that could potentially swing the sale - without making your sales letter longer than it needs to be.

Your close can make or break the sale. Ideally, you want to carry the enthusiastic prospect through to your order page, without any interruption.

If for some reason your reader still needs more information, it's instantly accessible on your FAQ page. Move your prospect from a mindset of visualized benefits to a state of definitive action, in order to reap those benefits. Get him beyond the hesitation stage and into action simply because that's the most certain way to get what he wants. That's the task of your closing paragraphs - it's your final opportunity to make an impact and achieve the desired response.

Charm prospects into action. Make it as enticing as possible and lead the way.

Emphasize the actual value and tangible benefits they get for such a comparatively small investment. Put forth your most alluring proposition. Promise the huge payoff that awaits their one small action. Point out the fact that the ultimate in leverage is to gain a maximum value for the minimum price, which is exactly what they're getting with your superb package.

Tips For Creating A Stronger, More Influential Close

Always sign your sales letter and have it scanned on to your web page. A different color is preferred, to set the signature apart from the rest of the text. With black text, a signature in blue works well. Blue adds warmth and personality to your message. A real signature is more effective than a fake signature created with a different typeface. It subtly tells prospects that your message is sincere and worthwhile. A simulated signature lacks personality and charm. It looks as though it's only there because it's supposed to be. Any genuine signature adds a sense of intimacy and individuality and the larger and more flamboyant the signature - the more personality it carries. But don't stop there. Add a by-line to your signature. Tell the reader a little bit about you in a context that's meaningful to your message.

For example, lets say you're a former police officer and you're selling a video about how to fight traffic tickets. You could increase the firepower of your message simply by adding a line to your signature.

> Bill McPherson
> Retired Sargeant, (23 years active duty)
> Durham Regional Police Department

You can add a similar detail to most any signature in just seconds… and increase your response as a result. It's almost like adding a footnote to a display ad. It's something that's sure to be noticed and it gives you a way to squeeze a little more persuasion into your sales letter.

Here are several more examples:

William Smith
Author and Product Developer

Chef Randall
Inventor Of The Turbo-Cooker

Sally Semenko
Former 6th grade teacher
Woodland Heights Public School

Andrew Laing
Co-founder of The Affiliates Club

Frank Kern
creator of MASS CONTROL and chief engineer of several other multi-million dollar product launches

Sameer Siddiqui
Author, Trainer and On-Line Trading Expert

Add A Powerful P.S.

"Just as important as the closing paragraphs of a letter is the postscript. Since it is generally the first part of the letter read thoroughly, it can entice a reader to want to find out more about your proposition."

-- Richard Hodgson

Why The P.S. Is Such An Important Component

The postscript or P.S. is among the few components of a sales letter that always gets read -- no matter what. It sits apart from the body copy of the letter and along with the headline and subheads, ranks among the most read pieces. Even skimming readers catch the P.S. every time.

Not only is it always noticed, but it's also one of the first things prospects see. This might seem a little unusual at first since the P.S. is the final element of the letter and could be located several pages beyond the headline. But think about how today's super-busy prospect checks out new websites, and you'll soon realize just how important your P.S. really is.

How Prospects Typically Read A Sales Letter

First, interested prospects land at your site in anxious anticipation. Online prospects generally have a good idea of what they're looking for… and know when they find it.

What drives prospects to your sales letter in the first place? The best prospects arrive from your lead-generation advertising. This could be a classified or display ad, postcard, mini sales letter, package insert, banner, ezine ad, search engine listing, or something else. Whatever it is… something about your listing or your ad drove them to seek you out on the web.

As your site begins to load on the prospect's monitor, he instantly begins his assessment. First of all, the prospect wants to be sure he is indeed at the right place - so, immediately, he begins looking for indicators to confirm this. That's why it's so important to link your lead-generation ad to your sales letter in a way that exemplifies congruence and consistency. Prospects want confirmation. If they don't find it quickly, they click away in search of treasure elsewhere. Use colors, headlines, offers and words that match your listing or ad - that's the best way to ensure an instant match. You want your prospect to be assured that he's found the right site. Keep your lead-generation tools and the first frame of your sales letter compatible.

Once prospects are reasonably assured they're on the right page, they either (1) bookmark the page for later reference, (2) skim through your letter, or... (3) read it until the interest wanes. It all depends on their personal schedules, reading preferences and the perceived relevance of your message.

Most readers conduct an initial scan of a page, looking to either qualify or disqualify your message as important and worthy of further reading. Everyone starts at the top with your main headline and sub-heading. This is a natural launching point. They then skim through the key areas that are clearly emphasized. These include all the sub-headings, bullet points, graphics, captions, and the P.S.

When the reader gets to the P.S… he knows he has to make a decision. Either he goes back to the top and starts reading the letter in detail, bookmarks the page for reference later, prints it out on paper, or he moves on to something else. The last option is the one you want to avoid at all costs… and the best way to do that is to employ a powerful, enticing postscript.

What's Wrong With Most P.S.'s?

Many postscripts lack emotional appeal. They're uninspiring and take for granted that the prospect is interested, enthusiastic, and receptive to the message.

If your P.S. creates a ho-hum reaction, you're wasting a powerful opportunity to arouse interest, intensify desire and create enough curiosity to get the reader to back up and take another look, or to go directly to the order form.

A flat, emotionless P.S. doesn't move anyone. It doesn't ignite passion or rekindle desire -- it just sits there.

As a postscript, it stands a good chance of being seen… as long as nothing has deterred the prospect before he gets there. But if your P.S. lacks appeal and fails to hook your prospect's interest, you're missing out on one of the most powerful and effective tools the sales letter writer has at his disposal.

If after reading your postscript the immediate response is "so what?" -- it's time to go back to the drawing board. Inject a powerful, emotional benefit and remind them of your time-sensitive, limited offer and your P.S. will have done its job.

How To Utilize A Postscript For Maximum Effectiveness

As an early read, the P.S. works to compel the prospect to delve deep into your letter. As a wrap up to your pitch, it's a driving force in motivating prospects to click through to the order page immediately.

Look at your P.S. as a stand-alone component of your letter. Does it pack a powerful punch? Does it deliver a benefit? Does it intrigue the reader to want to know more by referencing a detail from the body copy of your letter? It simply must do one of these three things -- or you probably need to overhaul your P.S.

Inspire interest and ad fuel to your prospect's desires. Captivate him with a timely message of compelling importance. Create a riveting sentence or two that keeps him glued to your message with undivided focus and attention

How To Make It Even Better

Drop in an extra bonus - almost as an afterthought -- in one final attempt to incite a positive action. Add an extra incentive such as easy financing or free shipping and handling. The postscript is an ideal spot to add one final goodie to an already appealing package.

It's as if you've gone to the wall for your prospect in order to present an offer he can't refuse. That one additional bonus might just be the thing that convinces the prospect to buy and buy now.

Another technique is to offer an upgrade package at an even greater discount. What you're actually doing is creating a favorable environment for the buyer to increase the amount of money he spends in the same transaction.

You've already done the selling job and the reader is anxious to go ahead and place an order. Suddenly, right before his eyes you give him an exclusive option to acquire your deluxe package at an even greater discount. It's too good to resist and many who just wanted the original package will upgrade on nothing more than the mention in your P.S. - provided it's alluring enough and they were already intent on buying anyway.

Just think of what this one option alone could bring to your bottom line. I've been experimenting with this technique for the past few months in selling my headline writing course. Results have been shocking, to say the least. The basic package sells regularly for $67... with the deluxe version going for $97. Nowhere in my sales letter is the deluxe version even mentioned. I only introduce it as an afterthought - in the P.S.

Results indicate that to date -- 37% of buyers opt for the deluxe version. In a single paragraph, I've increased my revenue per sale by over 30% -- 37 times out of 100. That's $1110 added directly to the bottom line profit for every 100 copies sold. Not a bad return for a mere mention -- after the fact. That's the power of a P.S. and what adding an upgrade option can do for you.

Key Ingredients Of Successful P.S.'s

Give your postscript "skimming appeal". Make it stand out visually as an important part of your message. Use it to captivate and intrigue prospects and pull them inside. Lead your prospect through to the order page.

Get right to the point and avoid excessive words. This is an important concept to keep in mind for all your copy... but it's particularly relevant to the postscript.

That's not to say that you shouldn't use a long P.S - quite the contrary. Just ensure that it's interesting to the reader the whole way through. Begin your P.S. as you would a headline. Use eye-grabbing words and action words to keep the reader mentally engaged and moving along. Always speak in terms of benefits, advantages and added value to the reader (your prospect).

Communicate the relative importance of the message contained within your P.S. Insist upon a sentence or two that clearly speaks to your ideal prospect about something you know is of primary importance. Nudge him into action -- either the action of being propelled into your sales copy to get the full story… or the action of proceeding directly to the order page where his desires can be realized by making a purchase.

Ensure that your P.S. is a separate entity, distinct from the rest of your text. Use a large font size or bold type for the "P.S." label. And always use UPERCASE characters. Space your P.S. slightly down from the signature line. Indent on the both the left and right to further create visual distinction and draw attention to your postscript.

Captivate your reader with interesting "hot off the press" news… or an insightful revelation that makes acquiring your package even more desirable. Provide an update of recent results obtained or an additional use for your product not mentioned before. This gets prospects thinking about new untapped opportunities that lie hidden, waiting to be discovered and utilized. It implies that the discovery of additional uses and applications are regular occurrences, making your offer even more outstanding than originally perceived.

Encourage clicking through to the order page and make it easy to do so by providing a live link within your P.S. Make it easy for prospects to get where they want to go - a destination they can reach faster and easier with your product.

Remind prospects of your best attributes - unique benefits, outstanding guarantee and an awesome, time-limited offer. Stress how much value they get for so little money. Do so in a way that anyone reading about it would certainly want to know more. Then give them the button to push to take the next step and proceed to the order page.

How To Make Sure Your P.S. Pulls Prospects In

Take your P.S. and record it on a separate piece of paper. Set it aside for a few days. In fact, this technique works best if you can forget about your entire sales letter for a day or two while you busy your mind with other important issues.

Then with fresh eyes, untainted by the kind of narrow-mindedness that tends to creep in when you're fully consumed by the creation of your sales letter, re-read your P.S. Now, play the role of your prospect. Put yourself in his shoes and review your postscript from this point of view.

Does it make you want to take positive action to find out more? Does it make you want to order now? Or… does it leave you uninspired? Does it arouse interest or curiosity… or does it seem boring?

If it passes this initial test, try it on others. Get their perspective. Think of your P.S. as one final kick at the can to get prospects interested in following through.

What About Content?

Use your P.S. to deliver major appeal in the form of benefits, offers, upgrades, or special bonuses. Enhance your proposition. Make it bigger, brighter, juicer, and generally more appealing.

Simply provide a new way for prospects to look at things and help him to justify the purchase in his own mind. Provide simple but sound reasoning. Allow your prospect a moment of introspection and self-evaluation. Then… provide the path that will get him there -- via your order form.

Some other P.S. strategies include:

- Provide a concise summary of the offer (if you haven't done so in the close)

- Emphasize the scarcity of the offer by way of an expiry date, limited quantity, or an impending price increase

- Use a testimonial to underscore the value of the product from an authority on the subject - one who's sure to be more objective than the marketer

- Remind prospects of the real value (high) vs. the actual cost (low)

- Refer to a comment made by a customer for emphasis - *"This would be a great deal at twice the price!"*

Another technique is to use one P.S. to encourage prospects to do a little self-evaluation. Get them to examine their life -- where they are now and where they'll be six months down the road.

You want the prospect who's thinking about your offer to look at your proposition from a fresh new perspective -- to see how it really does make sense and is absolutely risk-free.

Examples of Effective P.S.'s

P.S. Just last Thursday, I ran a small test for the Blueprint To Profits package. To tell you the truth, I was floored by the enthusiastic response! My fax machine has been spitting out orders all week... so I expect all remaining packages to be gobbled up in no time flat. You can RESERVE YOURS NOW by faxing me right away. That's the only way I can guarantee you won't be disappointed.

The last time I offered a Duplication/Marketing rights package, it sold out completely in just 6 days! But this offer is even better... so who knows how long they'll last. If you're even thinking about this one - I strongly urge you to take action immediately!

P.S. Don't risk being disappointed. Be one of the first 75 members by clicking here. Remember, you get all 18 full-length, profit-producing programs for a tiny fraction of what they sell for today. But it's only valid if you're one of the first 75 to take action. Don't miss it! This special offer won't be repeated. Ever.

P.S. With the amount of professional reading and client hand-holding you've got to do, you probably don't have much time to spend on those other important things. Things like… growing your business… offering new products and services to your clients… and enjoying the fruits of your labor.

BizWorth can help you grow your business and boost your profits, without taking up much of your valuable time. It's the ultimate small effort/high-payoff tool… and it's the perfect match for you. Why not add this solid profit stream to your business today?

P.S. The unique information found in my manual can save you months of labor-intensive research and frustrating trial and error learning. I've already done the 'grunt' work for you. Why not spend your time working out, instead? The choice is yours. Follow my proven bodybuilding system and you'll soon notice impressive results - I personally guarantee it!

P.S. Another writer described the special relationship between dog and master this way:

"He is your friend, your partner, your defender, your dog. You are his life, his love, his leader. He will be yours, faithful and true, to the last beat of his heart. You owe it to him to be worthy of such devotion."

What better way to honor the love, loyalty, and devotion of your dog.... than with a lasting treasure to be cherished forever. It's the ultimate tribute to a special friend - one you'll never forget.

P.S. -- My FREE REPORT gives you the best chance at success by doing something different. I've researched, tested, used, and proven these 15 secrets myself. Use them and watch your response rates soar! This FREE GIFT alone will spare you a lot of frustration and save you thousands of dollars in agency fees! Claim yours now by calling today.

P.S. -- Ready to put my guaranteed system to work for you? By acting now, you get the best deal ever - over $100 in bonus materials plus… my own personal donation to launch your "Burst Account today! Remember, you're fully protected by my triple, money-back guarantee.

This special offer, $100+ bonus pack and triple guarantee, is your opportunity to make more money than ever before, without doing any more work! It's remarkably easy to put this auto-pilot moneymaker to work for you. Once your monthly checks start rolling in, you'll be convinced that this is the most amazing moneymaking system ever!

P.S. -- If you're honestly interested in losing FAT and keeping it off for life, I urge you to move fast. Marcie McKinnon said that she would pay ANY PRICE for my plan after seeing her own shocking results. A marketing consultant told me I should be charging $49.95 for my information because it's works so well! That's a good idea so… maybe sometime soon. Your best bet is to take advantage of my dirt-cheap offer and get started today! Remember… It's risk-free!

What About Multiple P.S.'s… Do They Actually Work?

Having one P.S. certainly helps because it naturally attracts a high readership. If one works well, two can work even better. True -- both in theory and from practical experience. Gary Halbert is credited with being the first to use multiple P.S.'s in sales letters -- and he was among the most successful letter writers of all time.

Multiple P.S's allow you to accomplish several tasks at once. For example, you could use one P.S. to summarize your offer… a second to reference what a past customer or industry expert said about your product… and a third as a reminder that the offer will not last so your prospect better act fast or risk losing out altogether. Just be careful not to overdo it.

Make each P.S. well worth your prospect's time to read it. Don't just repeat the identical words you've already used in your copy -- or it may come across as being a sales gimmick.

Examples Of Multiple P.S.'s

P.S. -- Building a successful business on the web can be a difficult job. Just ask anyone who's tried. To make it on your own requires incredible patience, persistence, focus, resilience, adaptability, and skill. Can it be done? Absolutely! By why take the long road when you can take a safe and secure shortcut? That's what The Affiliate Club offers you - a shortcut to your success.

P.P.S. -- Remember, you're not just buying more information. What you're getting are the key ideas and action steps to accelerate your success. In addition, your membership entitles you to complete personal guidance and support --right down the line. But I can't hold this special offer open forever. Grab it now and take the first step towards your future prosperity.

P.S. -- Remember: This isn't simply another "how-to" program. It's a complete, turn-key, ready-to-profit business. It's everything you need to profit with an auto-pilot information marketing money-machine of your own! You get permanent Duplication and Marketing Rights to an amazing selection of hot-selling, high-value, high-profit products! You also get my step-by-step Marketing Tool Kit! And you get a full portfolio of winning ads and sales letters to duplicate my success! Plus, you get a huge bundle of additional goodies worth almost $2000 - yours FREE!

P.P.S. -- I was going to save this one... but what the heck. You've read this far, so I think you'd appreciate one more outstanding discount. So here's what I'm going to give you:

1. 7 Of The Hottest Ways to Get Rich On The Internet
 (8 tapes & manual)

2. Unlimited Duplication/Marketing Rights to the above... Plus...

3. The *Master Rights to: How To Create Killer Web Sites
That Sell Like Crazy! *Master Duplication and Marketing Rights enable you to resell reprint rights packages to anyone -- and pocket all the cash yourself!

These 3 extra surefire winners are worth another $2944.95 -- but they're yours for just $500 more! That's right! You can have the Deluxe Version of the Blueprint to Profit Package... including everything in the standard version... plus all 3 extras above for just $1997! Only 10 Deluxe Versions are available... so if you want this powerhouse package - be sure to claim it immediately! I'm not expecting them to last more than a few days!

P.P.P.S -- Just last Thursday, I ran a small test for the standard Blueprint To Profits package. To tell you the truth, I was floored by the enthusiastic response! The fax machine has been spitting out orders all week... so I expect all 50 packages to be gobbled up in no time flat. You can Reserve Yours Now by faxing back your order form right away. That's the only way I can guarantee you won't be disappointed.

The last time I offered a Duplication/Marketing rights package, they sold out completely in just 6 days! But this offer is even better... so who knows how long they'll last. If you're even thinking about this one - I urge you to take action immediately!

P.S. If you're hesitant for any reason, ask yourself: *"What have I done in the past year to seriously build my personal wealth?"* Since your satisfaction is 100%-Guaranteed, you risk nothing by responding immediately. The potential returns for you are unlimited. A big part of your future success will depend on your ability to choose the most promising opportunities. This special no-risk offer is one such opportunity. Don't miss out! Phone, fax, or mail the enclosed FREE BONUS OFFER COUPON -- TODAY.

P.P.S. The Special Bonus Report alone can save you thousands of dollars and unimaginable heartache and disappointment. It's yours FREE! But I must hear from you before the date shown on your reply coupon.

Information You Shouldn't Include In Your P.S.

Don't include any benefit that you don't own as an exclusive. In other words, if what you say about your product could just as easily be said of a competitor's product -- don't use that benefit in your postscript. You could very well use it in the body copy, but because it's not a benefit exclusive to your offer, it's not something that's worthy of the bright spotlight of the P.S. Benefits that aren't unique and exclusive, don't really belong in such an important area.

Another ingredient you might not want to feature in your P.S. is the price. Unless price is a major selling point, you don't want to point it out to prospects before you've had a chance to deliver your full package of benefits. If you reveal it here, it might be the second or third thing the prospect sees while skimming through your letter. Without seeing the full value of the package associated with the price, your prospect might leave before you've had the opportunity to unleash your powerful sales pitch. No entrepreneur or small enterprise can afford to take this kind of chance.

Key Points To Keep In Mind

Your postscript is a major component of your sales letter. It's a catalyst to action. As such, it has the ability to pull serious prospects in or to send them away. Make your P.S. a complete statement that can stand on its own -- like a headline. As a major weapon in your marketing arsenal, it deserves some attention.

Insert words into your P.S. that are designed to grab the attention and interest of targeted prospects and pull them inside. Use proven attention-grabbing words and phrases like:

New, Revealing, Free, Guaranteed, Astonishing, Shocking, Powerful, Phenomenal, How, How To, Breakthrough, Exclusive, Limited Offer, Only 47 Left In Stock, Just 47 Left In Stock, Urgent, Special, Time Sensitive, Announcing, Introducing, Fascinating, Exciting, Remarkable, Stunning, Amazing, Think About This, Important, Incredible, New and Improved, Fabulous, Fantastic, Revolutionary, Unique, First Time Offered, Super, Unmatched Anywhere, Riches, Fortune, and Success.

As with the rest of your sales copy, use the word You or Your as often as possible, without negatively impacting the flow of your copy. It's a magic word when it comes to sales letters as "you" speaks directly to the reader. It's the next best thing to calling your prospect by name.

Actually, calling prospects by name is easily accomplished by adding a simple script to your sales page. It might even be worth testing in your market. However, adding a personal tone to your message -- before readers feel that you know them -- could also work against you. It lacks sincerity and tends to make some people feel a little uncomfortable - and that's something all marketers need to be wary of. You might be better off saving the personalization technique for your follow-up communications, rather than using it in your website sales letter.

As in your headlines, you want your postscript to:

> Reach out and grab prospects by the jugular
> Target your specific market
> Deliver a concise, but complete message
> Stimulate and pull prospects inside
> Connect with readers on an emotional level

How Long Should The P.S. Be?

Make your P.S. long enough to have an impact and short enough to be easily read and understood. If you can deliver a wallop in a single line… do so. But if it takes a full paragraph to make it as strong as can be, than assign a paragraph to the task. The key is to make it as alluring as possible.

If your P.S. seems a little too lengthy (more than 4-5 lines, break it up into two, easy-to-read paragraphs. Better still, use a P.S., P.P.S., and a P.P.P.S. if necessary. That's the way to add distinction and make each point stand on its own whenever you've got two or more powerful statements to add at the end of your message.

Keep it as succinct as possible. Avoid excessive detail. Be direct with a single focus in each P.S.

The idea is to move your prospect to either read more of your proposition, or proceed directly to the ordering stage. You don't want him to stop and think about it. Nor do you want to introduce any element or detail that could dampen his highly charged enthusiasm. Simply add wood to the fire to continually build the intensity. Keep your ultimate destination in mind at all times and your focus on leading the prospect there.

How Prospects View P.S.'s

As a point of emphasis, your P.S. is usually one of the first things prospects see as they scan your page. They're looking for clues - clues that tell them to stay because your message is exactly what they're looking for… or clues that suggest their time is better spent at another site. To the skimming reader the headline might be the third or fourth key point he sees.

As the conclusion to your sales letter, the P.S. is your one final opportunity to twist your prospect's arm and guide him to the order form. It's your last-ditch attempt to persuade and influence prospects into action - action that is honestly in their best interest.

In this role, the P.S. takes on major significance. Deliver a weak P.S. message and you have to rely on the power of your earlier pitch to carry prospects through to the next step.

The danger here is simply that enthusiasm is fleeting. It's here in overflowing abundance one minute and gone the next. You've got to show prospects the way to get what they want when they're "hot" for the ultimate solution. Allow them to cool down and you decrease the chances they'll order at all. That's why the P.S. is so important and why you cannot afford anything but a powerful and compelling message that will keep them keenly interested while leading them into action.

Whether it's one of the earlier elements seen -- or the pivotal conclusion, your P.S. must compel further prospect interest and involvement.

Creating An Order Form That Finalizes The Sale

"Think about this: When you're considering an offer, don't you usually hang on to the order form and throw the rest away?

Most people are just like that. They think it over. And frankly, most of the time they're waiting for some "extra" money to come in so they can pay for it.

Once they come across that money, they (refer to) your order form, and take a second read through. Now this is where you're going to lose em... or sell em. Include all the elements needed to close the sale. Here again, all you're doing is trying to make it as simple as possible for your prospect to place their order."

-- Brian Keith Voiles

Making The Transition From Sales Letter To Order Form

The order form signals a change in both style and format. Immediately the copy shifts from the second person to the first person. Instead of a presentation of enticing benefits, promising guarantee, and special offer, it's all about action - getting your prospect to convert to a customer. The order page is where the prospect has to land in order to get everything promised in the sales letter copy.

Instead of talking about all the things *you* the buyer gets, it takes on the voice of the buyer himself -- "Yes, I want..." It's a seemingly minor point... but in reality, it's a crucial psychological shift where the prospect acknowledges and accepts the sale.

This shift to the first person also puts the prospect in the driver's seat - in total control of the outcome. It's his decision to buy or not to buy and the first-person copy confirms who's really in charge of the transaction.

Order pages are the ultimate destination. For the prospect, it's where he needs to go to get more of the good feelings he just experienced. For the marketer, it's the target page where the actual business transaction takes place.

The Lead Component

Start your order form with a concise headline. Don't just assign it the title of "order form"… give it some sales appeal as well. Sure, you want buyers to know instantly that they arrived at the right place to order. But keep the intensity and enthusiasm cranked up too. Reassure them that this is where they need to be to get the major benefit promised in the letter.

For example…

> "How To Get People To Listen -- Instant Order Form"

> "Here's Everything You Get Instant Access To When You Take Just 47 Seconds To Complete The Risk-Free Order Form Below!"

> "Your 100% No-Risk Trial Order Form"

> "You're just 3 Steps away from getting your success system -- *How To Write A Book On Anything in 14 Days or Less!* -- A Guide for Professionals!"

> "How To Write Headlines That Can Literally Make You A Fortune -- Your Instant Access Order Page"

Is an Order Form Headline a Necessity?

Using a headline on the order form may not be essential - but it does have its advantages. First of all, you can reinforce the ultimate benefit your package promises to prospects. It helps keep them on track and moving towards their solutions and dreams.

Secondly, having a headline provides continuity. It immediately ties the order page to the sales page the prospect just clicked from. It's confirmation that they arrived at their desired destination - right on schedule.

A generic "Order Form" title doesn't do this. It forces an additional search and confirmation by the prospect first, before he can proceed. Why not make it easier for your customers? The less they're forced to do, the greater the odds of them doing it. It's simply human nature.

What's The Best Way To Launch Order Form Copy?

Follow the headline with an action statement that begins with a simple box that can be checked off by the buyer. It should look something like this...

    YES, I want...

This simple action device is designed to involve prospects and signal the shift to an action-oriented phase - the necessary final step to the fulfillment of the solution. You want to move the prospect into action from the moment he arrives at your order page and this affirmative action step confirms the prospect's intentions to buy.

Next to the box, add the word "YES" in big, bold letters, followed by the major benefit your product delivers. Remind buyers of exactly what they're buying. As far as they're concerned, it's always about benefits over products.

It's always a good idea to recap the offer on the order form. Create a summary of your offer that includes all the elements the buyer gets. It's comforting and convenient to the buyer to see it all there in black and white. It's reassuring to be able to review all the ingredients he actually gets in return for your asking price. What might otherwise seem like a distant dream is placed right in front of him. The fact that it's repeated using the same language confirms in his mind that you're actually going to send everything described. It really is as good as the prospect first thought - "what a deal!"

Remind the buyer that he has nothing to fear with your ironclad, no-risk, money back guarantee. Assure him that everything will be to his delight... but if by any chance, he's not completely satisfied, you'll promptly refund every penny paid.

Introduce both the ordering and payment options. Make it easy to order using your customer's preferred method. If you don't provide enough choices, you're forcing buyers to behave in the way you want. It's much better to offer a selection of order and payment methods and give buyers the freedom of choice.

Make ordering as easy as possible via a secure order page. Also allow the order form to be sent by fax or mail. Be sure to accept orders by email too as it's the most convenient, expedient and lowest cost method - particularly for customers in different time zones and countries. If you're set up to take phone orders, do so. It's still a preferred method for those who feel safer dealing with someone they can actually talk to.

In terms of payment… credit cards are pretty well a *must* these days. And as far as credit cards go, it's better if you can accept at least those from the big three - Visa, MasterCard, and American Express. But don't limit yourself to credit cards only. Allow buyers to also use Paypal, money orders, cheques, direct electronic deposits, and cash transfers available from services such as Western Union.

Paypal and other online services make accepting credit cards quick, easy and painless - without the need for a merchant account of your own.

You want to make it easy for customers to buy. So, provide the most popular choices and let the buyer choose his own preferred methods. That way, the buyer maintains complete control. Make choice selection easy. Simply list each option beside a check-off box. Don't make buyers have to write in the brand of credit card or method of ordering. That's asking them to do more than is necessary and to do so certainly won't help response.

Another crucial element of every order form is the customer contact information. It's vital for shipping hard products and important for building a quality in-house list. It's also the part of the order form that involves the most work on the part of the buyer.

Make it as simple and straightforward as you can. Give buyers plenty of space to fill in details legibly. If your order form is being sent by fax or regular mail, most will fill it out by hand. Secure ordering details need to be entered via keyboard.

Be clear in your directions. Tell buyers what to do with their completed form. *"Click here to submit your order instantly"* is a specific directive. So too is this statement: *"To order by fax, simply print this form, fill in you name and address and fax it: 123-456-7890"*. In both cases, you're giving buyers specific, clear directions. Don't assume they will go ahead and do this on their own without your explicit reminder. If you don't lead them every step of the way, you create an opportunity for cash-paying customers to slip through your fingers.

Why take that chance? Tell them what they get… why it's worry-free… how to complete the order form… and where to submit it once it's completed. That's the kind of detailed guidance you need to maximize your response.

Be sure to thank customers for their order. It's also a good idea to be clear about when their order will be processed and when it will be shipped. If possible, provide an estimated date of arrival. Allow some leeway for any delays beyond your control, but do everything in you power to ship orders as quickly as they arrive. That's the best way to answer customer anticipation and keep problem shipments to a minimum.

Now… that's a lot of detail to include on one form. It requires an efficient use of space and the careful choice of words. If you need to use two standard pages to fit it all in and make it easily readable to all, so be it. If possible, arrange the design so that fax orders can be placed with a single sheet transmission. This helps keep the cost to the customer down to the bare minimum. Simply arrange the page so your customer's address and credit card information is grouped together. That's the key information you must receive as a merchant - the other stuff doesn't matter to you -- it's only there for the prospect. What you need is the credit card information and the complete name and shipping address of the buyer.

How To Improve The Responsiveness Of Your Order Form

Make sure your order form includes the important elements. Key components of a super-effective order form include:

Headline
Customer Order Acknowledgement
Summary of the Offer

Summary of Guarantee
Order Options
Payment Options
Customer Information
Directive
Merchant order acknowledgement/ shipping details

Begin to arrange them in sequence, beginning with the headline and following through to the order acknowledgement and shipping details. Arrange a layout that looks inviting and user-friendly to buyers. Make it easy for buyers to complete and move closer to their desired objectives.

Once you have all the components in place, look at each individually to see what might be done to enhance it. Headlines could be made more powerful by suggesting how much closer the prospect/ buyer is to the major benefit he's after. Now... the ultimate solution is just a click away.

The secret to fitting it all in is to refine each component to its essential elements. Rewrite your customer acceptance statement until you have it down to a powerful sentence or two. Limit the number of words in your offer summary. Simply touch on the guarantee without the explicit detail already covered in the body copy. Ask customers for only the most important address information to ensure your product gets there. That should help you to keep the order form as simple and straightforward as possible.

Group related elements together in a logical fashion. Your customer's order acknowledgement should include the guarantee and major benefit as one component of the order form. The various products and bonuses that make up the offer is another component. Customer information, order and payment methods is yet another. When you group related items together in this way, it makes it much easier to organize the page.

How you arrange the space on you order form can have a direct result on sales. It has to look appealing and easy to complete. Make it as easy as A-B-C. You must make the prospective customer comfortable -- and put his mind at complete ease. To improve the effectiveness of your order form -- simplify it.

If you've got plenty of testimonials at your disposal, consider placing one into an opening on your order form. The best order form testimonial is the one that describes your prompt service or how your package is even bigger and better than the buyer ever dreamed. By this point in time, the buyer has already made the decision to buy… but he still might feel a little apprehensive. An added testimonial is one more bit of evidence to comfort the buyer and confirm in his own mind that the decision to buy is the right one.

Elements Worth Repeating

Key elements worthy of repeating on the order form are essentially the primary components of your sales letter. It's the *Offer, Guarantee,* and the *Major or Ultimate Benefit* gained by customers that bear repeating.

Consider the order form offer summary a brief outline of all the products and incentives promised. It's like having everything from your shopping cart placed on the check-out counter in front of you, so you can make sure it's all there before you hand over your credit or debit card to the cashier.

The guarantee reminder is important for eliminating any lingering fears. A strong guarantee is a major selling advantage and reassures the prospect at the moment of truth as he opens his wallet. The fact that the guarantee is repeated adds power to your entire package. The perception is that you wouldn't restate a guarantee that didn't hold water and you wouldn't stress the guarantee if returns were high. Subconsciously, it projects an extra measure of self-confidence in your product.

 Benefits are what really move your customer to action and it's the *Ultimate Benefit* that makes the greatest impact. Ultimate benefits are what buyers get as a result of all the other benefits combined. It's the main advantage gained as apposed to all the individual benefits. You don't have the space to list half of them… but you can always repeat the Ultimate Benefit on any order form, since it's your strongest appeal.

How To Make Your Order Form More Universally Acceptable and User-Friendly

Stick to basic language - plain English -- or whatever language your market understands. Strive for simplicity and a look that says, "this is easy".

Continually refine your order form looking for ways to make it even more user friendly to anyone who might access your page from anywhere in the world. Make it as easy as 1-2-3… so all your buyer has to do is simply fill in a few blanks click on a button and - bingo - the order is on its way.

Essentially, the order form should facilitate buying. The easier it is for any prospect and the more it evokes positive feelings about you and your offer - the better. And the less effort and commitment required of the buyer, the easier it is to close the sale.

Review your order form repeatedly before it goes "live". Have someone else -- or better yet -- several people examine it as well.

Make sure you've got all the important elements covered and that it flows logically and smoothly. Insist on clarity and a single focus in your message. Spot any errors before they cost you money. In short, make your order form a selling piece in it's own right - independent and persuasive, with a single-mindedness of getting the order.

Add a link to an online currency converter from your order form. This enables the buyer to convert your listed price (generally quoted in U.S. dollars) and convert it to any world currency in real time. Many free converters exist - it's just a matter of choosing one and inserting a link. Currently, I use a converter from Yahoo… but some others tend to work just as well.

Since you're inviting prospects to take a trip away from your site, it's best to remind them how to return by using their browser's *Back* button so they quickly return to complete the order. The currency converter is simply a tool to help the prospect understand the cost in a currency he knows well and is more comfortable with.

Avoid overcrowding. Design your order form to be both pleasing to the eye and printer-friendly.

Keep text away from the outer edges and arrange your layout to be no longer than two pages in both letter format (North American standard) and the A4 size (British, European and Australian standard).

What Variable Options Should Be Included On The Order Form?

Payment, delivery, order method, and the product version available are the variables to include in the order form. Payment options are offered as a convenience and make the decision to buy a little easier. Mail delivery by air or surface routes, or overnight express by FedEx gives the buyer options based on urgency and budget. Accepting orders by phone, fax, secure server, email or mail allows buyers to make a choice based on convenience and comfort level.

Offering some options is a good thing. Most customers expect to have a choice in their method of payment. But offering too many choices in different areas is counterproductive.

Excessive choice means extra effort and could very well cause confusion and unnecessary delay - conditions that can only hurt response.

Offer a few multiple choice style options -- options that are easily made with a single stroke of a pen. That's about all you can and should ask the buyer to do. After all, you must get the buyer to enter his complete mailing address in order to fulfill shipment -- there's no way around that part. And doing so takes a few moments of the buyer's time and a little effort to enter all the pertinent details. Therefore... everything else should be easy as pie. Don't ask for more information than necessary. Make it quick and easy to complete the order process.

How The Order Form Can Reassure Anxious Customers

Stress your Guarantee. Shoehorn in a powerful testimonial. Provide explicit and specific details and create the look and feel that you've been around a while with thousands of satisfied customers.

Let's face it... new customers might still be a little apprehensive even after having arrived at your order page. Provide reassurance with your guarantee. Add an official looking graphic that visually signals your guarantee as soon as they arrive. Subconsciously, it tells prospects that they can order with complete confidence.

A key testimonial may look out of place on the order form... and that's exactly what you want. Why? Anything that seemingly doesn't fit the prospect's idea of a typical order form will stand out and draw the eye. And any element that's sure to grab attention is a key location to drop in a powerful testimonial.

These words get through and are taken to heart by the ready-to-buy prospect. They create the perception that this product must be exceptional - so good that they must have run out of places to put their customer comments and had to add them here, to the order form.

It's important to make sure the customer knows exactly what he receives from the transaction. That's why recapping the offer at the order stage is a good idea. This makes it easy for a quick review in support of their decision to buy today. Picture 5, 7, or even 12 items in all - each with a provocative title being offered at a price one would expect to pay for just one item. You create a "wow!" effect. Having a quick list of everything, including the main product, bonus items, premiums, and gifts provides additional comfort, security, and reassurance that what the buyer got excited about earlier is in fact, what he is about to receive.

But it's not enough to let them know what they get if they don't know when they'll get it. Give specific delivery information so they're not left wondering. With the order ready to be sent, your buyer is full of anticipation and excitement. He can't wait for your product to arrive. Providing a timeline gives buyers a point of reference and a more secure feeling knowing that within a short period of time, your package will arrive.

Confirm the order when it is submitted. Let people know you're actively on the case in real time and not passively accumulating orders until a quota is met before you send out the next batch.

Be professional, punctual and courteous. It's simple common sense. But unfortunately, it's something many online marketers overlook as trivial. But those who take the time to acknowledge every order and ship promptly start to forge positive relationships from the start.

Responding to order submissions as they occur gives you an opportunity to personalize your message - something you likely couldn't do earlier in the sales phase. Whether you use an automated response mechanism or a individually crafted acknowledgement, it's a definite plus to address the buyer by name - exactly as submitted on the order form.

Where Some Order Forms Go Wrong

Many assume that by the time they get to the order form, the sale is already a done deal and that the prospect will do whatever is asked of him. Some order forms are totally self-serving and not particularly buyer-friendly. Others are simply too confusing or require too much effort. It's easier to leave than to stick around and jump through hoops just to buy another product. View your order page as a prospective buyer would. Make the path to the prospect's desires as simple and hassle-free as possible.

Don't count sales until you receive them. Each moment in the sales parade provides a fresh new opportunity to strengthen the tie between prospect and product... or to scare him away. Your order form is a crucial step along the path. Don't stop selling until you receive the order in your hands.

It doesn't serve you to write splendid sales copy only to lead enthusiastic prospects to a confusing or complicated order procedure. In fact, ordering shouldn't be much of a "procedure" at all. Keep it straightforward and crystal clear. Make it irresistibly simple... a basic fill-in-the-blanks approach that's quick and easy.

Avoid anything that could be a distraction - including other offers other than up-sells -- to ensure prospects follow through and actually complete and submit the order. That's what it's all about. Any element that detracts from this purpose must be eliminated at once from your order page.

Problems With Secure Options and Third Party Providers and How To Overcome Them Quickly, Easily, and At Zero Cost

Secure ordering does help. It's a valuable option to offer at your site. But it's best to include other options as well. Make it part of your arsenal. But don't rely solely on the secure order option.

The problem is... that with most "secure order" services...

- You are severely limited as to the copy you can add to your page
- All order forms look alike -- giving you no distinct advantage
- There are little or no options on design or layout - you must use their templates, exactly as they're provided

Phase III

Review, Revise, and Edit To Make Your Copy More Effective

"If language is not correct, then what is said is not what is meant. If what is said is not what is meant, then what ought to be done remains undone."

-- Confucius

Easy Ways To Spot Errors

Set your completed sales copy aside for a few days. Get busy doing and thinking about other things and try not to think about your sales letter at all. Then with fresh eyes and an open mind, pick up your letter and read it aloud.

During the writing phase you'll have a tendency to get so involved in the project that sometimes even the most glaring errors are bypassed. The reason is that you've gone over your copy so many times that your eyes simply don't see it. Try it out and you'll see what I mean. Chances are you'll be at least a little surprised by what you didn't detect earlier. But that's okay. No need to beat yourself up over the small stuff. That's what editing is for anyway.

By setting your work aside for a few days and freeing your mind, you come back to the project with renewed energy, focus, and objectivity. Even though you may be pressed for time, I highly recommend following through on this technique.

When you do come back, read your entire letter aloud. Have a felt-tipped marker handy as you read. Whenever you stumble, pause, or trip over a word, place a small check-mark at the exact spot... and continue reading.

Don't worry about correcting each minor snag as you encounter it - simply reference the location and carry on reading aloud. It's quite remarkable just how many glitches you'll catch this way that you might not ordinarily, reading silently to yourself. When you get to the end, go back and look at each check-mark. Rework it until it sounds right. Replace big words with smaller ones. Shorten sentences so they flow off the tongue with greater ease. Do whatever it takes to smooth over the speed bump that first tripped you up.

You'll quickly see the value in reading aloud… so much so, that you'll want to rely on this practice for any future sales letters you write. You can enhance the efforts by having someone else read back to you. Ideally, take a 12-14 year old kid and have them read the letter to you -- while you follow along, marker in hand. Notice where they pause… and what they emphasize.

Listen for words they mispronounce. Question them on the material afterwards. Did it make sense? Do they know what you're selling and to whom? You want to be sure your message is written in a way that will be understood by anyone who could be considered prime prospect material.

Include these simple techniques in your editing and you will definitely aid readability.

How To Minimize Editing Time

Plan your work and then work your plan. Time spent in the early planning stages simplifies the process when it comes down to writing. It's simply a matter of doing your research to make the job easier.

Try writing a sales letter without a list of product benefits and a good understanding of the audience and it will take you a lot of time. But have such a list in front of you before you begin and it's simply a matter of revealing one benefit after another in an appealing way, proving your claims and putting an attractive offer on the table.

So step one to minimizing editing is to take the time to prepare first and build from a solid foundation of rich resource material.

Next, forget that you're *writing*. Think in terms of *selling* instead. If you own a digital recorder, or speech recognition software -- use it to "speak" your letter instead of trying to punch out words from a keypad.

Simply sell your prospect one-on-one. Communicate as though you were sharing an amazing discovery with a friend - something you knew in your heart of hearts was the perfect solution your friend had long sought. Share the benefits. Point out all the things that are special and unique and why your new friend is greater advantaged with your product -- than just about anything else in the world.

When you're finished selling, transcribe it to paper. Arrange it on the page so it looks as good as it sounds. With a solid rough draft in hand, simply enhance it by adding any elements you may have missed.

If you prefer to write your presentation, do so with the same enthusiasm. Remind yourself that you're not writing literature or a high school essay. You're writing to communicate… to persuade… and to influence prospects into action. You're writing to convince the reader to open his wallet and part with some of his cash.

An easy way to write a sales letter is to do so in segments. Don't try and tackle the whole job in one sitting. Think in terms of segments and knock off one segment at a time. Divide your letter up by the major components: Headline, Opening, Benefits, Offer, Guarantee, Close and the P.S. Then, write one segment at a time. Once you have them all, it's simply a matter of connecting the various segments in a smooth, orderly and logical fashion.

Other Things To Look Out For At The Editing Stage

Attaining maximum response is the overall objective. To achieve this result, you need to make your sales letter readable and as enticing as possible to prospects. Editing allows you to fine-tune your piece, making it more effective as a sales tool.

Editing is about getting rid of excess words and refining your message down to its most appealing and persuasive essence. It's about taking your best rough draft and polishing it up to make it even stronger and more persuasive.

Make your letter more appealing to the eye and more palatable to the emotions. You want it to be less intimidating and easier to read with shorter sentences and paragraphs.

Break your text up into bite-size pieces that are easily consumed and instantly processed in single gulps. Use plenty of sub-headings throughout your copy as well as the occasional enhancement such as a text box or image.

Make effective use of white space. Online, you don't have to cram as much text on to a single printable page as you might with a direct mail letter. Here, you can take the space you need… as long as it's inviting and interesting enough to keep the reader actively involved.

Here are some things to look out for when editing:

> More words than necessary
> Repetitive copy
> Weak or wavering copy that's not definitive
> Spelling mistakes, typos, and run on sentences
> Big words, long sentences and tiring paragraphs
> Continuous flow from paragraph to paragraph, section to section
> Any element that's not 100% truthful
> Boring, inactive copy
> Irrelevant sentences and graphic elements

Trim the fat. Take away any words, sentences, or paragraphs that don't belong. How can you tell what stays and what gets edited out? If it doesn't help sell, it doesn't belong. After all, it is a sales letter. You want to make your message as succinct as possible, without weakening the message. Fewer words means tighter copy. Trim anything that's unnecessary… but never sacrifice clarity to minimize the word count.

Eliminate areas of duplication within your letter. If you want to emphasize a key benefit, do so by adding it as an additional sub-heading or caption. If you repeat yourself in the body copy, prospects will recognize the material and be more inclined to cast your message aside. Redundancy does little to keep prospects on the edge of their seats, anxiously anticipating more.

Keep an eye out for words repeated within a single sentence. It's a mistake that's easy to make when you're deeply involved in creating mouth-watering copy, but it's something you need to correct before exposing your message to the public eye.

Clichés, jargon, and the latest buzzwords are all indicators of weak copy. Replace them with simple words and original anecdotes to drive home important points.

Change "You Could Be..." "You Could Have..." or "You Could Get..." to "Be..." "Have..." and "Get..." Instead of using the word "If"... use "When" instead. Be definitive in your descriptions and decisive in your claims. Don't waffle.

Some words may appear similar in meaning... but the impact they have on readers can be quite different.

Consider this...

> "Try our 18-Volume Set FREE for 30 Days."
> "Examine our 18-Volume Set FREE for 30 Days."

Only one word has been changed - but the impact is significant. "Examine" sounds like it involves effort and work - something that definitely eats up time. "Try" on the other hand, appears less daunting... less of a commitment. It's just one word... but the implications in terms of response, could be quite dramatic.

Spelling mistakes and typos convey an image -- one that's not particularly favorable to you, the vendor. It suggests sloppiness, a lack of attention to detail and an unprofessional presence. None of this serves you. So it's very important that you check and double check for this kind of glaring error. Get others to review your sales letter and order form with the goal of correcting these obvious blunders. It shows a level of care and attention commensurate with a serious enterprise - one that's intent on thriving.

Keep an eye out for sentences that run on too long. Split them up so they're easier to read. Keep it short and sweet. Don't be afraid to use one-word sentences - even one word paragraphs. One-word paragraphs are difficult to resist, thus ensuring your prospect reads further. Short words, short sentences and short paragraphs appear more inviting and require less effort to read.

Observe how your copy flows from paragraph to paragraph. Avoid interruptions and awkward areas that cause confusion. Let one paragraph lead naturally to the next. When necessary, use 'connecting links' to join one section to the next. Establish a smooth transition that's invisible to prospects.

Here are a few examples of connecting links you could use in your sales letters:

- But wait, there's more. Much more. You also get…
- One more thing you should know…
- And that's not all. Not even close. In fact…
- Now if all that sounds good… imagine how you'll feel when you…
- Hold On -- You're going to love this!
- And that's only the beginning…
- Here's the way it works…
- By the way…
- Guess what?
- Here's why you should act quickly…
- Want proof? Check this out…
- I'm serious. Really serious. In fact…
- Here's another gift for you…
- Let me show you exactly what I mean…

Scrutinize every word of your copy. Look for anything that possibly stretches the truth. If your testimonials aren't the exact words expressed by customers, make them so. Avoid the temptation to make alterations. Nothing is more sincere than the customer's true expression - complete with grammatical flaws and spelling errors. Don't try to fix it -- simply let it read exactly as written to you.

Be on the lookout for exaggerated claims. Review the accuracy of every statement you've made. You know in your heart if you've stretched the truth in your attempt to create compelling copy and every such instance needs to be edited out. Not only is it unethical to misrepresent your product, it's also a recipe for failure. If the product doesn't live up to your exaggerated claims, you'll be besieged with returns and refund requests.

Not only must every element of your sales letter be true… it also must appear to be true in the eyes of the marketplace. Anything that hints at trickery or deception needs to be removed. Benefit claims that cross the line of believability - whether true or not - need to be toned down so they seem realistic and within the grasp of average prospects. Avoid unsubstantiated hype altogether.

Wipe out boring copy with action-oriented writing. Activate your sales letter with occasional sentences of just a word or two. Make it easy to read without concentrated effort. Chances are, your prospect has other things on his mind. So, he'll appreciate your easy message and be more inclined to remember it and take positive action when he can sail right on through.

Eliminate the impediment of huge blocks of copy that look intimidating and time-consuming to wade through. Break it apart into short paragraphs that invite the reader to continue along on a promising and exciting journey.

Active writing is movement oriented. It keeps readers involved in your message by placing prospects in the experience now - not at some future point. Active writing is clear, direct, understandable and alive. It gains a momentum that carries readers along from one line to the next.

Keep your prospect involved with action words like:

Imagine, Profit, Discover, Unleash, Gain, Find, Learn, Think, Master, Get, Treat Yourself, Invest, Check, Luxuriate, Enjoy, Stop, Start, Improve, Boost, Acquire, Build, Generate, Accelerate, Win, Organize, Indulge, and Travel.

Use present-tense verbs so your prospect can feel the impact immediately. Change any future reference to the present and you'll boost the impact simply by adding an element of immediacy to the experience.

Delete anything that doesn't contribute to the sales effort. One of the goals of editing is to tighten up your copy by eliminating the unnecessary, redundant and ineffective components.

It if doesn't sell, it simply doesn't belong in your sales letter. Trim it down and clean it up. Eliminate wasted words, sentences, paragraphs, and entire sections if you have to. Just do whatever it takes to make every line interesting and compelling.

The same goes for any graphics you've included in your letter. If it's not relevant to your sales argument, than it doesn't belong. Focus your copy on the benefits your product delivers and on interesting ways to convey those valuable benefits.

Simple Ideas For Improving Readability and Flow

Improved readability means making your copy inviting and interesting. It's largely a matter of breaking it down into short segments and highlighting the most important points visually so they cannot be missed.

Inviting copy lures in readers. It doesn't challenge them or make them feel inadequate. Simple language that's interesting and compelling to the audience and processed without much conscious effort - that's what *inviting* copy is. Your words should be simple, interesting, and enticing enough to get prospects to go to the next line, paragraph, or section.

Forget all the rules you learned about proper sentence structure when writing. Concern yourself only with effective communication. Present a message that inspires non-stop reading, instead of the type that gets filed away for "someday" reading. The problem is that *someday* never comes. If your sales letter isn't read immediately… it might not be read at all.

That's why you've got to facilitate reading. Make it quick and easy to breeze through your letter… while turning up the appeal of your message with each sentence.

Keep it interesting by varying sentence length. Mix it up a little… but eliminate any excessively long sentences. Don't shy away from those short, one-word paragraphs as they have tremendous appeal and virtually guarantee that the next sentence will be read as well.

Draw extra attention to major benefits with sub-headings. Create interest-arousing mini-headlines that intrigue readers and make them hunger for more. Highlight key areas like testimonials, guarantees, and special offers with text boxes or frames. Establishing different formats for emphasis draws attention to those key elements, while breaking up the rest of the text, making it much more palatable, inviting and interesting to prospects.

Revise your letter to make it easier to get the essential and most appealing information on the first pass. Simple highlighting tools such as bold text and italics can be very effective in delivering your product's most appealing advantages quickly and powerfully. At the same time, these tools of emphasis help break up multiple pages of text, making it more interesting and less challenging to read.

Ensure that you get right to the point. Look for any areas - particularly at the beginning of your letter - where you might have attempted to set-up your proposition. Don't set the stage, get right to it and start selling from the first word.

Your entire message should flow smoothly and continuously - from one thought, idea, or paragraph to the next. Look for obvious breaks in the flow of your message and patch then over to make a seamless transition. The quicker and easier it is for your prospect to understand the essence of your message, the more likely he'll respond with an order.

Specific Ways To Emphasize Key Points

Editing gives you the opportunity to add points of emphasis. Draw attention to key areas including the headline, sub-heads, testimonials, bullet points, postscript, offer, summary, and guarantee. But you have to be careful not to overdo it. Over-use diminishes the effect you're attempting to create in the first place.

You can place key ideas in bold type
Italicize special paragraphs
Add an element of color such as RED to create contrast
- Employ bullet points help summarize key benefits and distinguish them from the regular body copy of the letter

Set your P.S. in larger type and make it bold

Indent individual paragraphs or entire sections of your letter
Use a text box to frame things like testimonials, guarantees, key points, case histories and offers

---

A key point to remember is to exercise continuity. If you italicize one testimonial, do the same to the others. This rule applies to subheads as well. Don't set one in bold type -- then use regular text for the next. Consistency aids readability and comprehension.

With online sales letters, you're best to avoid the underlining option as a tool of emphasis. The reason? Underlining is still a common method to indicate "live" links. Visitors have grown accustomed to spotting underlined phrases and sentences and automatically clicking on them in anticipation of further detail of interest.

If you use live links in your sales letter, you'll be sending prospects away from your sales letter - something you probably shouldn't do until they're ready to go to the order form. Using underlined text in your body copy that's not intended as a link could lead to confusion. As the online prospect clicks and sees nothing else loading… he might be puzzled, annoyed, or frustrated. At best, you've given him reason to pause by interrupting the flow of your letter. Your best bet is to avoid underlining altogether in the body copy and to use it only with caution in over-sized headlines only.

How To Make Reading Your Sales Letter A Less Daunting Task

Simplify reading by launching your copy with a simple, short paragraph. Use plenty of white space to frame your text and make it more appealing to the eye. Organize your thoughts so it's easy for anyone to understand the essential message -- quickly and easily.

Spend a significant amount of your editing time on the key elements - particularly the main headline and the opening few paragraphs. Tighten it up. Make it easy to get the prospect reading. Use massive appeal and short, enticing opening's to pull him inside. Play around with your opening. Try rewriting for more magnetic appeal in fewer words.

Use ellipses (…) in mid sentence to break it up and create anticipation and suspense. Combine this excitement with the irresistible appeal of enticing benefits and you'll leave readers hanging on to their seats in anticipation of your next statement.

Examples that make use of ellipses to keep the reader interested...

THOUSANDS HAVE BOUGHT MY HOME-MADE MANUALS
OVER THE PAST 3 YEARS. NOW, FOR THE FIRST TIME . . .
(Ken Silver)

Just suppose... that five years ago you had bought some well-located land. Think how different your life could be today...! (Robert Bartlett Real Estate)

I was just in the bathroom, reading a letter from my sister, when I got to the line... (Joe Vitale)

Short, riveting messages have power and magic. They arouse a sense of curiosity while continuing to build interest. In addition, they're easy to read in one quick glance as white space surrounds these small segments to help set them apart.

How To Strengthen Your Bullet Points

Many letters have multiple bullet points. But to simply provide one long list of bullets isn't the best way to make them jump out at readers. Here are 3 ways to boost the sales appeal and power of bullets...

1.   Prioritize
2.   Group together
3.   Emphasize

Prioritize your points by arranging them in descending order - from most significant to least.

Bundle bullets together into groups of manageable sizes. For example, try 5-12 bullet points per group. With anything more, it's best to split those into separate groups.

Emphasize your list in a visual sense that sets it apart from the rest of the text. Indent your bullets and use distinctive characters at the start. Avoid large lists where everything looks the same. One option is to bold text every other bullet point in the list, creating a distinct variation from the paragraph copy.

Remember Your Purpose While Editing

Spot errors, improve the flow, and make your sales letter more appealing to the eye. Your purpose is to enhance response and the way to do it is to make your sales letter as effective as possible.

Your prospect is constantly evaluating you and your product. Careful editing helps you discover errors, inconsistencies and weaknesses that could affect prospect opinions of you and your product - opinions that directly affect your results. Editing is about spotting potential turn-offs, distractions and challenges to your credibility. It's about making your entire sales letter as appealing and full of promise as possible.

The language of your letter should also match the language of the order form. The only difference is in format - from the second person to the first. Consistency lends believability to your words; inconsistencies raise concerns.

Editing can be challenging and frustrating at the same time. Just when you think you're finished… you'll often spot something else. But time spent polishing up your sales letter is time well spent. Multiple edits can be even more effective and help ensure maximum response.

Edit for readability, flow, eye appeal, and impact on the target audience.

When your sales letter looks appealing, is easy to read, flows seamlessly like a river traversing any terrain -- you've got something that can be worth a fortune to you. It impacts the reader on an emotional level and moves him into action. It's vitally important that you edit your letter with attention to every detail, before exposing your message to the public.

Design Enhancements

"Copywriting on the web, I came to realize, is like writing song lyrics. On the web, text and design need to compliment each other to create a good user experience - the way lyrics and melody need to compliment each other to create a good song."

-- Kathy Henning

Sales Letter Design 101

Keep it simple and basic so your page loads as fast as possible on an average computer system. Design the page from the prospect's perspective -- to facilitate buying. Serve your audience. Enhancing the design of your site means using proven techniques to add impact to your words and persuasive power to your message. Each aspect of the copy and design should work to funnel prospects through to the ultimate destination - the order page.

The best designs are simple, clean and effective. It should grow as a logical extension of the subject matter. Good design doesn't draw attention to itself... it simply makes the delivery of your sales message more dramatic and enticing. Design accentuates the words while laying low in the background.

Make your sales page appeal to busy people by:

> Loading quickly to your prospect's computer
> Instantly capturing attention and interest with a visually dominant headline
> Attractive color scheme and layout that's pleasing to the eye
> Making your letter seem like an easy read
> Delivering a high-appeal benefit or advantage

Simple and basic design means letting your words do the selling -- without the bells and whistles. Large graphic files, Flash presentations, elaborate backgrounds and animated images actually prevent your words from making an impact. These kinds of design features for the most part, make you look like an amateur. Most are large in size, so they take extra time to load. Not only that, but flashing images and colorful elements carry the prospect's eyes away from your words.

Every graphic element you're considering should make:

1.   Reading your sales letter easier
2.   The benefits even clearer to prospects
3.   Your page appear more inviting, alluring, and accessible

The First Thought You Want Running Through Your Prospect's Mind

As soon as prospects click on the link taking them to your sales page, the first thing they seek is confirmation. They want to know that they've arrived at the correct website. Your lead-generation ad, directory listing, search engine placement, or media exposure got them there in the first place by arousing desire.

The pump has already been primed, to some extent. The first thing prospects seek is the reassurance that they're where they're supposed to be… and they want to find out immediately. Nobody has time to waste, least of all, your prospect.

Connect the initial stimulus - the piece that motivated prospects to visit your site - to your sale page. Maintain the same theme and unique color scheme. Use words in your sales letter headline that relate to your ads and promotional pieces. The sooner your prospect makes the realization that he is in fact, exactly where he wanted to go - the better and the easiest way to do this is with similar colors and page layouts.

The second your website has been confirmed as exactly the site your prospect was looking for, he then begins an immediate assessment. Is it worth the time and effort? Is it reasonable to assume that this site really does offer the ultimate solution to the prospect's problem? Judgment begins instantly as clues are revealed.

If your page takes extra time to load on the prospect's monitor, you run the risk of losing that prospect before you begin. Flashy graphics and vibrant colors pull visitors away from your words... and it's your words that make or break the sale. A less than professional appearance lessens the prospect's confidence that you can deliver the kind of quality he's looking for.

A simple, straightforward page design loads quickly and keeps your prospect focused on the message - exactly the result you want.

Why It's So Important To Avoid Fancy Designs

You're sales letter is there to sell, not to look pretty. In order to sell, you've got to be prospect-centered... that is to say every element and every word should serve and be directed towards the prospect.

"Just because your ad looks good is no insurance that it will get looked at. How many people do you know who are impeccably groomed... but dull?"

-- William Bernbach

Your prospect has arrived at your site for a reason. You've promised a solution to a problem... or the path to a desire. That's all he's really interested in - his wants, needs, hopes -- and solutions to pressing problems. Respect the innermost desires of your audience. It's about them... not about you or your product.

Computers and connection times vary greatly. Most of your potential and loads of RAM. Not everyone has the advantage of broadband services with rapid download speeds. Some people rely on old modems and dial-up connections to Internet providers. With older computers and dial-up services, it takes time to get connected and still more time for even basic pages to load. Any site that's jammed with graphics and other bandwidth-choking elements is definitely not user-friendly to those with older computer systems.

It's simply easier for those prospects to click away to a site that's more respectful of their time and technical limitations. If your page takes too long to load, it's a sure bet that most prospects will flee - a result that can severely hamper the results you get from even the most sterling sales copy.

With today's available design tools, it's quite tempting to add features to your page. Chances are, you won't even notice any adverse effects if you have a reasonably fast PC and connection speed. But don't make the mistake of thinking that all your prospects have the same kind of equipment. They don't.

It's always a good idea to have a stripped-down, bare-bones version of your sales page. All you need is black text on a plain white background, without any added decorative touches.

Offer a link to this basic version on the first page above the fold, as your site loads. Give all users the opportunity to benefit from your message in an efficient way that meets their needs and is compatible with their equipment.

How To Make A Basic Sales Letter More Visually Appealing

The first thing you should do is add some white space to your text. Break up your body copy into smaller segments that are effortless to read, yet provide magical appeal. Frame your text with white space both horizontally and vertically. This helps by setting it apart and making it easier on the eyes.

Divide larger paragraphs into two or three separate ones, with adequate spacing between each. While a varied paragraph length is best to sustain interest, having any single paragraph longer than five lines is a deterrent for some readers. If it looks like it requires even a little effort, it could be enough of a reason for prospects to click away. Providing such reasoning is detrimental to both you and your prospect. But you can easily eliminate it by splitting your copy up and making it almost effortless to read.

White space provides much needed visual relief and makes the presentation of your information much more appealing. These small bite-size pieces are just enough to keep the prospect reading without tiring.

Allow for ample margins on both sides of the page. A column width of anywhere from 35 to 55 characters works best as it allows for an easy horizontal scan of the page, without strain. You can easily control the width of your website sales copy by setting the page up inside of a table. It's a simple function - one that's available with most site design programs

,or by editing the html code of the page.

Consider the natural flow of the eye as it scans and scrolls through your site. Pay attention to the things that get noticed first.

The top of the first frame that loads is where your prospect's eyes first land. This is what makes your headline such an important part of your sales piece.

Large objects get noticed before smaller objects… dark objects before lighter ones. Bold type draws the eye before regular type. And anything that's a little out of the ordinary naturally jumps out and commands attention. Use this to your advantage, but do so sparingly.

Think visually, one frame (approximately half a standard page) at a time. Each frame needs to sustain reader interest and involvement and must compel the reader to move on to the next frame or the next section. Break it down so your information is quick to arrive and easy to read and understand. It's all about making your pages prospect-friendly.

What Else Should You Keep In Mind When Organizing Your Site?

Whether your entire site consists of just a sales letter and order form, or it's a complex collection of various individual pages, keep your desired result in mind. You want results in the form of sales and converting prospects to customers is the task of your sales letter.

Additional page options include testimonials, product illustrations, company details, informative articles, or a *Frequently Asked Questions* section. Whatever the individual function, all roads should ultimately lead to the order form. And each page should have a similar look and feel to it, subtly connecting one to the other.

Create a funnel effect where each page of your site channels traffic in the direction you want prospects to travel. Include a navigational bar that introduces your pages in a logical, intuitive sequence. Use provocative headline links in the navigation bar -- rather than single word titles. Powerful headlines inspire clicks and enthusiastic action much more than uninspiring labels or button bars. And at the end of each page, provide a quick connection back to your sales letter or order form - depending on where they sit in the presentation sequence.

Simple Techniques To Aid Readability

Keep it simple with quick loading letters that look inviting and are easily readable. That should be rule number one.

Enhancements don't have to be complicated to be effective. In fact, you want to be careful not to overdo it. You want your points of emphasis to really stand out as unique elements that grab prospects and pull them inside.

Aid readability by establishing a strong contrast between the text and the background. Black text on a white background is the strongest possible contrast as they're at opposite ends of the spectrum. Any variation reduces the contrast somewhat. But as long as you stay close, your copy should remain easy to read.

If you want a slight variation, try black text on an off-white background color. One thing you should avoid at all costs is the reverse-type effect. It can work on occasion for small groups of words, but it's a major eyesore and a sure sign of a rank amateur to reverse your body copy from the standard -- dark text on a light background.

Establish visual attention-getters by employing simple techniques such as...

> bullet points
> bold text
> italics
> larger fonts
> numbered lists
> check boxes
> horizontal lines
> asterisks
> arrows
> text boxes
> indented paragraphs

Which Areas Should Definitely Be Emphasized?

Headlines
Sub-Headings
Testimonials
P.S.'s
Benefits
Guarantees
Offers

Your main headlines should be set in large bold type at the very top of your sales letter. Any sub-heading that follows should be noticeably smaller in size... but still larger that the body copy. Subheads may or may not be set in bold. If you use a super headline as a lead-in... it should be much smaller -- approximately the same size as the type in the body copy.

Always place testimonials inside quotation marks. Make it look as real as it is - the actual feedback of a living, breathing customer. Quotation marks are surefire attention-getters... so you might as well make the most of them.

A favorite tactic I use with testimonials is to set them in Italic type. Somehow the slightly angled positioning seems quite appropriate for the role. This effect tends to look a little better with a Serif font, than it does with Sans Serif.

With the P.S., I like to exaggerate the indentation and set the letters -- P.S. -- in slightly larger, bold type - around 14 points in size.

Benefits are best highlighted in bold sub-headings or as bullet points.

Guarantees can be featured in text boxes of various sizes, shapes, colors, and line weight. Another way to set your guarantee apart is by unveiling it next to an official-looking colorful graphic that cannot be missed.

Highlight offers by positioning them in a text box or indented column. One proven tactic is to use a numbered list itemizing every single product, premium, and bonus included in the package. The higher the number of items, the more impact the numbered list delivers.

What About Graphics?

Graphics can help make your sales letter more effective. The key is to not rely on photos, line drawings, or schematics to sell your product… but to use them sparingly to enhance the copy.

One thing you should always try to implement is a caption that runs alongside every graphic. Captions give you an opportunity to sell more of the sizzle and to have the kind of impact that a sub-heading enjoys. Graphics and the accompanying captions have a tendency to pull in large numbers of prospects, so use them for all they're worth.

Consider employing alternate image tags in your html code to reveal a miniature headline as the graphic loads. Should your prospect be surfing with a graphics-disabled browser, he'll still be exposed to your benefit-oriented verbal description.

The best photographs to use in your sales letter are those that:

- Show the product in action
- Trigger action/ movement toward sales copy -- rather than off the page
- Introduce happy buyers using or enjoying the product
- Unveil the benefits or results enjoyed as a result of ownership
- Present the entire package of products every buyer gets
- Reveal the identity of the product developer, inventor, author or discoverer

Use graphic images with restraint and caution. Any element of artwork adds substantial volume to the file size of your page. The larger the size - the slower it loads. Make each image as small as it can be without diminishing its effectiveness.

Choose images carefully. You want an image that contributes meaning or evokes strong feelings. If it fails to make an impact, if it doesn't 'speak' to the prospect, it simply doesn't belong in your sales letter. A poor selection can make your copy seem less important.

You should also choose the location of your image with great care. Place your image where it fits best. Tie the visual directly to your copy so its impact is immediate and unwavering.

If you're showing all the pieces included in your package for example, you should have the visual next to your offer. Here, prospects can see each piece described in your copy and get a better feel for the entire package. This technique is used extensively in infomercials - particularly those selling information products. They don't just show the main products - they show everything that's included, right down to the free bookmark.

What About Text?

Achieving consistency means using a single font for your body copy and perhaps a contrasting font for the headline. Avoid the temptation to use multiple fonts as any change midstream affects readability and interrupts the consistency of your communication.

For clarity and crispness, you can't beat black letters on a white or off-white background. This makes reading easier and less of a strain on the eyes. You could introduce a secondary color to accent your copy, but do so with caution. Always sign off with a color signature that's different from your text. Blue works best as the signature color - as long as it's a dark enough shade to contrast with the background color. You can also use secondary colors for sub-headings or bullet points. Just be sure not to overdo it.

For readability on paper, the ideal fonts are from the Serif family. Proven fonts include Times New Roman, Courier, and Century Schoolbook. For on-screen reading, it's hard to beat the crispness of San Serif fonts like Arial, Helvetica, and Verdana. It's simple, direct and straightforward.

Marketing from your website presents quite a dilemma. How does your prospect read your sales letter? Does he read it on his monitor… or does he print it out to make it easier to read on paper?

Personally, I briefly investigate offers from my monitor… and then print off sales letters from any I'm seriously considering buying. That way I can read at my leisure and scan for specifics much easier. Perhaps the ideal solution is to offer two versions of the same sales letter - one that's easier on the eyes when looking at a computer screen… and one that's more suited for reading on paper.

One option you don't see used much is an adjustment of the leading. "Leading" is the space between the lines of text. Typically, the leading is set as a standard default. Rarely is it altered -- despite the relative ease in doing so. But increasing the leading marginally can actually make the text easier to read.

Here's an example of sales copy with increased leading:

> "This is your invitation to get not just a 'sneak peek'... but ongoing access to in-depth, unedited, real world advertising test results -- exactly as achieved.
>
> It's a goldmine of precious, profit-producing information you can use to increase traffic to your site... build your own subscriber base... and skyrocket your sales and profits -- starting today!"

Make your column width one that's reader friendly. Few things cause more eyestrain and frustration than having to scroll horizontally across the page, from left to right, time and time again. Facilitating buying means making it as easy as possible to read and instantly digest your material. Narrow columns are definitely reader friendly. Why do think newspaper articles are so fast to read? The columns are as narrow as can be. I'm not suggesting you emulate a newspaper on your website. But I am suggesting making your column width a more manageable size - one that readers can quickly and effortlessly scan across.

Align your page to the left as most readers are used to this format. This text is written using the left-alignment option. Notice the strait line on the left of each paragraph. This provides a natural starting point for each line, making reading easier.

To center or right-align your page makes reading a much more arduous task. Both options position a ragged edge on the left of the paragraph, forcing the eye to find the starting point of each line. It seems awkward and unnatural. Justified text spaces the words to spread across the entire column -- regardless of word count. It creates straight lines on both sides of the column. The main problem with this option is that it provides no real rest area for the eye. This is another advantage left-alignment presents. The natural rest area falls at the end of each line and paragraph.

It's much more efficient and orderly to have a fixed starting point where the reader expects to find it - on the left-hand side of the page. This approach looks more appealing and readable than any other.

Headlines are an exception to the left-alignment rule. Setting these components apart with a center alignment helps distinguish these major benefit-oriented messages from the rest of the text. Since headlines are concise statements of major significance and appear far less than regular paragraphs, breaking the readability rule is acceptable.

Make your entire sales letter easy for readers to skim through. Make it "scan-enabled". Allow prospects to breeze through the entire letter effortlessly, without missing any key points. The secret is to maintain a clear direction and a prospect-centered approach while periodically unleashing a visual "grabber" - something that acts as a prospect magnet. That's the benefit of highlighted areas. Sub-heads, bullets, text boxes - anything that interrupts the flow of standard paragraph copy is effective in drawing eyeballs and interest.

Think of it this way...

So far, your prospect is interested enough to spend a few moments perusing your page. Something about your piece has warranted the spending of additional time. As the prospect scans the page, each major point of emphasis - bullets, sub-heads, text boxes, etc. - has the ability and allure to woo him in on a deeper level.

Now, instead of skimming through, he begins reading every word with interest and his enthusiasm soars.

The thing is... you never know which major point of emphasis will be the one that converts the mildly interested scanning prospect into a seriously qualified potential buyer. It could happen at any time - that's why it's crucial to consistently insert visual attention-grabbing elements throughout your sales copy. Plain text becomes boring quickly. But drop in distinctly different key points after every 3 or 4 paragraphs of body copy and you help sustain and boost reader interest.

Fine Tuning Your Design and Layout

After you've written and edited your copy and designed the sales letter for maximum visual appeal and impact, it's time to test how your page views in different browsers. Pay attention to how your page shows in both Internet Explorer and Netscape - the two most popular browsers in use today. What you see in one might not be the same as the other. It may take some tweaking of your html code to get the page to show the way you intended.

Strange things can sometimes occur to your page layout, seemingly without explanation. This can frustrate you to no end. Best to have someone with experience in this area do the tweaking for you.

Just make sure they don't change the marketing effectiveness of your sales letter. Let the "geeks" handle what they do best - but never let them modify the copy or design of your sales piece. With the information contained herein, you'll be much better equipped to create powerful and effective web site copy yourself.

Test for load times on various computer systems. Set up your sales letter on your site and see how it loads in your browser and on your screen. Once you're satisfied there, check it on a few other systems. Get others to access your web page from their computers -- and ask them to monitor how long it takes for the page to fully load. Pay particular attention to the time it takes on older, slower computers. Also keep an eye out for how it looks on different sizes of monitors.

Don't design your page to suit your new system, complete with giant screen and high-speed cable connection to the Internet. Not all your prospects have this same kind of speed, power, or size. You'd be much further ahead to design your sales letter - in fact, your entire site - to suit a system with much less capacity. Ultimately, you want to make your sales presentation clear and legible to every visitor arriving at your site.

Test different formats and layouts. The more varied your testing, the more universally appealing you can make your site.

How To Target Different Groups With Your Sales Letter

Always craft your copy and site to appeal to a specific individual audience. The more tightly-focused and narrow the niche, the better. Avoid the "one-size-fits-all" syndrome. If your product appeals to several distinct groups, address each individually.

This means a separate web site for each target market - rather than one all-encompassing site. It's dirt-cheap these days to build and host a basic site, so a limited budget should never get in the way of setting up multiple mini sites.

Each market is attracted by different benefits. What ranks as the number one, most alluring advantage to one segment, might have little or no effect on another.

For example, currently I'm working with a client to develop web sites for a food product. So far, we've identified 3 distinct groups as prime targets - 1) would be gourmet chefs, 2) time-poor family cooks, and 3) health enthusiasts.

The primary motives for each market are very different. Each has their own set of priorities, wants, desires, and challenges. So, each market requires a specifically targeted approach. If you were to use a single sales letter for all three groups, where would you begin? What benefit would you use first?

Your best bet is to narrow your focus. Maintain a single purpose and address your audience as though none other existed. Maintain a consistent layout and design on each page within the site. Make your product cater to these prospects exclusively. To try and fit every group into one site and appeal to them all is the opposite of target marketing. Reach out to all and you touch no one. But channel your site's direction on one specific group and you quickly gain a position of prominence in the mindset of that specific audience.

Testing Is A Major Key To Success

When you've composed your best effort, it's time to put it to the ultimate test.

The only accurate measurement is the result produced. Let the market decide with their wallets and purses. It's one thing for a prospect to indicate an interest in your product. But it's something else entirely to get him to spend his money to actually acquire it. When they do so in spades... you've got a winner. When results are disappointing, it's time to try different variations.

You can follow formulas, proven techniques, methods, and strategies all you like. You can produce a fine looking website sales letter from any computer. But if it doesn't generate cash sales, it isn't of much value to you. At least, not in it's present form.

"The most important word in the vocabulary of advertising is TEST. If you pretest your product with consumers, and pretest your advertising, you will do well in the marketplace."

-- David Ogilvy

Often the best results are achieved through repeated testing and tweaking.

Try different headlines, offers, guarantees and opening paragraphs. Experimentation, measurement, and careful analysis will help you improve your results, while providing valuable lessons that simply cannot be gleaned any other way.

It's important to take what you've learned here and apply it. Strive for continuous improvement. But only test one variable at a time. That's the only way to be sure that one particular adjustment could alter your result.

Headlines and offers are the places to begin testing, as they often hold the greatest potential for changing results.

Common Mistakes

"There is only one thing more painful than learning from experience and that is not learning from experience."

-- Archibald McLeish

Mistake #1: Lack Of Preparation

Most marketers are so anxious to get out there and start making sales that they fail to do adequate preparation up front. It's easy to find a product to sell…and you can hardly blame anyone for wanting to kick-start sales. After all… making sales is what it's all about. And each sale generates revenue… profit… and a valuable customer.

But not taking the time to adequately understand the marketplace and fashion your 'solution' to best address inherent *wants* will cost you much more in the long run. The frustration will drive you crazy as you struggle to understand why more people aren't buying your terrific product.

Find a hungry market and then feed them exactly what they want. Many people have it backwards. They work 10, 15, or 20 years in a particular industry and become highly skilled, competent specialists in their field. Next, they use what they know to develop a product. Offering a product online is an easy way to get started in business - and so off they go, in search of Internet riches. They hang their shingle, launch a website and wait for all the orders to come pouring in. But this approach is akin to putting the cart before the horse. Unfortunately, they've got it backwards.

A better approach would be to first find a market with unmet desires. Find a market that's anxious for solutions and benefits… shape your product and package your offer to fulfill those desires and then, test it. Fine-tune your offer until you get it right and sales take off. It's a strategy that's both simple and scientific. But it does work.

Your efforts are usually wasted when you fail to target your audience… when those people you're attracting to your site aren't qualified prospects… and when you're lead-generation systems aren't pulling enough prospects to your sales message.

Mistake #2: Presenting A Confusing Message

Again, the lack of preliminary work is most often to blame for this mistake. The preliminary work in this case, is the outlining of a sales letter plan before writing.

A plan forces you to think things through. It helps you organize your ideas, data, benefits, bonuses, and the sequence of your presentation. Planning helps ensure you've covered all the key elements and that your sales letter isn't sorely lacking any important component.

Ineffective letters lack structure and proper structure means arranging various elements for impact, interest, and effortless understanding. Gather all the information you need at the research stage and then lay it out in logical order. Construct your letter by simply going from point A to point B to point C, according to your priority sequence - always from the prospect's point of view.

Deliver every key point, right on schedule. Maintain a single direction that leads prospects on a straight path right to the order form.

Mistake #3: Wasting Your Visitor's Time

Few things are more annoying to busy people than having someone else waste their time. Considering how precious a commodity time is in today's society, to waste other's time is to be disrespectful and inconsiderate.

How do online marketers waste their visitor's time? The most obvious answer is telling a story in a roundabout way. When you don't get right to the point or you go off on a tangent, you're wasting your prospect's time - time they can never get back.

Pay attention to details. Minimize the time it takes for your sales letter to appear on your prospect's screen. Avoid extra clicks by dividing your sales letter into multiple pages. Each page takes additional time to load and only adds to your prospect's frustration. He feels out of control, not knowing how many times you're going to force such delays upon him. With each required click, you're actually creating another interruption and an invitation to move on. Provide a straight trail to the prospect's desired destination.

Don't beat around the bush. Don't waiver or wander. Be direct and benefit-oriented. Lay out benefit after benefit and present your "news" in a logical order that makes sense immediately. Follow the simple plan as outlined in this text and deliver multiple, appealing benefits... prove those benefits... introduce your offer and guarantee... and compel your prospect to proceed to the order page.

Mistake #4: Lacking Credible Proof

Product developers are anxious to get their new creations out into the marketplace. So they whip up a sales letter and launch it in cyberspace, before getting usable feedback from users. Again, they jump the gun... but their copy is missing one of the most important elements -- credible testimonials.

Sure it takes time to gather feedback. But collecting customer comments should be an ongoing process for every entrepreneur and business owner. Testimonials are powerful proof that your product delivers what you claim in your sales copy. The fact that someone else who has tried your product has such positive things to say, carries a lot of weight with new prospects.

Testimonials bring instant credibility by presenting evidence that your product works and works well. Get your product in the hands of others and solicit their feedback. The sooner you do so, the sooner you'll gather the credibility and believability you need to sell unlimited quantities online.

How do you get testimonials for a new product? Ask known experts if you can send your new product to them. Explain that's it's brand new and that you're seeking opinions on it. Most will gladly oblige, if they have the time to do so.

Offer sample products or review copies to 20 to 50 people in your industry or community. Explain upfront that you're very interested in what they have to say about your product. Another technique is to sell the first 50 or 100 units or copies at an exceptionally low price, to those who are willing to answers a few questions about it afterwards. Don't inundate them with page after page of questions - limit yours to one or two key questions. I know one service provider who includes the requirement of customer feedback as part of any price proposal.

As soon as you hear back from someone, make a duplicate copy and ask their permission to use it in your marketing materials. Most people are happy to help you because they genuinely benefited a tremendous amount from your product.

Mistake # 5: Not Being Clear About What It Is You're Offering

Uncertainty leads to confusion and confusion leads to inaction. There is no other possibility. If prospects aren't absolutely certain about what it is you're proposing, they certainly won't take action to acquire it. Promote your package as the ultimate solution and be crystal clear in listing all the components that are included.

Keep it simple. You've heard that before. But it's a rule that's so often violated that I've chosen to repeat it. Prospects have a lot on their minds. 'Busy-ness' is a common condition in our society. So you must be absolutely clear about the specifics.

Let prospects know in no uncertain terms what you're going to do for them, what it is they get, why they'll be further ahead by accepting your offer, and how to order now. Walk them through it step-by-step. Guide your prospects to the solution they desire and make it as uncomplicated as possible.

Mistake #6: Uninspiring Copy That Focuses On The Product

Talk about products and you'll quickly turn off prospects. It's not the product that people are interested in anyway… it what's it does for them.

Talking about products and their features is boring. Instead, give readers plenty of benefits that are right on target to match their desires and to solve their problems. Benefits create and sustain interest - features do not. When you're talking about products, do so from the prospect's perspective. Put it in terms that are meaningful, interesting, and valuable to them. In other words, stress the benefits.

Address your prospect and all the things that matter to him as an individual and you'll quickly gain his undivided attention. A product directed presentation is nothing more than a sales pitch - something any merchant could offer. But a prospect-centered communication reaches the audience on an emotional level about specific and important problems, anxieties, wants and aspirations.

Focus your sales letter on the *wants* of your ideal target prospect. Present simple solutions that are quick, easy, affordable, and immediately applicable to your buyer's life. Offer helpful advantages with unmistakable clarity. Engage prospects by being genuinely concerned for their well being, knowledgeable about the market, and serious about your ultimate solution.

Keep your prospect interested by staying on track. Stick to the topic that's number one on every prospect's list: himself.

Boring copy is unmoving - stagnant. It just sits there. But compelling copy is vibrant and alive. It evokes clear, vivid images that are interesting and exciting. Good sales copy uses action words and promotes continuous movement and involvement.

Mistake # 7: A Short Message That Doesn't Do An Adequate Selling Job

Yes, prospects are busier than ever these days. Yes, it's important not to waste their time with excessive verbiage and meaningless meanderings of thought. But leave anything important unsaid and it will cost you untold numbers of lost sales.

Consider your sales letter your one and only opportunity to influence and persuade prospects to action - an action that is decidedly in their best interest. It's your one chance to convince prospects - some who may have never even heard of you before - to part with some of their money based on the promise of something far greater in return. For some, buying requires a major leap of faith. It demands they step outside of their established "comfort zones".

It behooves you to capitalize on every tool to win over hesitant prospects. Anything less than your absolute best effort simply won't do. You've got to have a great product, an alluring offer and a sales letter that makes the investment impossible to resist.

Website sales letters can be long - most of mine run from 8 to 26 pages in all. Regardless of size, your message must never be boring. As soon as your reader's interest wanes, he's gone. But keep him on the edge of his seat with benefit after benefit, a dynamite offer, impressive, no-risk guarantee and a powerful reason why acting now is clearly worthwhile, and your prospect will read every word with interest, enthusiasm and intense desire.

Mistake #8: Failing To Pull Prospects In From The Start

Ineffective headlines inevitably lead to poor results. If your headline doesn't reach out to your target market with a direct, benefit-oriented appeal designed to captivate their attention and activate interest, the rest simply doesn't matter. Without a powerful and provocative headline, prospects won't even reach your body copy. It's the headline that grabs them and causes them to sit up and take notice because it's exactly the kind of thing they've been searching for.

Your headline is your primary sales tool. It's the most important element of any ad, brochure, postcard, or sales letter in any environment.

Headlines that push the prospect's hot buttons are headlines that get noticed and compel further reading. Those that lack a strong focus and massive appeal are simply passed over. The headline is the first thing prospects see. It can be likened to a traffic sign. A green light tells prospects to proceed immediately. Amber injects an element of caution where prospects are on extra alert looking for obvious potholes. And a red light means there's nothing of value or importance down this road - so, it's probably best to try another route by clicking away.

Unleash your biggest bang in the headline. Pull out all the stops. Utilize your most valuable attributes in an arresting and alluring way. Hold nothing back for if your headline doesn't attract eager, interested prospects, surely nothing else will either. That's why it's so important to summarize your most magical appeal into one sentence and vault it to the top of your sales letter.

Mistake #9: A Weak Close

It takes a strong sales letter to move your prospect to the point where he seriously considers making a purchase. But you cannot afford to drop the ball at this stage. Unfortunately, many sales letters conclude without a powerful close, falsely assuming the sale is a done deal.

The close is all about making the sale between the ears of the prospect.

He needs to convince himself that buying makes good sense. If he hadn't seriously considered buying, he never would have come this far. It's the task of your close to finalize the deal by winning conscious acceptance on the part of the prospect.

What hampers many closing paragraphs is this: they fail to stress the cost of inaction. Remind the prospect of the pain he feels now -- without your solution firmly in hand. Agitate his anxiety a little. Let him know that for things to change in his life, he must instigate those changes.

Nobody is going to magically drop the solution in his lap. But by making a purchase today, he's being proactive and moving forward. To let this opportunity slip by is to pretty much keep things the same way. *Is this really what you want, Mr. Prospect?*

Be direct in your description of value and benefit to the buyer. Avoid vague descriptions that are open to interpretation. Give prospects something solid to chew on. That means making every benefit tangible, so prospects can clearly see what they get out of the transaction.

Present solid "reasons why" buying now is the most intelligent way to respond to your sales proposition. Make your offer even more appealing to those who respond immediately, knowing that any delay multiplies the chances they won't buy at all.

Mistake #10: A Site That Doesn't Facilitate Easy Buying

Any entrepreneur whose site doesn't make the buying experience quick and easy is shooting themselves in the foot. Many sites require too much effort from the prospect. Multiple clicks are one such annoyance. So too, are slow loading pages, difficult ordering procedures, multiple pop-up windows, and anything else that complicates or delays the prospect on route to his goal.

Give prospects what they want without undue delay. Let them know what you have to offer in your headline. Insist on a basic design that's compatible and quick to load on slower computers. Make your site easy on the eyes and a comfortable place to spend some time.

Unfinished pages are another problem. Nothing pushes me over the edge more than to click on a link and wait for the page to load, only to discover some cute graphic proclaiming the page to be "under construction".

If you're not ready to sell, don't go live in cyberspace and announce your site. Why? Your prospects are ready to buy now. Sending them to your half-finished site is only going to annoy and frustrate people. Some will vow never to return -- not the kind of start you want. Test your pages. Edit extensively. Only when all systems are 'go' should you launch your site.

Mistake #11: A Sales Letter That Doesn't Effectively Calm Prospect Fears

Some sites raise red flags from the beginning. An unpolished look… poor layout or color combinations… or someone claiming a level of expertise that seems questionable -- are all caution signs.

Online prospects are an intelligent group as a whole. You may fool some people on occasion, but why would you even try? Your goal should be long-term success and continuous growth. There's no room for anything that's the least bit deceptive, dishonest or amateurish.

Online business continues to grow exponentially worldwide -- due to lower costs and easy accessibility. Unfortunately, so too are the numbers of crooks and quick-buck artists that operate in cyberspace. Everyone knows about it and most are on the lookout for shady business operators. What does all this mean to you? Well, your prospects probably don't know you, so you're at a disadvantage right away.

Offer a rock-solid guarantee to reassure prospects. Let them know that you're willing to shoulder any risk, so they have nothing at all to worry about.

Start to establish a relationship with your pool of prospects by adding personality to your copy and a short bio and photograph to your site. Create the impression that you're here to stay awhile and that you're not some fly-by-night operator out to make some quick cash. You want buyers to feel safe and secure in the knowledge that should they ever have a problem, it will be handled quickly, efficiently and to their satisfaction.

Mistake #12: A Lack Of Uniqueness

To be effective online, you've got to stand out from the crowd. But one of the challenges is that the crowd is forever growing. It doesn't matter what industry you're in. If someone else isn't pursuing the exact same prospects you are, they soon will be. Competition is inevitable - so get used to it.

You've got to really emphasize what makes your product totally unique. It's not enough to be as good as the rest… you've got to be better - much better. What is it that's new or exciting about your product that others don't offer? That's the kind of thing you need to stress early in your sales letter. Not just what makes it unique, of course… but what this means to the prospective customer. It's all about how he benefits from your distinct advantages.

You've always got to strive to maintain an edge over the competition. Anticipate future needs and desires in the marketplace. Keep an eye on what others are doing. Innovate and experiment. Focus your sales letter on the unique attributes your product offers.

"Learning from your mistakes is smart. Learning from the mistakes of others is wise."

-- Unknown

Conclusion

So there you have it… everything you need to know to create a powerful direct response sales letter - whenever you want. Use this book as a framework for getting started and learn all you can as you progress. But more importantly, put your knowledge into practice.

Just one effective online sales letter can generate years of impressive cash flow. It's a powerful moneymaking tool available to anyone with a product to sell… and an idea for turning that product into a big idea. It's about developing a proposition with huge appeal to a carefully selected market. It's a matter of influencing action (and putting money in your pocket) by helping people get the things they want.

Robert Collier put it this way…

"For the ultimate purpose of every business letter simmers down to this: The reader of this letter wants certain things. The desire for them is consciously or unconsciously the dominant idea in his mind all the time. You want him to do a certain thing for you. How can you tie this up to the thing he wants, in such a way that the doing of it will bring him a step nearer to his goal?"

Begin with your goal in mind. Identify your marketing objectives before you begin crafting your letter.

Always keep an eye on the result you're after - winning maximum response. Pay close attention to the bottom line results. In order to succeed, you need to generate response, sales, delighted customers, and profits. Writing sales letters may be a creative or artistic expression, but the ultimate objective is all business. Never lose sight of this. From your perspective, it's about making sales.

Gather all the facts and background information you can. Understand everything about your product, your potential customers, the likely competition, sales trends, and buyer preferences. Do this and you'll uncover the most promising product strengths, advantages, and unique benefits -- while being able to capitalize on the weaknesses of competing forces.

Extract the facts and bring those facts about your product to life. Establish vivid images that clearly describe your product's benefits and pile one benefit on top of another. Be patient. Resist the temptation to go for the sale early on. Don't stop selling until you've revealed every conceivable benefit of value. The more informative your sales letter is, the more persuasive it tends to be.

Tailor your product to the specific market you intend to reach. This customized market approach makes it easier to demonstrate to prospects that yours is ideally suited for them and provides a better solution than any alternative.

What you say to potential customers is more important than how you say it. Strive to *communicate* - rather than *write*. Focus on the message more so than the delivery. Design is a secondary element relegated to a supporting role. It's not about drawing attention to the messenger (your website or sales letter) - it's about influencing a single prospect with your words because he stands to gain so much in the process.

Your sales letter is an advertisement written to sell your product. But you don't want it to been seen as advertising rhetoric. Make it informative and interesting. Give it news value. Tell a dramatic story to captivate readers and involve them in your words.

 Be simple, direct, inviting, and memorable. Make your proposition different from others. Create a message that interests, informs and persuades prospects to actually do something to improve their lives in some way. Make it easy for prospects to read along. The more they read, the more absorbed they'll become by your message.

Establish your strongest advantages early. Launch your message with a big idea and expand on the idea throughout. Grab your prospects attention and interest in the first frame of your sales letter and don't let go until they've convinced themselves of the benefits of action.

"Advertising: the science of arresting the human intelligence long enough to get money from it."

-- Stephen Leacock

Make your message of supreme importance and urgency to the prospect. You've got to get him to want to spend time reading the letter now and they only way to do that is to make it crucial significance, because of the potential reward or solution.

Follow the sequence outlined in this book -- from the headline to post-script. Appeal to the self-interests of your prospects. Know what they want and what it is they perceive they're buying. Sell them on the benefits. Offer up solid proof that your product does all you claim and more. Promise a guarantee and present the most appealing offer you can to get prospects to bite.

Your financial rewards lie in your effectiveness at serving and influencing other people.

You will profit to the extent that you help others get what they want and are able to persuade them that your product is the best of all available options. Use the tools as outlined and you'll soon reach your own pinnacle of sales letter success.